# The Tinder-b
# Assembly Book

## Starting points, stories, poems and classroom activities

compiled by Sylvia Barratt

with drawings by Lisa Kopper
and with a subject index to
fifteen A & C Black song books

## A & C Black · London

First published 1982 by A & C Black (Publishers) Ltd
35 Bedford Row London WC1R 4JH
© 1982 A & C Black (Publishers) Ltd
Reprinted 1984

ISBN 0-7136-2169-9

Phototypeset by MS Filmsetting Ltd,
Frome, Somerset
Printed in Great Britain by William Clowes Ltd,
Caxton Works, Beccles, Suffolk

# Contents

# Self

# Others

# Surroundings

# Times of difficulty

# Celebrations

# Introduction and aims

The material in this book has been selected to help children find out about themselves, their relationships and their environment. The approach can be thought of as pre-religious. Its aim is towards the development of moral and spiritual awareness and it is hoped that it will provide a foundation for the study of religion. Such an approach can either be used as an alternative to the traditional assembly or along side it.

The five sections of the book are *Self, Others, Surroundings, Times of Difficulty*, and *Celebrations*.

## Self

In *Self* the themes explore what it is to be a human being by investigating different aspects of the personality: appearance and characteristics, emotions and needs. The emphasis is on the individual, showing that while everyone has strengths and weaknesses and behaves well and badly, everyone is of equal value. Investigating the different kinds of needs that we all share – physical, emotional, social and intellectual – helps children to build a more complete picture of themselves and their place in the world. They begin to appreciate that we are all interdependent, one with another. In exploring emotions the teacher will need to encourage the children to talk frankly about their feelings. To do this it will be necessary to accept the children's personal accounts uncritically – a child is unlikely to admit to feeling angry if the teacher has expressed disapproval of angry behaviour. Encourage the children to examine and assess their own emotional reactions and the causes and effects of them, and allow them to make their own evaluations.

## Others

In *Others* the themes explore the children's close relationships with other people and the relationships between human beings and other living things. Having looked in the first section at the children's own needs and emotions, in *Others* the emphasis is on encouraging the children to think about and sympathise with other people's points of view.

## Surroundings

The aim of the third section – *Surroundings* – is to encourage the children to realise and observe more closely the effects on them and others of the immediate surroundings: the social structure of the home and school, the neighbourhood in which they live, and the basic elements of the environment – water, air, sun, and so on. In this way it is hoped they may appreciate their own immediate surroundings and go on from this to a greater understanding of the wide variety of environments in which people live. Throughout the section and in the last theme particularly the influence which the natural world has on the children's survival and well-being is stressed and they are encouraged to think of ways of caring for their surroundings.

## Times of difficulty

The three themes – *Separation, Death* and *Disappointment* – covered in *Times of Difficulty* are ones of which most children will have some experience. These experiences can be very frightening for children coping with them alone, and the recognition in assembly that they are experiences which are shared by others can be very reassuring. Young children experience unhappiness for a variety of reasons: moving house and leaving friends, separation from parents, the death of someone they love, their parents' divorce, and so on. Quite often they welcome the opportunity to gain more understanding of times which can be of major concern to them by talking about their experiences, expressing feelings and discussing circumstances and causes. The teacher can provide occasions when children, if they wish to do so, can take part in discussing dispassionately their times of difficulty. Clearly the children's rights to privacy in matters which may be deeply felt should be respected. For this reason very little classroom follow-up is suggested, although some children may themselves initiate more discussion on some issues.

## Celebrations

It will be helpful to start with the children's own experiences when exploring the subject of celebration. Almost all children have birthday celebrations of one form or another and these can be celebrated regularly in school. Aspects of birthday celebrations are common to many festivals (lighting candles, giving presents, eating special food, giving cards) and can lead on to the exploration of other traditional celebrations such as Halloween, Diwali, Christmas, and so on. The selection of festivals is not comprehensive but it shows how a festival may be approached and it is hoped that it will encourage teachers to investigate other festivals such as Chanukah, Eid, Easter – particularly those which may not be included here but which may be celebrated by children within the school.

# Some suggestions

The approach of the book is particularly intended for teachers who believe in the importance of working through the interest and experience of the children. While enough material is provided for the teacher to make a selection for assembly with very little preparation beforehand, it can also be used as a starting point for the teacher's and children's own ideas which may go beyond what is provided and lead to a very full treatment of the themes accompanied by useful and involving classroom preparation and follow-up.

You may wish to use one theme for a day or a week or for a longer period according to your own and the children's needs – the material does not constitute a set number of assemblies. In any one assembly you may like to take one of the starting points, follow it with a story or poem and discussion, and finish with one of the songs given in *Tinder-box*.

Alternatively an assembly might follow from a classroom project based on one of the themes presented by the children themselves. Written work could be read out, paintings displayed, and the children might dramatise one of the stories. It should be noted that while some of the starting points are best suited to presentation by a teacher, many are devised to involve the children themselves in the presentation of their own assemblies.

In addition to the stories and poems provided, a list of resources is given at the end of each theme.

The material covers a fairly wide range of age and ability and whilst for younger children many of the poems will be directly within their experience others are intended to extend their thinking and may require a little explanation from the teacher.

For help and suggestions in compiling this book I would like to thank Brenda Harrison, Inspector for Religious Education, Cambridgeshire; John Elliot of the Cambridge Institute of Education; the staff past and present of Milton Road Infants School, Cambridge: Jenny Bell, Margaret Chattrabhuti, Jane Glover, Alison Kitchener, Barbara Nye, Sheila Pittson, Penny Sherwood, Ann Stonell; Mary Babington of Torriano Infants School, London; Elizabeth French and the staff of Westgate Hill Infant School, Newcastle upon Tyne; Chris Hoggarth; John Laws and Pam Bell of St Anthony's C of E Primary School, Newcastle upon Tyne; C. A. Lumsden of Ravensworth County Junior School, Cleveland; Sheila Shaw of Abbey Primary School, Leicester. Particular thanks to Steve Hoyle, Advisory Teacher for the Inner City Project at the Lambeth Teacher's Centre, London, to Sue Wagstaff and to my editor Sheena Hodge for their many helpful suggestions.

Sylvia Barratt

# Me

## Objectives
☐ To think of ways of finding out about ourselves
☐ To consider what it feels like to be "me"

Although children are keenly interested in themselves, they often have an incomplete understanding of all but their more obvious features and ways of behaving. This theme takes a general look at self-awareness.

## Starting points
○ Ask the children to tell you the name of someone they know better than anyone else, perhaps a friend or an adult who cares for them. Suggest that there are people they know better still – themselves. Discuss some of the things they know about themselves – their likes and dislikes, things which annoy them or make them really happy.

○ A class can make a giant-sized passport for display and discussion in assembly (see classroom activities). It could be for a child, a teacher or well known character from real life or literature. The name can be omitted so that the other children have to guess who it is. What does it tell us about the person? What doesn't it tell us?

## Classroom activities

### Language
☆ Discuss with the children how they get to know themselves – by looking in a mirror, by comparison with others, by listening to other people's views of them, by thinking about themselves. (An important point to make is that the opinions of others are not necessarily accurate or true and can in fact be contradictory.)

☆ Ask the children to write about things they like and dislike about themselves. (It is very important to accept these disclosures without critical comment of any sort.)

## Me, I'm myself

Me, I'm myself,
No one's like me,
And I'm not like anyone
I'm just myself
Little old me.
I'm not quite sure what
makes me different,
I suppose it's in my ways
No one's the same
especially me.

*Pat Kirk*

What is good about being yourself? (No one else like you in the world, you are special, unique. You know more about yourself than anyone else does.)
Do you think you would like to be someone else?
If you suddenly changed into someone else by magic, what would be difficult about it? (You would feel wrong, have no memory of person's past, miss people you love.)
What things make a person different from other people? In what ways are people the same?

## The cat who thought he was a tiger

It is important to get to know yourself really well. This cat made a lot of mistakes at first:

This is the story of a cat who thought he was a tiger. His four brother and sister cats and the children, Hank and Carolyn all lived together in a little house, but he lived alone in the big back yard – because he thought that's what other tigers did.

They all ate together, but he ate grass – because he thought that's what other tigers did. They all slept together, but he slept in a tree – because he thought that's what other tigers did. And they all played together, but he played with his shadow – because there were no other tigers in the big back yard. Then – because he thought that's what other tigers did – he joined the circus. He ate cotton candy – which made his whiskers sticky. He slept in a pile of sawdust – which tickled his nose. And he played with balloons – which always broke. One day he wandered into the animal tent and there he saw – A TIGER.

"Hello there, tiger," he said. "May I play with you?"
"What? You play with ME." The tiger roared with laughter.
"Why can't I play with you?" asked the cat. "You're a tiger and I'm a tiger."
"You? A tiger. No you're not," said the tiger, "You're a little cat."
"I am?" he said. "Yippee," he shouted.
He left the circus and ran down the road. He jumped over the fence, through the big back yard and into the little house. His four brother and sister cats and Hank and Carolyn all gathered around him. "I am a cat," he said. And everyone was simply delighted.

Now the cat who knows he's a cat plays with his brothers and sisters and eats with his brothers and sisters and sleeps with his brothers and sisters.

*Polly Cameron*

What are tigers like? How are they different from cats?
Why was life difficult for the cat because he thought he was a tiger? (Slept outside on his own, had no friends, balloons burst, etc). Sometimes people make mistakes about themselves. They think they can't do something when they can if they try, or they think they are good at everything when they may have a lot to learn. Are you like this sometimes?
How can you get to know yourself better? (Think about what you are like, listen to what others have to say about you, accept that there are good and bad things about everyone.)

4

## Cherry Alive

Children have a special way of looking at the world:

"I am cherry alive," the little girl sang,
"Each morning I am something new:
I am apple, I am plum, I am just as excited
As the boys who made the Hallowe'en bang:
I am tree, I am cat, I am blossom too:
When I like, if I like, I can be someone new,
Someone very old, a witch in the zoo:
I can be someone else whenever I think who,
And I want to be everything sometimes too:
And the peach has a pit and I know that too,
And I put it in along with everything
To make the grown ups laugh whenever I sing:

And I sing: *It is true; It is untrue;*
I know, I know, the true is untrue,
The peach has a pit,
The pit has a peach:
And both may be wrong
when I sing my song,

But I don't tell the grown ups: because it is sad,
And I want them to laugh just like I do
Because they grew up
And forgot what they knew
And they are sure
I will forget it some day too.
They are wrong. They are wrong.
When I sang my song, I knew, I knew!

I am red,
I am gold,
I am green,
I am blue,
I will always be me,
I will always be new!"

*Delmore Schwartz*

The little girl is saying that being herself and alive is exciting. When do you feel as alive, happy and excited as Cherry? Children have a very special way of looking at the world. They enjoy things which grown ups don't even notice anymore. Do you think grown ups enjoy things the way you do? What don't they enjoy?
Do you think you will change as you grow older?
Do you ever imagine that you are someone or something else?

## Me

As long as I live
I shall always be
My Self – and no other,
Just me.

Like a tree.

Like a willow or elder,
An aspen, a thorn,
Or a cypress forlorn.

Like a flower,
For its hour,
A primrose, a pink,
Or a violet
Sunned by the sun
And with dewdrops wet.

Always just me.

*Walter de la Mare*

☆ Make an official-looking passport. Show the children a real one first and after discussion get them to make their own. They can insert a photograph of themselves or paint a self-portrait.

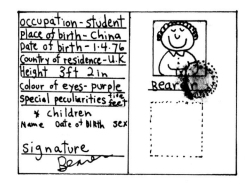

### Drama
☆ Dramatise the story of *The cat who thought he was a tiger*.

### Songs
*Tinder-box:* 1 I've got a song, 2 Halfway down

### Stories
*The Birds and Hetty* B. McFarlane (Cheshire Publishing Pty Ltd)
*The Boy with Two Eyes* (Basil Blackwell *Rights of Children* series)
*Daniel the Reluctant Duck* D. Burt (E. J. Arnold)
*Dinah the Dog with a Difference* E. de Fossard (E. J. Arnold)
*Fish is Fish* L. Lionni (Abelard-Schuman/Puffin)
*Flat Stanley* J. Brown (Methuen)
*I Want to be a Fish* R. Harris (Kestrel)
"The Little Girl Who Changed Her Name" by Ivy Dubois from *The Faber Book of Nursery Stories* ed. Barbara Ireson (Faber)
*Lucille* A. Lobel (World's Work)

### Information Books
*Benjamin Books* series: *I'm special, I have a name, I was born, What is a person* P. Egan (Church Information Office)

### Filmstrip
*Me* (Philip Green Educational Ltd)

# Appearance

## Objectives
☐ To take a closer look at our appearance
☐ To explore and respect diversity in appearance
☐ To think about facial expressions and what they tell us
☐ To consider times when appearances may be deceptive
☐ To encourage confidence in appearance

Very often children are unaware of the details of their appearance: they may not be able to describe the colour of their eyes or the texture of their hair. They may not be aware that they respond to facial expressions and gestures, nor appreciate fully the effect their own smiles, frowns and movements have on others. They are sometimes hurt by thoughtless teasing and need help to appreciate their own and others' individual worth.

## Starting points
○ Display a large picture of a child's face or draw one in assembly with the children's help. (Provide the outline and let different children add eyes, eyelashes, eyebrows, etc). Display a number of faces showing different skin colours and features. Alternatively, ask the children to look at someone else's face – their neighbour's, or your own if you are brave enough. Encourage them to observe closely and describe the features of the face.

○ Make a display of photographs of people of different ages, appearance, ethnic origin, etc. Discuss the similarities and differences between them in terms of age, sex, size, colour, and so on. Try to encourage respect for the diversity of people's appearance.

## Noses

Parts of the face look strange if you look at them closely:

I looked in the mirror
and looked at my nose:
it's the funniest thing,
the way it grows
stuck right out where all of it shows
with two little holes where the breathing goes.

I looked in the mirror
and saw in there
the end of my chin
and the start of my hair
and between there isn't much space to spare
with my nose, like a handle, sticking there.

If ever you want
to giggle and shout
and can't think of what
to do it about,
just look in the mirror and then, no doubt,
you'll see how funny YOUR nose sticks out!

*Aileen Fisher*

What does the poem say about noses?
Feel your nose. What is it like?
Why do we have noses?
Why do you think they are on your head and not on your feet?

## Horrible things

Faces can express our feelings:

"What's the horriblest thing you've seen?"
Said Nell to Jean.

"Some grey-coloured, trodden-on plasticine;
On a plate, a left-over cold baked bean;
A cloak-room ticket numbered thirteen;
A slice of meat without any lean;
The smile of a spiteful fairy-tale queen;
A thing in the sea like a brown submarine;
A cheese fur-coated in brilliant green;
A bluebottle perched on a piece of sardine.
What's the horriblest thing *you've* seen?"
Said Jean to Nell.

"Your face, as you tell
Of all the horriblest things you've seen."

*Roy Fuller*

Describe how Jean looked as she told Nell about the horrible things.
Why was Jean looking horrible?
What other feelings do we show with our faces – our expressions? (Happiness, anger, fear, etc). (You could make the point that sometimes we can't tell what a person is really thinking from their expression. For instance, they may be looking angry but really be feeling sad. When this happens we need to talk to the person to understand their real feelings.)

# The giant child

Appearances can be deceptive. The child in this story is a giant who gets mistaken for a grown up:

Once there was a child who had lost his parents. He walked all over the world looking for them. He stopped at every village and asked if anyone had seen his parents, but nobody had. One day he came to a village where everyone stared at him. They had never seen anyone so large before.

"I am so hungry," said the boy. "Could you give me some food? I only want a little."

The villagers gave him as much as he could eat. When he was full, he thanked them and said, "Now I must be on my way and look somewhere else for my parents."

The people stopped him and said, "Oh no! You have eaten so much, you must pay us for your meal."

"But I don't have any money," said the boy.

"In that case," said the mayor of the village sternly, "you will have to work to pay us instead."

"How can I work?" said the boy. "I am only a child."

"Nonsense!" spluttered the mayor. "You are far too big to be a child. You can't fool us. We can all see you're a giant. Anyone as big as you can do more work than any of us."

He was a good boy and always did what he was told. He worked very hard all day. The work made him hungry again, so the villagers gave him more food. That night he slept in the big barn. The mice and the dog felt sorry for him.

The next day he had to work again to pay for his supper and his bed. Each day he was more and more worn out by the work. It was not really surprising since he was only a child. The harder he worked, the more he ate. The more he ate, the harder he had to work to pay for the food. The villagers were delighted with their giant. Since he did all their work, they didn't have to do anything

themselves. But the children of the village were worried. They could see how thin and unhappy the giant was. They felt sorry for him. "We must help him," they said. They saved some of their food and gave it to him for his lunch and supper. He was grateful, but he was still very hungry. They told him funny stories and jokes, but he was so tired that nothing would cheer him up. In the end the children decided to do their friend's work, so that he could have a rest. Now the hard work wore the children out. They fell asleep at the table. They could not stay awake at school and they were even too tired to play. The parents were worried because their children were so sleepy. The doctor didn't know what was wrong. "What have the children been doing?" he asked.

The parents decided to find out. They followed the children to the fields and saw them doing the giant's work. They were just wondering what to do when ... they heard loud footsteps. They hid among the trees and saw a giant man and woman who had come to the village in search of their son. Now the villagers were ashamed of the mistake they had made. Their giant really was a child, just as he had said. The parents were delighted to see their son again and carried him safely home. The villagers went back to their work and never made any child work too hard again.

Why did the villagers think the giant child was a grown up?
Do you ever decide you know what people are like when you first meet them? Are you always right?
What should you do? (Get to know them better, talk to them, listen to them.)
People all look very different, some are very tall, some very small, some dark, some fair. Do you think it is right that someone should be treated differently because they look different from you?

○ Explore different hair types, styles, care and head dress: ask the children to feel their hair – is it short or long, straight or curly, smooth or rough; demonstrate hair styling – experts could be invited into the school to do this, or a display of photographs could be prepared showing a variety of historical and present day styles; explore traditional and present day head dresses and hats; discuss hair care.

○ Use "Horrible things" as the starting point for mime. A class could prepare a mime of different feelings and challenge the children in assembly to say what they are. With older children the importance of expression and gesture in communication can be emphasised by using them inappropriately, e.g. someone could shout in a very angry way at someone else that they are really pleased to see them.

**Classroom activities**

**Language**

☆ With the children's help make a collection of words describing different expressions – glum, happy, anxious, sad, and so on.

☆ Ask the children to describe a smile or a frown. What happens to the mouth, nose, cheeks, eyes, eyebrows? They might use words like twinkle, curve, light up, darken, crease, crinkle.

## Mathematics

☆ Get the children to look in a mirror or consult with friends to decide what colour their eyes are. Make a block graph of the results for the class. Repeat for hair colour, height and weight.

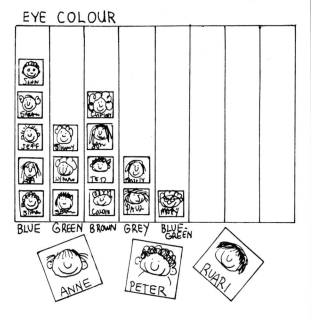

EYE COLOUR

BLUE  GREEN  BROWN  GREY  BLUE-GREEN

## Art

☆ Ask the children to paint a self-portrait. Encourage them to look carefully in a mirror and make the picture as accurate as possible. Include eyelashes, eyebrows, nostrils, chin, ears, skin colour, and so on.

☆ Each child can choose a special occasion or festival and paint a picture of themselves in the clothes they would wear for it. Make a class collage of the paintings.

☆ To encourage careful observation, ask the children to describe the appearance of the person who took assembly that day – their physical appearance and the clothes they were wearing. The younger children could draw a picture and the older ones could write a description. Ask the person to come into the classroom. How do the children's descriptions compare?

# The mouse with seven tails

Many children suffer from teasing because their appearance or behaviour differs from others:

This is a story about a little mouse who had seven tails. Listen to how his life became a misery!

On his first day at school, he wore his best and most beautiful clothes, but everybody laughed at him when they saw his seven tails:

"Oh look! Oh look!" chanted the children in the playground "Look at his seven tails!"

All day the mouse cried, until his eyes were sore and red. After school, he ran home weeping bitterly and threw his satchel across the floor. His worried mother cuddled him and asked, "What happened little one? Did someone scold you? Did you fall down?"

The little mouse sobbed as he told his mother his sad story. "Those seven tails make a fool of me. I don't want to go to school!"

"Don't cry or worry little one," his mother said, "just study hard and do your sums."

But the little mouse cried, "No! Never!" So his mother brought out the sharp scissors, and snip! One tail fell off.

The mouse smiled, and the next day he went to school laughing and jumping, shaking his six tails. But in the playground the children laughed even more. "There goes the mouse with his six long tails!" And the mouse could only cry.

One by one, he made his mother cut off all his tails. When the last tail had gone he was sure in his mind that no one would tease him. Once again, he went to school, happy and cheerful. But the children laughed, clapped and whistled, their faces full of joy.

"He has no tail! Look!" they cried, "The mouse without a tail!"

The mouse cried more than ever and sobbed in his mother's lap, "Now I'll never return to school."

"Laugh with the children" advised his mother, "and soon everyone will play with you."

This time, he listened to his mother, and went to school more confident.

The children still teased him, but, to their surprise, the mouse began to laugh and play with them. Now, no one teases him and everyone likes him. Our little tail-less mouse laughs, plays, jumps – and studies.

*Traditional Indian folk tale retold by Niru Desai*

# I'm afraid of a man who looks strange

Down my road there's a man who limps. He's got a walking stick and wears a big coat and hat. Some of the other children say he's a wicked old man.

When he comes walking along the street we run into a doorway at the foot of a staircase and hide until he has passed.

I get so frightened that he will follow us.

I've told my mum but she says he's just an ordinary man with a bad leg. I'm still afraid of him though.

Why did the children say the man was wicked?
Did they really know he was wicked?
How do you think the man felt when the children ran away?

Why was the mouse teased?
Have you ever been tormented because you were different – new to school, wore different clothes, had a different accent, behaved in a different way?
What other things do you get teased about?
What can you do to help someone who is being teased? (Don't take part yourself, stop the teasing, say something friendly, ask the child to play.)
What did the mouse do to stop the children laughing at him?

## My face

My face isn't pretty,
Nor is it quite plain –
I suppose it's an ordin'ry
Face in the main.

My mum says, "If even
You had your hair curled,
You wouldn't exactly
Be a Miss World,

But cheer up, my lovely,
Don't look glum all the while –
You'd look so much nicer
If only you'd smile!"

*Author unknown*

## The most beautiful child

They all lived together in a great, glorious forest –
all the birds of the air. There were small birds and
tall birds and grumpy birds and happy birds, and
beautiful birds – and none of these was more
beautiful than Mr Peacock, or so they all said. His
fantastic tail, glossy back and bright feathers made a
sight magnificent to behold – magnificent! And who
was the ugliest bird? Mrs Owl, no doubt; with her
podgy, fat figure, and big staring eyes, she was
surely the ugliest of them all – so they all said.

One day as Mrs owl was going to school to take
her child her lunch, she passed by Mr Peacock's
house.

Mr Peacock said: "Where are you going, Mrs
Owl?"

"Oh, I'm off to school to take my child her
lunch."

"Could you take my child his lunch too?" said
Mr Peacock.

"Very well," said Mrs Owl. "But how will I
know which is your child?"

"Oh," laughed Mr Peacock. "Just look for the
most beautiful child there and give it to him."

"Right," said Mrs Owl, and off she waddled to
school, carrying the two parcels. She arrived just as
the children had finished their lessons and were
starting their playtime. Mrs Owl found her child,
and gave her lunch. Then Mrs Owl began to look
for the most beautiful child in the playground.

She looked at each bird carefully. She compared
one with the other. She lined them all up and
examined each one from every point of view.
Eventually, after a long time, she returned home.
On the way, she met Mr Peacock again.

"Ah, I see you delivered his lunch to my
beautiful child. Did you find him easily? I'm sure
you did."

"Well," said Mrs Owl, "I arrived at the school
and gave my child her lunch, and then I did as you
told me. I started looking for the most beautiful
child there."

"Oh good," said Mr Peacock, "so you did find
my child."

"Well," said Mrs Owl, "not exactly. I looked and
looked, and compared one child with the other, to
see which was the most beautiful. And really, Mr
Peacock, I couldn't find any child there who was
more beautiful than mine!"

*William Papas*

Do you sometimes wish you looked different?
Would you rather play with someone who looked glum and complained a lot or
someone who was friendly and smiled?

**Songs**
*Tinder-box*: 2 Make a face
*Subject index*: Clothes, Parts of the body

**Stories**
*The Boy with Two Eyes* (Basil Blackwell *Rights of Children* series)
*The Elephant with Rosey-Coloured Ears* B. Resch (Black)
*The Fabulous Hat* J. Hickson (Puffin)
*Frances Face Maker* W. Cole (Magnet)
"My hair is horrible" from *Ginnie* by Ted Greenwood (Kestrel/Lions)
*New Shoes* B. Gilroy (Macmillan)
*No Two Zebras are the Same* Andersson (Lion Publishing)
*Party Pants* W. Mayne (Hodder)
*Which is Willy* R. Bright (World's Work)
*Wriggles: The Little Wishing Pig* P. Watson (World's Work)

**Information books**
*Let's Read and Find Out* series: *Straight hair, curly hair* A. Goldin, *Your skin and mine* P. Showers (Black)

**Filmstrip**
*Clothes* (Philip Green Educational Ltd)

9

# Physical abilities

## Objectives
☐ To consider how we experience the world through our senses
☐ To think of the things we can do with our hands
☐ To explore the different ways we move using all parts of our body

## Starting points
○ Ask the children to imagine they are standing outside by themselves in the early morning. What can they hear, see, smell? They go to pick something up. What is it? What does it feel like? They go to find something to eat. What does it taste like? To do all these things they have to use their senses, which help them to understand the world. With the children's help list the senses:

> We see with our eyes
> We hear with . . .

○ Prepare a cassette of everyday sounds. Can the children guess what they are?

○ A class can make a feely bag for assembly. Fill it with items of different texture, shape and weight – fur, feather, soap, wood, bread. Blindfold volunteers to come up and describe what they can feel. Can the others guess what it is?

○ Describe simply the body's skeleton, joints and muscles and how they help us to move. Display a picture of a skeleton – or a real one if possible dressed up for fun. Alternatively, choose a child to demonstrate the different ways the body can move.

○ With the children list some of the things we can do by moving different parts of our body:

> With my legs I can kick, run, skip . . .
> With my hands I can pick things up, draw . . .
> With my mouth I can eat, talk . . .

○ Ask a class to present a skipping display using the rhymes given here or others they know.

○ Traditional dances could be presented either by children learning them in the school, or by inviting a local dance group to give a demonstration.

○ Ask a group of children to prepare a display of gymnastics or music and movement.

## Seaside

Barefoot on the hard wet sand
Run and run,
The world is just awake, stretching
In the sun.
As far as we can see, the beach lies
New and clean
Shining with stones and shells, jewels
For a Queen.

Look, a starfish rocking gently
In a pool.
Catch it – put it back again
Safe and cool.
Play until the tide comes up
Foaming white
To wash the sand smooth again
In the night.

*Jennifer Andrews*

What senses would you have to use to do the things in the poem? (Touch – feeling wet sand, sunlight. Sight – seeing the sea and starfish.)
What else would you be able to hear/smell?
What else do you do on the beach?

## Favourite colour

I love a kind of pinky-red
And I cheer when it appears,
I see it most on brother Ned
When the sun shines through his
  ears.

*Elizabeth Hogg*

What is your favourite colour?
Why do you like it?
How does it make you feel? (Happy, warm, excited . . .)

## Hearing and seeing

The spider made friends with the millipede. One day while they were sitting together the millipede said, "My dear, did you know that human beings are deaf? When I stamp my thousand feet they can't hear even one of them."

The spider answered, "Really! And did I ever tell you that they are blind as well? When I've spun myself a new house, a human being will walk straight through it!"

*Traditional African*

## The Loser

Mama said I'd lose my head
If it wasn't fastened on.
Today I guess it wasn't
'Cause while playing with my
  cousin
It fell off and rolled away
And now it's gone.

And I can't look for it
'Cause my eyes are in it,
And I can't call to it
'Cause my mouth is on it
(Couldn't hear me anyway
'Cause my ears are on it),
Can't even think about it
'Cause my brain is in it.
So I guess I'll sit down
On this rock
And rest for just a minute . . .

*Shel Silverstein*

## This is the hand

This is the hand
that touched the frost
that froze my tongue
and made it numb

this is the hand
that cracked the nut
that went in my mouth
and never came out

this is the hand
that slid round the bath
to find the soap
that wouldn't float

this is the hand
on the water bottle
meant to warm my bed
that got lost instead

this is the hand
that held the bottle
that let go of the soap
that cracked the nut
that touched the frost
this is the hand
that never gets lost.

*Michael Rosen*

Hold out your hand and look at it
carefully. Why is it useful to have a
thumb that is separate from your other
four fingers?
How many places do your fingers bend?
What was the person in the poem able
to do with his hand?
What else can you do with your hands?
(Make things, help other people, express
feelings.)

## The Sycamore Tree

"I think I can,"
Said Mary Ann;
"I'm sure you can't,"
Said Mary's aunt:
"It all depends,"
Said Mary's friends.
So Mary's mother
And sister and brother
Discussed the matter
With one another.
They whispered together
Arguing whether
They should agree
To let her climb
The Sycamore Tree.
They thought that they oughtn't
To give their permission
For the tree was in such a
Neglected condition.
But while they were talking
Without a stop
Mary Ann
Had climbed to the top,
And there she balanced
(Without permission)
At the tippermost top
In a topply position!

*Jonathan Always*

Have you ever tried to do something
you found a little difficult or frightening?
(Jump further than ever before, cross a
road on your own, etc.)
Did anyone try to stop you or help you?
How did you feel when you had
managed it on your own?
Is there something that you would like
to do that you haven't tried yet?

## Skipping rhymes

Granny in the kitchen,
Doing a bit of knitting,
In came a burglar
And pushed granny out.

Each peach, pear, plum,
Apple juice and bubble gum.
Lick it once, lick it twice
Each peach, pear, plum.

Please, Miss, my mother, Miss
She sent me round to tell you this,
That I, Miss, won't, Miss,
Be at school tomorrow, Miss.

My mum's a secretary,
She was born in February,
If you think it's necessary,
Look it up in a dictionary.

As I was going to Turkey
As I was going to the fair
I met a Cinderella
With flowers in her hair.
Oh twisty twisty baby
Twisty all you can
Twisty like a masha
And twisty all you can
Rumba to the bottom
Rumba to the top
Turn around and turn around
Until you make a stop.

*Traditional*

○ Explore different ways of communicating which
use movement – mime, semaphore, sign language,
hand movements in Indian dance, and so on.

**Classroom activities**

**Language**
☆ After discussion ask the children to choose one of
their senses and to use their imagination to write an
account of how this sense helped them to do
something brave.

☆ Finish the following sentences:
I like to see (an ice-cream)
I like to hear (pop music)
I like to smell . . .

**Mathematics**
☆ Make a class book of record movements:
Tom can skip 128 times
Ann can run on the spot for 3 minutes
Gabrielle can bounce a ball 62 times

Ask the children for other ideas. Encourage them to
make accurate measurements and records of the
movements using stop-watches where necessary.

**Science**
☆ Find out about skin. What are its qualities? (Keeps
us waterproof, regulates our temperature, protects us
from the sun.)

**Art**
☆ Observe a friend's eye very closely. Draw a large
detailed picture of it using coloured crayons.

☆ Paint a picture of someone moving very fast
(dancing, running, jumping).

**Projects**
☆ Extend the work done with the feely bag to the
other senses. You could use shoe boxes attractively
decorated and containing the following:

*Smell* – bottles containing vinegar, peppermint,
perfume, and so on. Ask the children to think of
words describing the different smells.

*Hearing* – bell, whistle, chime bar, plastic egg boxes,
paper, button box, clock, and so on. Think of words

## Mr Wolf and his tail

One day Mr Wolf was out walking when some big dogs began to chase him. They chased and they chased, and they nearly caught him. But luckily Mr Wolf suddenly saw a cave in the mountain. It was just big enough for him to get inside, and he dashed in quickly. The cave was too small for the big dogs to get in, so they had to stay outside.

Mr Wolf panted and panted, "Huh-huh-huh," till he got his breath back. Then when he felt better, he thought he had been very clever to get into this cave. So he began to talk out loud. "Feet, feet," he said. "What did *you* do to help me to get into this cave?"

"Why, we jumped over the rocks and the rivers, and we brought you here," said his four feet.

"So you did," said the wolf. "*Good* feet!"

"And what did *you* do?" he said to his two ears. "What did *you* do ears, to help me?"

"Why, we listened to the right, and we listened to the left," said his two ears. "We heard where the dogs were coming, so we could tell you which was the right way to go."

"So you did," said the wolf. "*Good* ears!"

"And what did *you* do to help me eyes?"

"Why, we looked," said his two eyes. "We pointed out the right way. We found this cave."

"So you did," said Mr Wolf. "*Good* eyes."

Then Mr Wolf said, "What a fine fellow I am to have such good feet, such good ears, and such good eyes. I *am* clever." And he leaned over to pat himself on the back. When he did this, he saw his tail. "Oh," said Mr Wolf. "Oho! And what did *you* do, tail? I bet you did nothing at all. You just hung there on the end of me, expecting me to carry you along, and you did nothing at all to help. Why, I bet you nearly let the dogs get hold of me. What *did* you do?"

The tail was so cross at being spoken to like this, that he said, "I'll tell you what I did. I waved to the dogs to tell them to come on and catch you!"

"You *bad* tail!" shouted Mr Wolf. "You bad, bad tail!" And he turned around and bit it as hard as he could. Then he shouted very angrily, "Get out of here at once! You bad old tail! Get out of this cave!" And he pushed his tail out of the cave. But when he pushed his tail out, of course, he went out with it. And the big dogs were waiting outside, listening to every silly word, and they caught him.

*Traditional, retold by Leila Berg*

Every part of the body is useful for something. Why do we have feet, hands, hearts, skin, hair, eyelashes …?

to describe the sounds.

*Sight* – make a treasure box of items to stimulate imaginative discussion and writing. Include jewellery, exotic ornaments, coins, old photographs, maps.

*Taste* – sweets, toothpaste, onion, flour, variety of fruit drinks. Get the children to experiment by closing their eyes or holding their nose while tasting. Can they tell what the tastes are? Can they tell the difference between tastes while holding their noses?

☆ Base a classroom project on the physical abilities of a number of animals, birds or fish, comparing them with those of humans. One or more of the following aspects could be covered – movement, sight, respiration, ability to endure different climatic conditions. Use the *Guinness Book of Records* or *Book of Comparisons* to find out more unusual facts but also investigate the more obvious abilities which animals have and which humans don't, and vice versa.

### Songs

*Tinder-box:* 4 Kaigal-Hands, 5 I've got a body, 28 Slowly walks my grandad, 39 Sound song, 40 Mysteries

*Subject index:* Action songs, Dancing, Hobbies and sports, Parts of the body, Senses

### Stories

*Huff the Grumbling Pigeon* E. de Fossard (E. J. Arnold)
*The Little Hippo* H. D. Schwartz (Evans)
*The Little Wood Duck* B. Wildsmith (Oxford)
*Moving, Doing, Building, Being* M. Macdonald (Andersen)

### Information books

*Body Book* C. Rayner (Deutsch/Piccolo)
*Book of Comparisons* (Diagram Group Sidgwick & Jackson)
*Caspar Books* series: *Caspar's Ears, Caspar's Feet,* etc. Tourneur/Crampton (Burke)
*Funny Facts* series J. L. G. Sanchez and M. A. Pacheo (Evans)
*How We Play* A. Harper (Kestrel)
*Let's Read and Find Out* series: *Find out by touching, Follow your nose, How many teeth, The listening walk* P. Showers, *My five senses* Aliki (Black)
*Science 5–13* series: *Ourselves* (Macdonald)

# Learning, dreaming and imagining

## Objectives
☐ To think of the things our brains help us to do
☐ To think about the need to learn
☐ To think how we learn through enquiry and experimentation

## Starting points

○ Discuss with the children what their brains are capable of – thinking, storing up memories, imagining, helping them to make choices and decisions. Does the brain ever stop working? What happens at night when they go to sleep? Does it stop working then?

○ Use the song "The world is big the world is small" as the basis for an assembly by illustrating and dramatising the words. Discuss who teaches the children – parents, teachers, sisters and brothers, friends. How do they learn – through reading books, talking to people, imitating them, listening to the radio, watching television, playing games, travelling.

○ Dramatise the story of *The blind men and the elephant*. Prepare a collage of the elephant or make a large painting of it for display.

○ Ask a group of children to prepare an assembly based on the poem "I wonder". Discuss the poem in class and invite the children to make a list of questions which they find difficult to answer. These can be written out in felt tip pen, displayed and read out in assembly by the children. Involve the other children through discussion.

○ Invite classes to demonstrate a project or new skill they have been learning.

## Anancy and common sense

Anancy is the trickster hero of Caribbean folk stories. Sometimes spider, sometimes man, he is guileful, treacherous and lazy, but also playful and even lovable. In this story his behaviour is at its worst:

Once upon a time, Anancy, feeling very greedy for power and wealth decided to collect all the common sense there was in the world. He thought that everyone would then have to come to him with their problems and he would charge dear for his advice. So, he set out to collect all the common sense in the world.

He collected and he collected, and all that he found he put in a large calabash. When he could find no more common sense, he sealed the calabash with a roll of dry leaves. Then, he decided to hide all the common sense, at the top of a very high tree, so that no one else could get at it.

Anancy tied a rope to the neck of the calabash, tied the two ends of the rope together and put the loop over his head, so that the calabash rested on his stomach.

He started to climb the tree, but found that the calabash was getting in his way. He tried again and again, but all in vain. Suddenly, he heard someone laughing behind him, and looked around to see a little boy.

"Stupid fellow," cried the little boy, "if you want to climb the tree, why don't you put the calabash behind you?"

Anancy was so annoyed to hear this little bit of common sense coming from a little boy, when he, Anancy, thought that he had collected it all, that he flung the calabash at the foot of the tree and broke it.

And so, common sense was scattered in little pieces, all over the world, and nearly everyone got a bit of it.

Anancy is the cause.

*Traditional Caribbean, retold by Louise Bennett*

What do you think having common sense means?
Was Anancy using his common sense when he climbed the tree? Why? Why not?
Can you think of a time recently when you were very sensible?

## I wonder

I wonder why the grass is green
And why the wind is never seen.

Who taught the birds to build a nest
And told the trees to take a rest?

Or when the moon is not quite round,
Where can the missing bit be found?

Who lights the stars, when they blow out,
And makes the lightning flash about?

Who paints the rainbow in the sky,
And hangs the fluffy clouds so high?

Why is it now, do you suppose,
That Dad won't tell me, if he knows?

*Jeannie Kirby*

We often ask difficult questions because we are curious to understand the world. Have you ever wondered why the grass is green or why the wind is never seen? How could you find out?
Some questions are very difficult to answer but we would still like to know the answers. Can you think of some questions like that? (The discussion might lead into thinking about science – what is science? What sort of questions can we answer using science? What questions can't we answer?)

## Classroom activities

### Language

☆ Ask the children to write a story about an imaginary incident in which they saved someone's life by using their common sense.

☆ Talk about *your* earliest memory then ask the children to discuss and write about theirs.

☆ Discuss what it would be like to lose your memory. What would you be unable to do? What difficulties might you find yourself in?

☆ Use the Anancy story as the starting point for a discussion about the different types of stories the children read or are told – fables, folk tales, fairy stories, science fiction, fact.

### Problem solving

☆ Give the children open-ended problems to solve:

Design a machine for helping you to get up in the morning.

List the ways you could cross the road without your feet touching the ground.

Design a spring-cleaning machine.

Point out to them that they need to use their imaginations and intelligence to solve problems.

## Leon and the Sumwitch

Leon tumbled out of bed, jumped into his clothes and ran into the kitchen. He gobbled down a glass of milk, seized a bread and set off down the road. He was late for school.

Leon's teacher was very cross when he got to school. "Good *Afternoon*" she said – though she knew perfectly well it was still the morning. Leon grinned at her and found his sum book.

At first he thought the sums were too easy, "Baby Sums!" he snorted, but he soon found the work harder and he got fed up. He began to talk to his friends about the Dracula film he'd seen.

"Quiet! Get on with your work!" warned the teacher.

"Yes, miss!" Leon agreed with a smile and he tried to get started again.

But somehow he just couldn't seem to get into the swing of things. The adding up didn't add up properly and the take aways just wouldn't subtract. Soon he was talking to his friends again and getting into even more trouble.

So when home time came Leon had to sit with his head down while all his friends went home. Even now Leon kept on fussing and when the teacher came to look at the sums he'd still only done half of them.

"Why you so late from school?" his mum asked when Leon got home.

"I was helping my teacher, mummy," Leon lied.

"And what did they teach you at school today?"

"Oh I did a lot of sums at school today, mummy, and I got every one right!"

That evening Leon watched television with his brothers. At last he went to bed and fell into an untroubled sleep. But sometime in the dead of night Leon shot bolt upright in his bed. His hair stood on end. There was somebody in his room!

At the foot of his bed Leon saw an old woman dressed in a mysterious green cloak. The cloak was covered in all sorts of mathematical signs. In her hands she held a large green canvas bag.

"Do you know who I am, Leon?" she asked in a horrid voice.

"Nnnnnnnnnnnnnnnnnnnnnnnnnnnuh Noooooooooooooooooo!" chattered Leon.

"I am the SUMWITCH," she announced. "Children who work hard at school and who do their sums properly have nothing to fear from me. But children who are lazy and get their sums wrong and waste time I always catch and punish!"

As she spoke she shook the green sack all over Leon's bed and hundreds and thousands of sums tumbled out and spilled over onto the floor. "This is my gift to you," she cackled. "You have to do all these sums by morning, *and get them right*, and still not be late for school in the morning. *And if you fail*, I'll cough up some more!"

And just to prove she meant her words she coughed violently and a rather unpleasant, yellow long division sum landed on Leon's pillow.

Leon was worried. He sat up all night and filled fourteen books with sums. In no time at all it was morning and time for school. As soon as he reached the classroom he showed his teacher the sums.

"My oh my! Leon! What is this? You have done all this work at home! Well, my oh my ... this is very good!"

During the day Leon worked very hard. He got almost every sum right by checking and double checking. Just once he made a stupid mistake and just once he heard an invisible cough behind him that sent a shiver up his spine. A sticky multiplication problem landed, SPLAT! on his page.

From that time Leon has always done his best and he always checks and double checks his sums to make sure they are right!

*Steve Hoyle*

Why do we need to learn mathematics?
Do you find it difficult to work hard sometimes like Leon?
Do you think it was good that Leon had a Sumwitch? Why? Why not? Is it right to scare people into doing their work? What would be a better way of getting them to do it?

## The blind men and the elephant

There were six blind men – all of them very clever and very eager to learn more.

One day a boy ran to them calling, "There's an elephant in town! Come and see! Come and see!"

"What *is* an elephant?" they asked themselves and hastily followed the boy who led them to the market place.

In his hurry to meet the elephant the first blind man blundered straight into its huge, solid side. At once he shouted, "Goodness me! the elephant is like a wall!"

"No it's not!" said the second blind man. He had found the elephant's tusk. He felt its length, its smoothness and sharp end. "The elephant, quite clearly, is like a spear!"

The third blind man, meanwhile, had taken the elephant's long squirming trunk in his hands and declared, "The elephant is like a snake."

Each in turn found a different part of the elephant's huge body. The fourth blind man bumped into a leg and was certain the elephant was like a tree. The fifth touched the elephant's ear and was convinced that the animal must be like a fan. The sixth found its long thin tail and was determined it must be like a rope.

And so they argued on and on. They argued all day and they argued all night. Each was convinced that he was right and that all the others were wrong.

*Traditional Indian folk tale*

Late last night
I lay in bed
driving buses
in my head

*Michael Rosen*

What do you imagine before you go to sleep at night?

Who do *you* think was right? Were *any* of them right? Were they partly right? Are you ever sure you know the right answer to something and that everyone else is wrong?

## Magic

Sandra's seen a leprechaun,
Eddie touched a troll,
Laurie danced with witches once,
Charlie found some goblins' gold.
Donald heard a mermaid sing,
Susy spied an elf,
But all the magic I have known
I've had to make myself.

*Shel Silverstein*

Do you think Sandra really saw a leprechaun?
If she didn't really see one what might she have done? – dreamt it, thought she saw it, imagined it.
When do you make things up/use your imagination? (Pretend games, creative writing.)
When do you dream?

### For fun

☆ Devise a school treasure hunt with clues for the children to solve.

☆ Play memory games.

### Songs

*Tinder-box:* 6 Can anyone tell me that? 25 Let's pretend, 33 The world is big, the world is small, 40 Mysteries, 58 New things to do
*Subject index:* Sleeping and dreaming

### Stories

*Catkin the Curious Kitten* E. de Fossard (E. J. Arnold)
*The Children and the Silly Kings* (Basil Blackwell *Rights of Children* series)
*Dragon at the Gates* C. Lastrego and F. Testa (Black)
*Clouds* P. Blakeley (Black)
*Frederick* L. Lionni (Abelard-Schuman/Lions)
*Imagine If . . .* H. Heine (Dent)
*Mr Meebles* J. Kent (Hamish Hamilton/Puffin)
*Monty Mouse Looks for Adventure* E. de Fossard (E. J. Arnold)
*Robert's Story* L. Berg (Macmillan)
*A Story A Story* G. Haley (Methuen)
*When the Wind Stops* C. Zolotow (World's Work)

### Filmstrip

*Without Words* (Philip Green Educational Ltd)

I somtimes imagine elephants with wings flying in the night
Elephants red elephants,
With no trunks.
Richard Wadsworth
7.

# Growing and changing

## Objectives
☐ To give children some understanding of the changes in themselves from birth to their present age
☐ To think of some of the day to day changes taking place around us
☐ To think of future changes in ourselves

Whilst this section mainly encourages the children to think of themselves as they are now, it is also necessary to draw attention to the rapid changes they have already undergone since birth, and to the changes yet to come. This helps them to understand themselves and the way their view of the world changes.

## Starting points
○ Make a display, either on a wall or free standing, of children's baby photographs (guess who this is), baby clothes, toys and utensils. Explain to the children that we are changing all the time because of getting older and because of the things that happen to us – our experiences. Explore with them what it is like to be a baby and what babies can and can't do. You could ask a mum or dad to bring their baby into the school and show the children how it is cared for – bathed, fed, nappies changed, etc.

○ Discuss the changes the children have experienced since being babies – learning to talk, walk, dress themselves, ride bicycles, starting school. What will they be able to do when they are teenagers, adults?

○ Ask the children about the things they notice are changing around them from one moment to the next and from day to day – the clouds, the weather, seasons, new children arriving in school, new teachers, pop charts, new lessons.

○ Discuss how adults change – they have stopped growing but they go on changing. Having children changes them. Suggest that the children ask their parents how their life has changed since having children. What happens to people as they grow old? – their hair might go white or grey, they may walk more slowly. Invite an old person into school to talk about life when they were very young. Encourage the children to ask their own parents or grandparents about their lives.

## The End

When I was One,
I had just begun.

When I was Two,
I was nearly new.

When I was Three,
I was hardly Me.

When I was Four,
I was not much more.

When I was Five,
I was just alive.

But now I am Six, I'm as clever as clever.
So I think I'll be six now for ever and ever.

*A. A. Milne*

Think of the ways you have changed since you were a baby.
What can you do now that you couldn't do then? – walk, talk, read, run.
What will you be like when you are a year older?
What will you be able to do?
Do you like the age you are now?
Can you stay the same age? Why not?

## Growing up

| | |
|---|---|
| When I was seven | When I was older |
| We went for a picnic | We went for a picnic |
| Up to a magic | Up to the very same |
| Foresty place. | Place as before, |
| I knew there were tigers | And all of the trees |
| Behind every boulder, | And the rocks were so little |
| Though I didn't meet one | They couldn't hide tigers |
| Face to face. | Or *me* any more. |

*Harry Behn*

## Secrets

Some questions they won't answer.
   I ask, "Why not?" They say
"Because you would not understand.
   You will some day."

But there are things I've noticed
   That I can't talk about –
The shapes of hands, or faces;
   A fear; a doubt.

"A penny for your thoughts," they say;
   But though they're old and grand,
I cannot talk – because they would
   Not understand!

*Edward Lowbury*

## Capability Tim

I wish I could whistle,
I wish I could wink,
I wish I could wiggle my ears,
I wish I could ride
A two-wheeler like Tim,
With a bar and a bell and real gears.

*Elizabeth Hogg*

Are there things you wish you could do which you can't yet? What? Why can't you do them yet?

Getting older and bigger makes a difference to the way we see things.
What had happened to the picnic place when the child went back to it?
What had happened to the child?
Did the child think it was more fun to be seven? Why? Why not?

# The smallest Christmas tree

The little tree was sad because it was too young to go to town with the other trees and take part in the Christmas celebrations:

It was getting near to Christmas and a little fir tree was standing all alone on the hillside and he was weeping. His little branches were drooping and he was a sad sight.

A kindly bird was flying by and he hovered above the little tree and asked "Why are you crying? Aren't you going to the town for Christmas?"

"No I'm not. They say I'm too small for Christmas," sobbed the little tree.

He told the bird how all his big brothers had begged him to grow up quickly and become a real Christmas tree in time to go to the town. And in the end they left him alone and went to be Christmas trees themselves. And so the little fir tree was lonely. "Oh how I wish I was bigger," he wept. "Then I could have gone with the other fir trees to be a Christmas tree."

Hearing all this the bird became worried and thought he should do something to help. "In the town I have a friend, a donkey, and he knows all about Christmas. Perhaps he can help." And the bird flew away.

In a little while a fox passed by on his way to town for Christmas. The fox asked the little tree why he was standing alone on the hillside. And again the little fir tree said he was too small to be a Christmas tree and wept more bitter tears.

Meanwhile the little bird and his friend the donkey were hurrying along towards the hillside. "It's a long way," brayed the donkey "and I'm missing all the getting ready for Christmas in the town." And he grumbled as he trotted along.

"Here we are," said the bird as he landed by the tree. And the donkey stared for never had he seen such a little fir tree.

"Can I help you?" asked the donkey politely.

"Oh I wish I weren't so little. I shall never be able to see Christmas in the town," sobbed the little tree.

"Don't cry, little tree," said the donkey. "Look, the lights are being lit on the Christmas tree in the town. Everybody is getting ready. They're wrapping up presents and hanging stockings by the fireplaces for Father Christmas. They're getting the turkeys and the puddings ready and soon the carol singing will begin. Please don't cry little tree," said the donkey. "Perhaps next year you will have grown big enough to see Christmas."

So the little tree dried up his tears. "Yes, maybe next year I'll be big enough." And he and the donkey and the bird went to sleep. It was still and cold and quiet and the snow began to fall.

And then it was Christmas Eve. The snow glittered in the sun and the world was all white. And there amid the whiteness stood the smallest and prettiest Christmas tree you could ever see. The donkey and the bird started to sing their favourite carol. All the animals from near and far came to join in.

Soon everyone was gathered around the smallest Christmas tree in the world. And it was a starry snowy Christmas Eve on the hillside. Christmas had come to the little tree and with so many friends around him, he wasn't lonely any longer. And the little fir tree wasn't sad any more. He'd had his own special Christmas on the hillside with so many friends. And trees, like babies, grow and he thought he would be big enough by next year to go to see Christmas in the town.

*Peggy Blakeley*

Why was the Christmas tree sad?
Have you ever been sad or angry because someone said you were too small to join in something exciting?
What things are you still too young to do?

○ Sing *Puff the magic dragon* and talk about its meaning.

## Classroom activities

### Language

☆ Explore the concept of changes in time through the children's own experiences:

*A day of time* – write about and make collages of the things the children do from the time they wake up in the morning until they go to bed at night. You could divide the children into twos each working on one activity of the day – getting up, washing, breakfast, working in school, playtime, and so on. Make an ordered labelled display. Clock faces can be added by the children to show the appropriate time.

*A week of time* – ask the children to describe and illustrate the days of their week. They could describe the previous week saying what sort of day each was and what happened during it, e.g.

> Wednesday was a wonderful day.
> Granny came to visit.

Each child can make up their own week. Draw each day on a circle of stiff paper or card and string them together from the ceiling in order of days.

*A year of time* – make a class collage of paintings showing seasonal changes, festivals, holidays and school terms, or separate collages for each month.

☆ Read the poem *Crossing the bridge* to stimulate discussion and written work about travelling by imagination or magic from this world into another. What would the children like to find there?

☆ Make up poems about the things the children could or couldn't do at different ages using the structure of *The End*:

> When I was one I sucked my thumb
> When I was two ...

## Science
☆ Find out about the life-cycle of the butterfly and make a collage of it showing the various stages of development:

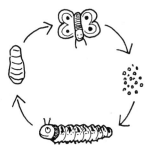

☆ Grow peas, beans, seeds and pips. Watch their growth and record changes with drawings, measurements and graphs.

☆ Observe the changes in daylight and the position of the sun by measuring shadows or making a sundial.

## Art
☆ Make a class collage of an apple tree in spring, summer, autumn and winter:

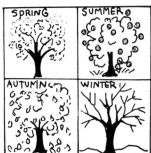

Some things change quickly ...

## Today

Today is a day
different from any other day
that has ever been;
a day when the birds
are singing differently,
the clouds are slowly fitting together
like a jig-saw puzzle
and the sun falls in patches
around me.

I
also am different.
I have also a strange new feeling
inside me,
a feeling mingled and strange
undescribable.
That is why today is different.

*Cathy Thomson, aged 12*

Can you think of some of the ways that today is different from yesterday? (Weather, school work, dinner).
The things which happen to you from day to day make you feel different. Can you think of a time when you felt like this? How do you feel on your birthday and then on the day after?

... others change very slowly.

## Moving mountains

There was an old man who lived in the north of China. Some people called him silly. "You silly old man," they said. "What are you doing with that spoon?"

"I'm clearing away the mountains" said the old man. "They're in the way."

The people laughed. "That's silly," they said. "You'll never do that!"

"No," said the old man, "I'm too old. But I will give the spoon to my children, and they will give it to their children, and they will give it to their children, and they will give it to their children, and they will give it to their children, and that way the mountains can be moved."

*Traditional Chinese*

Some things change very slowly – you can't see yourself growing but you are. How do you know? (Finger nails and hair need cutting, you grow out of shoes and clothes.) What other things take a long time to change? (Trees take a long time to grow, the seasons change very slowly.)
You wouldn't try to move a mountain and certainly not with a spoon but there are things which we try to do which are so difficult or tiring we have to do them little by little. Can you think of something like this?
Like the old man in the story we have to pass some tasks on to our children. (You could explain that it took hundreds of years for enough people to believe that it was wrong to send young children to work in the coalmines before this was changed.)

Some changes are very frightening . . .

## Brownies

I felt lonely and new
Why did I ever come?
Know-one forced me to
I was being stupid.

All these new faces
All in the same uniform
I was different
From the other Brownies

The children were different
Their belts slipped down
Their ties were tatty and crooked
They had different coloured shoes.

We had new games
New things to work at
New things to see
Brown Owl was new.

It was terrible
There was not a single friendly face
I thought it was ghastly
But I soon got used to it
I love it now.

*Susan Mangam, aged 9*

Why didn't the girl like her new brownie pack?
Why do you think she came to like it in the end?
Are you ever afraid of doing something new or going
somewhere different? Why don't you like it?

… others are exciting.

## Crossing the bridge

I cross the bridge and leave behind
The world I know.
A place without surprises –
As ordinary and dull
As Monday morning
Or a pair of old school socks.
But over there – who knows?
It's unfamiliar territory.
A land of possibilities,
Shining maybe with magic and with miracles,
Where objects gleam and people smile.
Every bridge I cross
Might take me somewhere good.
New bright things might be found
And old dull things be lost.
I won't know till I've crossed.

*George Moore*

When do you feel bored? What do you wish would happen?
Can you imagine coming to a bridge you had never crossed
before? What would you like to find on the other side?
What did the person in the poem think might be found on the
other side?
What exciting things can you think of to do when you next
feel bored?

☆ Observe the transition of a bud into a flower and
draw or paint each stage.

**Project**
☆ Ask the children to collect information about their
lives to date enlisting the aid of parents if possible.
Include such items as how old they were when they
got their first teeth, walked, spoke their first words,
started nursery school. Include anecdotes about
funny or naughty things they did as toddlers, their
pets, favourite toys, and so on. Record these details
in books or make charts.

**Songs**
*Tinder-box:* 7 Song of the clock, 46 I went to the
cabbages, 49 Puff the magic dragon, 58 New things to
do, 65 One two three
*Subject index:* Days of the week, Growing and
changing, Seasons, Times of the day

**Stories**
"Bad Harry and the haircut" and "My Naughty Little
    Sister and the big girl's bed" from *All About My
    Naughty Little Sister* D. Edwards (Methuen)
*Barney Bipple's Magic Dandelions* C. Chapman
    (Warne)
*The Happy Owls* C. Piatti (Ernest Benn)
*Julia's Story* L. Berg (Macmillan)
*Once upon a time* B. Gilroy (Macmillan)
*Throne for Sesame* H. Young (Deutsch)

# Hobbies and skills

## Objectives
☐ To think of the things we do for enjoyment
☐ To explore special skills and interests
☐ To think about why we enjoy them

Our special interests and hobbies tell us a lot about ourselves. Children can learn to understand themselves better through examining the things they most enjoy doing.

## Starting points
○ Prepare a display of photographs of people of all ages using special skills – athletic, artistic, musical, technical, and so on.

○ Talk to the children about hobbies mentioning all kinds of things from collecting matchboxes to horse riding. Ask the children about their hobbies and special interests. Which hobbies are currently the most popular? Who has an unusual hobby? What would they like to do when they are older? What do their older brothers and sisters, mums and dads do?

○ With the children's help set up a display of popular hobbies (stamp collecting, train spotting, football), and ask children who take part in them to explain what they involve and why they enjoy them.

20

---

when I first tryed to do some cooking my dad said go and get the flour and I said its to high but he said have a try. and I stood on tip toe and with my little finger I pulled it down it fell down and spilt on the floor now I am taller and can reach it.

Katy Cosh. 6.

Wen I firts tried to swim I sank to the bottom and gurgled and I came up agein and spluttered But now I can swim properly

Tristram Hunt

Have any of you started a new hobby? What do you like about it? What do you find difficult about it? Are you getting better at doing it?

Are any of you learning a new skill like riding a bicycle or learning how to cook? Are you finding it difficult at first? How can you get better at it?

## Mark and his pictures

It can take a long time to learn how to do something really well, and you may have to try again and again:

Mark tore up his drawing. It never came right. All the lovely, exciting pictures he had in his head never seemed the same on paper. And when he showed his family –

"The paper's too big," said his father.

"The drawing's too small," said his mother.

"I can't see anything at all without my glasses," said his grandmother. "And I never know where they are!"

"Wait until you go back to school," called his friends. "They will teach you how to draw. Come and play!"

Mark shook his head. He wanted to draw now!

"I'll try to draw a shipwreck," he said stubbornly, "With a storm and raging waves."

But though he tried – and tried – and tried – it wouldn't come right. It was stiff – and it was dull!

"Oh," said Mark. And he tore the drawing up. "Oh," cried Mark. And he jumped on it. "Oh! Oh! Oh!" shouted Mark in a fury. And he ran out of the room and out of the house away into the garden. And he lay on his stomach under a bush.

"Whoosh!" said the wind. "I can help you! It's no good shouting and stamping, though: that's no way to learn. Now watch closely." And the wind began to blow.

The trees were blowing wildly and excitedly – bending, curving, swaying in the wind. The leaves were tossing and quivering all together – the clouds were drifting and racing in the sky. The flowers were nodding and shaking all their petals – seeds were floating everywhere and the grass was bending flat.

Mark ran to the water and noticed how it rippled – flowed and splashed and raced with the movement of the wind. In the roadways it was different for the houses were so strong. But fences shook and the tiles blew off, papers flew and doors slammed shut!

"I'm a whirlwind!" cried the wind. "A tearing huge tornado! I'm a gale, a gust, a summer breeze! I'm very restless, changing, moving. And that's what you need in your pictures! MOVEMENT! The movement of the wind! Now, go home and try!"

And Mark ran all the way back to his house, seized the paper and pencil and drew . . . and it was better!

For a while Mark was content. He found now that he could make things look as if they were moving in his drawings, and so they were never stiff or dull. But they still didn't look right, either. Once again he tried – and tried – and tried. But the pictures wouldn't come right. "Oh!" said Mark. And he crumpled them up. "Oh!" cried Mark. And he threw them out of the window. "Oh! Oh! Oh!" shouted Mark in a fury. And he ran out of the room and out of the house into the drizzling rain.

"Pitter patter! What's the matter?" said the rain. "I can help you! Now watch closely."

And the rain began to pour. Raindrops slanting down like arrows – making circles in the puddles. Puddles round and square and oblong, short and long and wide and narrow. Bouncing up like tiny fountains from the pavement, roads and paths.

"I'm a tumbling, thundering waterfall!" cried the rain. "I'm a whirlpool in the sea! I'm a wave – a ripple on the sand – a fountain and a shower! I make patterns by the hour on windows, roadways, everywhere. And that's what you need in your pictures! PATTERN! Now go home and try!"

And Mark ran all the way home and, wet as he was, seized the pencil and paper and drew. It was much, much better!

For a while Mark was very happy and he drew a great many pictures. They were full of excitement and the movement of the wind. They had good design and the pattern of the rain. But there was *still* something wrong. This time Mark didn't tear them up. He didn't even shout or cry. He just went thoughtfully into the garden and sat on the grass. And all he said was, "I wish I knew what to do."

"Hullo!" said the sun, coming out from behind a cloud. "I can help you! But it's no use just wishing. That's no way to learn. Now watch closely."

And the sun shone brighter, and brighter and brighter. And there was colour everywhere! Bright green grass and dark brown earth. Deep blue water sparkling with golden light. Brilliant flowers and scarlet berries, grey-green trees and purple fruit. Roof-tops brown and red and black, shining windows and whitest paint. Long grey streets and sunny gardens – gayest clothes and books and toys. Everywhere Mark looked was colour, bright and vivid, clear and strong.

"I'm flames and fire!" cried the sun. "I'm a ball of burning gold! I make the rainbow in the rain and the shadows on the ground. I'm strong, I'm bright, I'm beautiful, I'm the colour of the world! And that's what you need in your drawings. COLOUR! Now go home and try!"

And Mark ran all the way home, laughing in the sunshine and he seized his pencil, his paper and his paints: and he painted. And it was a really good picture.

And when he showed his family –

"That's fine!" said his father. "I'm proud of you!"

"That's wonderful!" said his mother. "You are clever!"

"Good gracious!" cried his grandmother. "It's so bright and beautiful I can see it without my glasses."

And Mark ran happily into the garden to join his friends.

*Carol Odell (slightly abridged)*

○ Ask an adult who has an interesting hobby or special skill (a footballer, rock climber, sitar player, weaver) into school to talk about it to the children. Ask them to bring some of their equipment to show to the children. They could explain what their hobby or skill involves, how they train for it, how much time they spend on it, what problems are involved, what is exciting about it.

○ Ask someone from the local library or community centre to tell the children about local facilities for hobbies and skills.

**Classroom activities**

**Language**

☆ Get the children to describe and illustrate their own or a family hobby or pastime.

☆ Visit a bakery, pottery, football ground or other place where the children can watch people using special skills. Describe the visit and illustrate it.

☆ Ask older children to give a detailed description in writing of the rules, techniques, background and history of a hobby or skill they enjoy or would like to take part in. Choose one or two of the children to present their work to the class.

**Mathematics**

☆ Make a hobby graph.

☆ With the children make a list of their interests and hobbies. After discussion put these in sets marked Alone and With others. At the intersection include things that can be done both alone and with others, (see page 30).

**For fun**

☆ Make a matchbox collection – see how many different items can be collected inside one matchbox.

## My Brother Bert

Pets are the Hobby of my Brother Bert.
He used to go to school with a Mouse in his shirt.

His Hobby it grew, as some hobbies will,
And grew and GREW and GREW until –

Oh don't breathe a word, pretend you haven't heard.
A simply appalling thing has occurred –

The very thought makes me iller and iller:
Bert's brought home a gigantic Gorilla!

If you think that's really not such a scare,
What if it quarrels with his Grizzly Bear?

You still think you could keep your head?
What if the Lion from under the bed

And the four Ostriches that deposit
Their football eggs in his bedroom closet

And the Aardvark out of his bottom drawer
All danced out and joined in the Roar?

What if the Pangolins were to caper
Out of their nests behind the wallpaper?

With the fifty sorts of Bats
That hang on his hatstand like old hats,

And out of a shoebox the excitable Platypus
Along with the Ocelot or Jungle-Cattypus?

The Wombat, the Dingo, the Gecko, the Grampus –
How they would shake the house with their Rumpus!

Not to forget the Bandicoot
Who would certainly peer from his battered old boot.

Why it could be a dreadful day,
And what Oh what would the neighbours say!

*Ted Hughes*

Do any of your hobbies get a little out of hand? What do you think Bert wanted to be when he grew up? What would you like to be?

## Johnny's pockets

Johnny collects
Conkers on strings,
Sycamore seeds
With aeroplane wings,
Green acorn cups,
Seaweed and shells,
Treasures from crackers
Like whistles and bells.

Johnny collects
Buttons and rings,
Bits of watch,
Cog wheels and springs,
Half-eaten sweets,
Nuts, nails and screws.
That's why his pockets
Bulge out of his trews.

*Alison Winn*

What kind of things do you like collecting?
Where do you keep them?
Where do you find them?
Why do you like those things so much?
What would you like to collect next?

# Anger

## Objectives

☐ To consider what makes us angry and why
☐ To explore how it feels to be angry
☐ To think about the consequences of being angry
☐ To discuss alternatives to reacting angrily

Anger is an important emotion to explore with young children. Sometimes they may get so angry that they lose control to the point of feeling murderous – a frightening experience which they may welcome sharing.

## Starting points

○ Set up a display of the children's artwork depicting anger (see classroom activities).

○ Talk to the children about the times when *you* get angry – with them, other people, yourself or whatever. Talk about what it feels like and what you do about it. Explain that everyone gets angry sometimes, adults as well as children. Ask them what makes *them* angry.

○ Ask a group of children to prepare an angry dance – stamping feet, slamming doors, shaking fists.

○ Another group of children could perform a piece of music describing anger (see classroom activities).

An eight-year-old girl describes how she felt when she was very very angry:

### Anger

I was angry and mad,
And it seemed that there was hot water inside me,
And as I got madder and madder,
The water got hotter and hotter all the time,
I was in a rage,
Then I began to see colours,
Like black and red,
Then as I got madder and madder,
My eyes began to pop out of my head,
They were popping up and down,
It was horrible,
And it would not stop,
I was steaming with anger,
Nobody could not stop me,
Then it was gone,
And I was all-right,
Horrible, black, madness.

*Yvonne Lowe, aged 8*

How does the girl describe her anger?
Can you think of a time when you felt as angry as this?
Can you think of a way to describe it?
Why do you think the girl didn't like feeling angry? (Anger can be frightening – you can feel out of control.)

When I am **angry** I get a headache and get hot and cross I feel so grumpy that I want to pull mummy's leg off and Run away and I feel like to throw potatos on the ground and squashing them.

Nina Baldry 6

### The Two Giants

Sometimes friends fall out with each other for very small and silly reasons:

Once, long ago, two Giants lived in a beautiful country. In summer it was warm, and in winter the land was even more beautiful under snow.

Each day the Giants walked together among the mountains and through the forests, taking care not to step on the trees. Birds made nests in their beards, and everywhere the Giants went, thrushes and nightingales sang.

→

## Classroom activities

### Language

☆ Ask the children about times when they have been angry and what happened as a result. They could write about or draw a cartoon strip of the events which led up to the incident and what happened after.

☆ With the children list the things which make us angry and discuss why they annoy us. Collect them together in an Angry Book with a different item and illustration of it for each page.

☆ Make a collection of words and phrases that describe anger, e.g.

| | |
|---|---|
| a bear with a sore head | steamed up |
| seething with rage | fiery tempered |
| blind with anger | furious |

Discuss why they are effective. The children can write them out in bold print using felt tip pens and mount them on a display of their written work and paintings.

### Mathematics

☆ Make a set of the things which annoy us and things which make others angry with us. Discuss which of them would fit into an intersection. (See *Fear*.)

One day while paddling in the sea, the two Giants found a pink shell. The shell was very bright and both Giants admired it.

"It will look lovely on a string round my neck," said the Giant called Boris.

"Oh no! It will be on a string round *my* neck," said Sam, the other Giant, "and it will look better there."

For the first time in their lives they began to argue. And as they did the sun went behind a cloud and the cloud became bigger and blacker. The wind blew and blew and the waves and clouds grew and grew. It began to rain. The more the Giants argued, the colder the day became. The waves swept higher and higher up the beach.

The Giants were furious and threw stones at each other as they ran towards the mountains to escape the flood. Soon the whole country was covered by water except for the tops of two mountains, which became the only islands in a wide, cold sea. Boris lived in one and Sam in the other.

It was cold. They liked snow, but it never snowed. Each day was just dull and terribly cold.

They grew more angry than ever, and instead of stones they now threw huge rocks at each other.

After both Giants had been struck many times on the ear and nose and the tops of their heads, their anger knew no limits. The sea was dotted with rocks which the Giants had thrown, and one day Sam decided to use these rocks as giant stepping-stones. He waited until Boris was asleep, then picked up his huge stone club and climbed out of his mountain. Sam leapt on to the first rock. Then he leapt on to the second rock. As Sam reached the third rock, Boris opened one giant eye. He saw Sam, snatched his club and, whirling it round his head, jumped out of his mountain and began leaping from rock to rock towards his enemy. The whole world shook as the two Giants charged towards each other.

Suddenly both Giants stopped. Sam looked at the feet of Boris. Boris looked at the feet of Sam. Each Giant had one black-and-white sock and one red-and-blue sock. They stared at their odd socks for a long time. Gradually they remembered the day the sea had covered the land. In their haste to escape the flood, the Giants had got their socks mixed. Now they could not even remember what they had been fighting about. They could only recall the years they had been friends. They dropped their clubs into the sea, and laughed and danced.

When they returned to their islands, each found a small white flower and felt the sun warm on his shoulders. The sea began to recede. Flowers grew where the water had been. The birds returned to the islands. Soon the two mountains were separated by nothing but a valley of trees. The country was large and beautiful once more.

*Michael Foreman (slightly abridged)*

Do you think the two giants had a good reason for getting so angry?
Can you remember getting angry with someone because you wanted something they had first?
Have you stopped being friends with someone because you quarrelled over something silly? What did you quarrel about?
When do you think it is silly to get angry? (When someone hurts you by mistake, when you don't win a game, when people tease you.)
When do you think it is *right* to get angry?

## The Ugsome Thing

An old woman keeps her temper when everything around her goes wrong:

There was once a monster called the Ugsome Thing. He was round and fat and scaly and he had long teeth twisted like sticks of barley sugar. He lived in a castle and had many servants to wait on him.

The Ugsome Thing had a magic power, and if he could make anyone lose his temper, that person became his slave and had to obey him. Now, as he went through the village near his castle, he passed a cottage garden which was full, on a Monday, of the whitest clothes he had ever seen. He decided to make the old woman who lived there come and do his washing. It would be very simple. He only had to make her lose her temper and she would be in his power.

So one Monday morning, when her clothes-line was full of the whitest wash possible, he cut the line with his knife and the snowy clothes lay tumbled on the dirty grass. Surely that would make her lose her temper.

When the old woman saw what had happened, she came running out of the door, but instead of losing her temper she said quietly, "Well! Well! Well! The chimney has been smoking this morning and I'm sure some smuts must have blown on my washing. Anyway it will be a good idea to wash it again. How lucky that the line broke just this morning and no other!"

So she picked up armfuls of the dirty clothes and went back to the wash-house, singing as she went.

The Ugsome Thing was very angry and he gnashed his barley sugar teeth, but he soon thought of another idea to make her lose her temper.

On Tuesday the Ugsome Thing visited the old woman again. He saw that she had milked her cow, Daisy, and that the milk stood in a pan in the dairy. He turned the whole pan of milk sour. Surely that would make her lose her temper. When the old woman saw the pan of sour milk she said. "Well! Well! Well! Now I shall have to make it into cream cheese and that will be a treat for my grandchildren when they come to tea. They love having cream cheese on their scones. How lucky the milk turned sour today and no other!"

On Wednesday the Ugsome Thing turned all the hollyhocks in the old woman's garden into thistles but instead of losing her temper she made pin-cushions stuffed with thistledown. On Thursday the Ugsome Thing tripped the old woman up and hurt her knee but instead of losing her temper she

enjoyed a restful day lying on the sofa making a quilt. On Friday the Ugsome Thing made her drop a basket of eggs but she made scrambled eggs, her favourite food, for dinner.

Now the Ugsome Thing was very angry indeed and he gnashed his barley sugar teeth, but he soon thought of another idea to make her lose her temper. This idea was a very nasty one, because he was very, very angry indeed. On Saturday the Ugsome Thing set the old woman's cottage on fire. Surely that would make her lose her temper. The flames shot up the walls and soon the thatched roof caught fire.

"Well! Well! Well!" said the old woman. "That's the last of my old cottage. I was fond of it, but it was falling to pieces and the roof let in the rain and there were holes in the floor."

When the Ugsome Thing came along to see if the old woman had lost her temper, he found her busy baking potatoes in the hot ashes, and handing them round to the village children.

"Have a potato?" she said to the Ugsome Thing, holding one out on the point of a stick.

It smelled so good that the Ugsome Thing took it and crammed it into his mouth whole, because he was very greedy, and some of it went down the wrong way. He choked so hard with rage and hot potato that he burst like a balloon and there was nothing left but a piece of shrivelled, scaly, greenish skin.

By this time, most of the people in the village were lining up to have a baked potato, and while they waited they planned how they could help the old woman.

"I'll build the walls of a new cottage," said one.

"I'll make the roof," said another.

"I'll put in the windows," said a third.

By the time all the potatoes were cooked and eaten, her friends had promised the old woman all she needed for a new cottage.

*Ruth Ainsworth (slightly abridged)*

**Dance and drama**

☆ Discuss how we express our anger in our movements, actions and facial expressions and try demonstrating this in dance and mime.

**Art**

☆ Discuss what colours the children would use to depict anger, e.g. red, orange or purple. Ask them about the reasons for their choice. Paint angry figures, faces or patterns using the angry colours.

**Music**

☆ Taking the words and phrases describing anger which you have collected (see above) discuss how they might be represented musically. Ask the children for suggestions of instruments or voice sounds they might use for "steamed up" or "fiery tempered". Bring their ideas together to form a short piece of angry music.

**Songs**

*Tinder-box:* 9 The angry song, 53 Why does it have to be me

*Subject index:* Anger

**Stories**

"The fairy doll" from *All About My Naughty Little Sister* D. Edwards (Methuen)

*I Was So Mad I Could Have Split Book* G. Frisen and P. Ekholm (Black)

# Happiness and sadness

**Objectives**

☐ To think about the things which make us feel happy or sad

☐ To consider how it feels to be happy or sad

☐ To think of ways of helping other people and ourselves to feel happy

Initially, it may help young children to understand the feelings of happiness and sadness by contrasting them.

**Starting points**

○ Make a display of children's paintings and written work describing things which make them happy or sad (see classroom activities).

○ Discuss with the children how they are feeling today – happy or sad? How many of them are feeling happy because something good is going to happen? What is going to happen? How many of them are feeling sad because the day started badly – someone was cross with them or they fell on the way to school? What other things make them sad? What things make them happy?

○ Dramatise the story of the *The Little Brute Family* illustrating how a "little good feeling" can change us all from feeling miserable to feeling happy.

## It is grey out

It is grey out.
It is grey in.
In me
It is as grey as the day is grey.
The trees look sad
And I,
Not knowing why I do,
Cry.

*Karla Kuskin*

Do you ever feel sad without knowing why?
What is grey outside?
Is this a good description of the way you feel when you are sad? Do you feel grey inside?
Can you think of other ways of describing your sadness?
What can you do about sadness? (Wait for it to pass, do something you know you will enjoy.)

## June 9th

I feel lonely when I have to play by myself.
And no one wants to play with me.
It's as though I had the plague or something.
My mum and dad are always telling me off,
My brothers and sisters run away when they see me,
I'm not wanted,
Why is it always me?
Why? why? me?

*James McFadyzean, aged 9*

Have you ever felt like this?
Why do you think no one wants to play with the boy?
What could he do to feel better? (Help his mum and dad, think of something to do on his own.)

Simple things can make you feel happy:

## The friendly cinnamon bun

Shining in his stickiness and glistening with honey,
Safe among his sisters and his brothers on a tray,
With raisin eyes that looked at me as I put down my money,
There smiled a friendly cinnamon bun, and this I heard him say:

"It's a lovely, lovely morning, and the world's a lovely place;
I know it's going to be a lovely day.
I know we're going to be good friends; I like your honest face;
Together we might go a long, long way."

The baker's girl rang up the sale, "I'll wrap your bun," said she.
"Oh no, you needn't bother," I replied.
I smiled back at that cinnamon bun and ate him, one two three,
And walked out with his friendliness inside.

*Russell Hoban*

What did the bun look like? Why did it make the boy feel happy?
What kind of things do you like to eat? Why do they make you feel happy?
What other things make you feel happy? (A sunny day, playing a game, reading a funny story.)

## I get very frightened when my mum and dad quarrel

Grown ups get cross sometimes too:

I get very frightened when my mum and dad quarrel. I don't like it when they shout or are rude to each other. I cry and try to make them stop.

Sometimes I hide in my bed and pull the eiderdown over my head so that I can't hear anything.

When my mum and dad have made it up, we are very happy. Then I am glad I've got such nice parents.

Sometimes it doesn't help to cry ...

# The sad story of a little boy that cried

Once a little boy, Jack, was, oh! ever so good,
Till he took a strange notion to cry all he could.

So he cried all the day, and he cried all the night,
He cried in the morning and in the twilight;

He cried till his voice was as hoarse as a crow,
And his mouth grew so large it looked like a great O.

It grew at the bottom, and grew at the top;
It grew till they thought that it never would stop.

Each day his great mouth grew taller and taller,
And his dear little self grew smaller and smaller.

At last, that same mouth grew so big that – alack! –
It was only a mouth with a border of Jack.

*Author unknown*

Do you ever cry? When? Why?
Do you find it difficult to stop crying?
Do you feel better afterwards or worse? Why?

When I feel happy I sometimes play with my friends and when I feel angry I push a table against the door and then I sulk.

Sophie King. 7

... other times it does.

# Tear-water tea

Owl took the kettle out of the cupboard. "Tonight I will make tear-water tea," he said. He put the kettle on his lap. "Now," said Owl, "I will begin."

Owl sat very still. He began to think of things that were sad. "Chairs with broken legs," said Owl. His eyes began to water. "Songs that cannot be sung," said Owl, "because the words have been forgotten."

Owl began to cry. A large tear rolled down and dropped into the kettle. "Spoons that have fallen behind the stove and are never seen again," said Owl. More tears dropped down into the kettle. "Books that cannot be read," said Owl, "because some of the pages have been torn out."

"Clocks that have stopped," said Owl, "with no one near to wind them up." Owl was crying. Many large tears dropped into the kettle.

"Mornings nobody saw because everybody was sleeping," sobbed Owl. "Mashed potatoes left on a plate," he cried, "because no one wanted to eat them. And pencils that are too short to use."

Owl thought about many other sad things. He cried and cried. Soon the kettle was all filled up with tears.

"There," said Owl. "That does it!" Owl stopped crying. He put the kettle on the stove to boil for tea. Owl felt happy as he filled his cup. "It tastes a little bit salty," he said, "but tear-water tea is always very good."

*Arnold Lobel*

What did the owl think of to make himself cry?
What makes you feel sad?
What makes you feel better?

## Classroom activities
### Language
☆ Discuss the good things which happen to us – the things which make us happy, excited or contented. Ask the children to think of the contrasting things which make us sad:

> Praise makes us happy ... makes us sad
> Being loved makes us happy ... makes us sad

☆ Ask the children to choose one thing which makes them really happy or really sad then write about it and illustrate it. You could give younger children a structure to help them:

> Happiness is a (birthday present, a warm cuddle, a sunny day)
> Sadness is ...

☆ Make up a recipe of sad things for making *Tear-water tea*.

### Art
☆ Ask the children to use their imaginations to draw or paint a picture of the "little good feeling" from *The Little Brute Family*.

☆ Make happy and sad masks for display in class or assembly.

☆ Make smiley badges which can be reversed to give a frown:

27

## The Little Brute Family

A little good feeling shows the Brutes how to enjoy themselves:

In the middle of a dark and shadowy woods lived a little family of Brutes. There were Papa Brute, Mama Brute, Brother and Sister Brute and Baby Brute. Baby Brute howled between spoonfuls. Brother and Sister Brute kicked each other under the table, and Mama and Papa made faces while they ate.

After breakfast Papa Brute took up his sack and went off to gather sticks and stones. Mama stayed home to thump the furniture and bang the pots and scold the baby. And Brother and Sister pushed and shoved and punched and pinched their way to school.

In the evenings Mama served a stew of sticks and stones, and the family ate it with growls and grumbling. Then they groaned and went to sleep. That was how they lived. They never laughed and said, "Delightful!" They never smiled and said, "How lovely!"

In the spring the little Brutes made heavy kites that bumped along the ground and would not fly. In the summer they flung themselves into the pond and sank like stones but never learned to swim. In the fall they jumped into great piles of leaves and stamped on one another, yelling. In the winter they leaped upon their crooked clumsy sleds that took them crashing into snowbanks where they stuck headfirst and screamed.

That was how they lived in the dark and shadowy woods. Then one day Baby Brute found a little wandering lost good feeling in a field of daisies, and he caught it in his paw and put it in his tiny pocket. And he felt so good that he laughed and said, "How lovely."

Baby Brute felt good all afternoon, and at supper when his bowl was filled with stew he said, "Thank you." Then the little good feeling flew out of his tiny pocket and hovered over the table, humming and smiling. "How lovely!" said Mama, without even snarling. "Delightful!" said Papa, forgetting to growl. "Oh, please," said the little Brutes together, "let it stay with us!" And Papa smiled and said, "All right."

When Papa Brute went out for sticks and stones the next day, he found wild berries, salad greens, and honey, and he brought them home instead. At supper everyone said, "How delicious!" because it *was* delicious, and everyone said, "Please" and "Thank you." And they never ate stick and stone stew again. Then the little good feeling stopped wandering and stayed with the little Brute family.

When springtime came the little Brutes made bright new kites that flew high in the sky, and in the summer they swam beautifully. In the fall they gathered nuts and acorns that they roasted by a cozy fire when winter came. And in the evening they sang songs together. The little good feeling stayed and stayed and never went away, and when springtime came again the little Brute family changed their name to Nice.

*Russell Hoban*

What was life like for the Brute Family before they met the little good feeling?
How did it change their behaviour?

## What a day

What a day,
Oh what a day.
My baby brother ran away,
And now my tuba will not play.
I'm eight years old
And turning grey,
Oh what a day,
Oh what a day.

*Shel Silverstein*

**Songs**
*Tinder-box:* 10 Poor child, 49 Ladybird, 50 Puff the magic dragon, 57 Maja pade – Let's all be happy
*Subject index:* Celebration, Happiness, Sadness

**Stories**
*The Happy Owls* C. Piatti (Benn)
*I Should Have Stayed in Bed* J. M. Lexau (World's Work)
*Miserable Aunt Bertha* J. V. Lord and F. Maschler (Cape)
"The Well-off Kid" from *The Goalkeeper's Revenge* B. Naughton (Heinemann)

**Information books**
*How We Feel* A. Harper (Kestrel)

# Fear

## Objectives
☐ To consider what kinds of things are frightening and why
☐ To explore how it feels to be frightened
☐ To differentiate between rational and irrational fears
☐ To consider times when fear is fun
☐ To discuss ways of facing fear

Whilst they can list many of the causes for feeling afraid, few children have given much thought to the way it actually feels to be afraid, or what kind of physical changes to the body fear produces. Most do not realise that being afraid can sometimes be useful or indeed that slight fear can be fun, even though they often choose to read frightening stories or play games designed to make them feel scared.

## Starting points
○ Talk about the things which frighten *you* then ask the children about their fears. Some fears may seem silly to others but are nevertheless very real. Try to encourage respect for other people's fears. *Lion at school* could be used as a basis for a discussion on this – the little girl was not afraid of the lion but she did fear the bully. The bully on the other hand was terrified of the lion.

○ Get the children to imagine themselves in a frightening situation and ask them how they would feel. For example – Imagine you are in a cold, dark place at night. It is so dark that you can't see where you are. You can hear strange noises but don't know what they are. You are alone and lost. How do you feel? What do you think is going to happen?

○ A class can prepare a background tape of spooky noises to help create a scary atmosphere in assembly or to accompany a reading of *Shadows* or *In the dark* (see classroom activities).

○ Ask a fire safety officer, coastguard or traffic policeman into the school to talk to the children about real dangers they have need to fear and how to behave sensibly in dangerous situations.

## Shadows

I can feel someone is here;
My stiff head turns round, as a black shape follows
   me.
Timidly I walk, it's following me.
My dry throat tells it to go away
But nothing it replies;
Panic strikes me,
My legs want to walk,
I am still.
No use, it's still there.
Then my wet frightened body slithers into bed,
   under the cover.
I am alone.

*Kamala Panday*

## In the dark

One night I was going along
   the street
And I heard a big crash
So I ran and all the stars
   began to disappear
And I ran more and more and
   then the lights along
   the street went out and
   I did not know what to
   do, I heard footsteps
   coming towards me.
And I saw a shining torch
   behind me so I screamed
   and I woke up, and all
   it was, was a dream.

*Julie Cashman*

What is the child in the poem frightened of?
What things are you frightened of at night-time?
Why are you scared of some things at night when you're not scared of them in the daytime?
How do you feel when you are frightened?
What do you like about night-time?

## Bump

Things that go "bump!" in the night,
Should not really give one a fright.
It's the hole in each ear
That lets in the fear,
That and the absence of light!

*Spike Milligan*

When I Am In Bed
When I'm in bed I dream about dragons
They scare me in my dream
Dragon goes puff puff puff
And he puffs flames over my bed
Matthew Robins 5

## Classroom activities

### Language

☆ Discuss how it feels to be frightened. What happens to us? e.g.

> we scream and cry
> our hearts beat faster
> our hands get hot and sweaty
> we shiver and shake
> we can't breathe properly
> we can't think quickly

☆ Ask the children to write about one of the following:

> The time when I was really frightened
> My worst nightmare
> When I like being frightened

☆ Write a horror story

### Mathematics

☆ Make a set of things which are afraid of us – mice, insects, birds – and a set of things we are afraid of – ghosts, angry parents, high cliffs. Make the point that many things we fear may also be afraid of us. Make an intersection of the two sets for this category. Mount two large intersecting circles on sugar paper, ask the children to draw the things they want to include then pin their pictures into the circles.

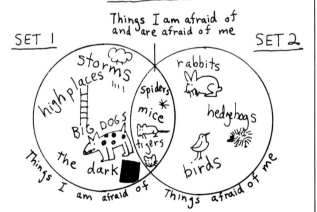

## The playground (extract)

Fear of falling:

Just where the river curled out to meet the sea was the town playground, and next to the playground in a tall cream-coloured house lived Linnet. Every day after school she stood for a while at her window watching the children over the fence, and longing to run out and join them. She could hear the squeak squeak of the swings going up and down, up and down all afternoon. She could see children bending their knees pushing themselves up into the sky. She would think to herself, "Yes, I'll go down now. I won't stop to think about it. I'll run out and have a turn on the slide," but then she would feel her hands getting hot and stomach shivery, and she knew she was frightened again.

"Why should I be so scared?" she wondered. "If only I could get onto the swings and swing without thinking about it I'd be all right."

*Margaret Mahy*

## Ants live here

> Ants live here
> by the curb stone
>     see?
> They worry a lot
> about people like
>     me.

*Lilian Moore*

Why are the ants worried?
If you were an ant what would you be worried about?
When is it sensible for you to be afraid? (Crossing a busy road, talking to strangers, playing beside a river.)

What do you think Linnet was frightened of?
What would help Linnet to stop feeling frightened?
Can you think of things you have been frightened of doing?
What do you think grown ups are frightened of?

## I'm scared to cross the road on my own

I'm scared to cross the road on my own. My mum and dad have told me how dangerous it is, and when I try to cross there are always cars.

Even though they are right at the other end of the street, they drive so fast that I haven't got time to cross.

When mum is with me she holds my hand and we always use the zebra crossing. Even then I'm afraid when a car is coming. What if the driver hasn't seen us and runs us over!

How can you stop being frightened of crossing the road? (Learn the Green Cross Code – go through this with the children.)

# Lion at school (extract)

*Once upon a time a little girl, who didn't like going to school because she was afraid of being bullied, met a lion. They made friends with each other and the lion went to school with her for the day:*

All that morning the lion sat up on his chair next to the little girl, like a big cat, with his tail curled round his front paws, as good as gold.

He didn't speak unless the teacher spoke to him. He didn't growl, he didn't roar. At playtime the little girl showed the lion how to drink milk through a straw.

He finished his milk up. They went into the playground.

All the children stopped playing to stare at the lion. Then they went on playing again. The little girl stood in a corner of the playground, with the lion beside her.

"Why don't we play like the others?" the lion asked.

The little girl said: "I don't like playing because some of the big boys are so big and rough. They knock you over without meaning to."

The lion growled. "They wouldn't knock ME over," he said.

"There's one big boy – the very biggest," said the little girl. "His name is Jack Tall. He knocks me over on purpose."

All the big boys were running about, and the very biggest boy, Jack Tall, came running towards the little girl. He was running in circles, closer and closer to the little girl.

"Go away," said the lion. "You might knock my friend over. Go away."

"Shan't," said Jack Tall.

The little girl got behind the lion. The lion began to swish his tail: *Swish! Swash!* Jack Tall was running closer and closer and closer. The lion growled. Then Jack Tall saw the lion's teeth as sharp as skewers and knives. He stopped running. He stood still. He stared.

The lion opened his mouth wider – so wide that Jack Tall could see his throat, opened wide and deep and dark like a tunnel to go into. Jack Tall went pale.

Then the lion roared.

He roared and he ROARED and he **ROARED**.

All the teachers came running out to see what the matter was. All the children stopped playing and stuck their fingers in their ears. And the biggest boy, Jack Tall, turned round and ran and ran and ran – out through the playground – out through the school gates – along the streets. He never stopped running until he got home to his mother.

The little girl came out from behind the lion.

"Well," she said, "I don't think much of *him*. I shall never be scared of *him* again."

On Monday morning the little girl started in good time for school, because she was looking forward to it. She arrived in good time, too.

She did not see the lion.

Later on, in the playground, the biggest boy came up to the little girl.

"Where's your friend that talks so loudly?" he said.

"He's not here today," said the little girl.

"Might he come another day?" asked the biggest boy.

"He might," said the little girl. "He easily might. So you watch out, Jack Tall."

*Philippa Pearce*

Why did Jack Tall stop bullying the little girl?
Can you think of times when you have been frightened in the playground? Why were you frightened?
How do you think you should behave when you are playing with other children at school?

## Art

☆ Make masks of faces which are frightening or frightened.

☆ Paint a frightening situation.

## Drama

☆ Discuss how people act and look when they are being frightening or are frightened. Divide the children into pairs, one to be frightening and the other frightened.

☆ Arrange the children in a circle. Get each child in turn to make frightening or frightened sounds or statements.

☆ Base a short play on *Lion at school*.

## Music

☆ Experiment with voices and instruments to make a short piece of scary music. Begin by discussing sounds which are frightening. You could use the poem "Shadows" to stimulate the children's ideas.

## The adventures of Isabel

Isabel met an enormous bear,
Isabel, Isabel, didn't care;
The bear was hungry, the bear was ravenous,
The bear's big mouth was cruel and cavernous.
The bear said, Isabel, glad to meet you,
How do, Isabel, now I'll eat you!
Isabel, Isabel, didn't worry,
Isabel didn't scream or scurry,
She washed her hands and she straightened her
    hair up,
Then Isabel quietly ate the bear up.

Once in a night as black as pitch
Isabel met a wicked witch.
The witch's face was cross and wrinkled,
The witch's gums with teeth were sprinkled.
Ho ho, Isabel! the old witch crowed,
I'll turn you into an ugly toad!
Isabel, Isabel, didn't worry,
Isabel didn't scream or scurry,
She showed no rage, she showed no rancor,
But she turned the witch into milk and drank her.

Isabel met a hideous giant,
Isabel continued self-reliant.
The giant was hairy, the giant was horrid,
He had one eye in the middle of his forehead.
Good morning, Isabel, the giant said,
I'll grind your bones to make my bread.
Isabel, Isabel, didn't worry,
Isabel didn't scream or scurry.
She nibbled the zwieback that she always fed off,
And when it was gone, she cut the giant's head off.

Isabel met a troublesome doctor,
He punched and he poked till he really shocked her.
The doctor's talk was of coughs and chills
And the doctor's satchel bulged with pills.
The doctor said unto Isabel,
Swallow this, it will make you well.
Isabel, Isabel, didn't worry,
Isabel didn't scream or scurry.
She took those pills from the pill concoctor,
And Isabel calmly cured the doctor.

Isabel once was asleep in bed
When a horrible dream crawled into her head.
It was worse than a dinosaur, worse than a shark,
Worse than an octopus oozing in the dark.
"Boo!" said the dream, with a dreadful grin,
"I'm going to scare you out of your skin!"
Isabel, Isabel, didn't worry,
Isabel didn't scream or scurry,
Isabel had a cleverer scheme;
She just woke up and fooled that dream.

Whenever you meet a bugaboo
Remember what Isabel used to do.
Don't scream when the bugaboo says "Boo!"
Just look it in the eye and say, "Boo to you!"
That's how to banish a bugaboo;
Isabel did it and so can you.
Boooooo to you.
                                    *Ogden Nash*

Who did Isabel meet? What were they like? What did they threaten to do to Isabel? How did Isabel behave?
Have you found ways to stop being frightened of things like bad dreams and the dark?
What can you do next time you feel frightened?

**Songs**
*Tinder-box:* 11 All alone in the house, 37 City beasts, 61 Halloween is coming
*Subject index:* Fear, Ghosts, Halloween

**Stories**
*Albin is Never Afraid* U. Lofgren (Macdonald)
*Bears in the Night* Berenstain and Berenstain (Collins)
*Black Dog* C. Mattingley (Bodley Head)
*The Book Mice* T. Knowles (Evans)
*Can I Cross the Road?* (Church Information Office Benjamin Books)
*Creepies* H. Hoke (Franklin Watts)
*Creepy Creatures* B. Ireson (Beaver)
*Devil-in-the-fog* L. Garfield (Constable Young Books)
*The Ghost Diviners* E. Mace (Deutsch)
*The Ghost Downstairs* L. Garfield (Puffin)
*Ghostly Experiences* S. Dickinson (Lion)
*Grimbold's Other World* N. S. Gray (Faber)
*Haunting Tales* B. Ireson (Puffin)
*Jeremy Mouse* Althea (Dinosaur)
*Lost in a Shop* R. Parker (Macmillan)
*My Brother Sean* P. Breinburg (Bodley Head/Puffin)
*Not What You Think* S. Weigel/G. Marsh (Dent)
*The Owl Who Was Afraid of the Dark* J. Tomlinson (Methuen/Puffin)
*Sally-Ann in the Snow* P. Breinburg (Bodley Head)
*There's a Crocodile Under My Bed* I. and D. Schubert (Hutchinson)
*There's a Nightmare in My Cupboard* M. Mayer (Dent)
*What Are You Scared Of* H. Larsen (Black)
*Where the Wild Things Are* M. Sendak (Bodley Head)

I like fairy tales because they are scary They make me have nightmares. But I dont care. Hannah Davies 6

# Food, shelter, exercise and rest

## Objectives
☐ To think about the need for food, shelter, rest and exercise
☐ To consider why we need them

Encourage the children to think about some of the things their bodies need for health, strength and in order to work well.

## Starting points
*Food*
○ Make a display of photographs or children's paintings of foods which contain protein, vitamins, fats, sugars, and roughage. Discuss why we need food – it gives us energy, keeps us warm, protects us from illness, without it we would die. Explain about the particular foods which are necessary to strengthen the bones, keep the skin healthy and so on. Ask the children how they feel when they haven't eaten for a long time. How does it feel to be hungry? How do they feel when they have just eaten well?

○ Make a grocery display with food from as many different parts of the world as possible. Use the display to stimulate discussion about the origin of the food, how it is grown, how it gets to the shops, how it is cooked. You could use empty food packets, photographs and real food if possible.

○ With the children's help make a list of dishes, e.g. spaghetti bolognese, rice and peas, hamburgers, shepherd's pie, fufu, cous cous, pancake roll, curry. Ask the children if they know what ingredients are used to make them, how they are made, and what they look and taste like.

○ Prepare simple foods in assembly and share them with everyone, e.g. drop scones, popodoms, peppermint drops.

○ Discuss why certain foods are eaten or avoided on special occasions or by certain people. Why are eggs special at Easter, pancakes on Shrove Tuesday? What is a vegetarian? What does *kosher* mean?

---

## Everybody said no!

The food we eat takes a long time and a lot of hard work to grow:

Mrs Mudd had a very big family. She had a husband called Mr Mudd. She had four big children called John and Sally and Dick and Betty. She had a dog called Jackson and a cat called Hoover. And she had a baby called Little Joe. Mrs Mudd had to work very hard looking after them all.

One day, Mrs Mudd bought an apple tree in the market and brought it home.

"Look at this lovely little apple tree!" she said to her big family. "Would anybody like to help me plant it in the garden?"

But everybody said no! Mr Mudd was very busy reading the newspaper. John and Sally had to do their homework. Dick was brushing his teeth. Betty was washing her doll. Jackson was trying to bury his bone under the sofa. Hoover was watching the goldfish swimming round in the bowl. And Little Joe was just too little. So Mrs Mudd had to plant the apple tree all by herself.

In the summer the sun was very hot and the earth dry and hard. The leaves on the little apple tree began to droop and wilt.

"Look at our poor little apple tree!" said Mrs Mudd to her big family. "Would anybody like to help me water it?"

But everybody said no! Mr Mudd was busy snoozing in a deckchair in the garden. John and Sally were painting a picture. Dick had to polish his shoes. Betty was knitting new pink socks for her doll. Hoover was climbing the lilac tree. And Little Joe was too little. So Mrs Mudd had to water the apple tree all by herself.

In the autumn the apple tree was covered in big juicy apples. "Look at all the apples on our apple tree!" said Mrs Mudd. "Would anybody like to help me pick them?"

But everybody said no! Mr Mudd was very busy watching a football match on T.V. John and Sally were playing snakes and ladders. Dick was combing his hair. Betty was sewing a new skirt for her doll. Jackson was asleep under the sofa. Hoover was dipping his paw in the goldfish bowl. And Little Joe was too little. So Mrs Mudd had to pick the apples all by herself. Soon Mrs Mudd had picked a whole basketful of apples. She took them into the house.

"Look at this lovely basketful of apples!" said Mrs Mudd to her large family. "Would anybody like to help me bake a nice apple pie for supper?"

But everybody said no! Mr Mudd was very busy writing a letter to his bank manager. John and Sally were cutting out pictures from a magazine. Dick had to tidy his bedroom. Betty was dancing with her doll. Jackson was chewing his bone on the rug. Hoover was cleaning his whiskers. And Little Joe was still too little. So Mrs Mudd had to bake the apple pie all by herself.

When the pie was ready she took it out of the oven. It was piping hot and golden brown and smelt delicious. Mrs Mudd carried it into the living-room.

"Look at this lovely apple pie!" she said to her big family. "Would anybody like to help me eat it?"

And everybody said **yes!**

*Sheila Lavelle (slightly abridged)*

What did Mrs Mudd have to do for the apple tree to grow strong and bear apples?
How long did it take for the apples to grow?
What other things do you need to make an apple pie? Where do you think the ingredients come from? Where are they grown?
What other things do you think Mrs Mudd's family ate?
What is your favourite food? Where does it come from? How is it made?

*Shelter*

○ Discuss buildings using a display of photographs or slides if possible. Show as wide a variety as you can. What is the building the children are in now? What is it used for? What other kinds of building are there? What are they used for?

Discuss why buildings in this country often have thick walls and sloping roofs. When are the children most glad to be indoors? Discuss the kinds of materials used to make buildings – bricks, concrete, wood, tin, mud, grass, snow, skin. Why are different materials used in different climates. Why would mud bricks be unsuitable for this country?

○ Make a display of clothes designed for different climates and seasons – a group of children could dress up in them. Discuss the fabrics used to make them – wools, tweeds and furs for cold climates, cottons and silks for hot climates.

*Exercise*

○ Make a display of photographs of athletes. Discuss why we need exercise. How do we feel without it?

○ Get a group of children to perform a dance game, e.g. *Brown girl in the ring* or *The farmer's in his den*. What do they enjoy about games? Why are playtimes important? What would it be like if they had to stay sitting down all day long?

*Rest*

○ Display children's paintings of a dream they have had and talk about the need for sleep. Scientists have tried to find out what happens when we don't get enough sleep. After two nights we become very tired and find it harder and harder to stay awake. We make mistakes, forget things, and get cross with friends. Finally we cannot stay awake any longer. Our bodies need sleep in order to work well.

## Miss T

It's a very odd thing –
    As odd as can be –
That whatever Miss T eats
    Turns into Miss T;
Porridge and apples,
    Mince, muffins and mutton,
Jam, junket, jumbles –
    Not a rap, not a button
It matters; the moment
    They're out of her plate,
Though shared by Miss Butcher
    And sour Mr Bate;
Tiny and cheerful,
    And neat as can be,
Whatever Miss T eats
    Turns into Miss T.

*Walter de la Mare*

What do you enjoy about eating? How do you think the food you eat changes into you?

## Christmas dinner

Almanzo bowed his head and shut his eyes tight while Father said the blessing. It was a long blessing, because this was Christmas Day. But at last Almanzo could open his eyes. He sat and silently looked at that table.

He looked at the crisp, crackling little pig lying on the blue platter with an apple in its mouth. He looked at the fat roast goose, the drumsticks sticking up, and the edges of dressing curling out. The sound of Father's knife sharpening on the whetstone made him even hungrier.

He looked at the big bowl of cranberry jelly, and at the fluffy mountain of mashed potatoes with melting butter trickling down it. He looked at the heap of mashed turnips, and the golden baked squash, and the pale fried parsnips.

He swallowed hard and tried not to look any more. He couldn't help seeing the fried apples'n'onions, and the candied carrots. He couldn't help gazing at the triangles of pie, waiting by his plate; the spicy pumpkin pie, the melting cream pie, the rich, dark mince oozing from between the mince pie's flaky crusts.

He squeezed his hands together between his knees. He had to sit silent and wait, but he felt aching and hollow inside.

All grown-ups at the head of the table must be served first. They were passing their plates, and talking, and heartlessly laughing. The tender pork fell away in slices under Father's carving-knife. The white breast of the goose went piece by piece from the bare breast-bone. Spoons ate up the clear cranberry jelly, and gouged deep into the mashed potatoes, and ladled away the brown gravies.

Almanzo had to wait to the very last. He was youngest of all, except Abner and the babies, and Abner was company.

At last Almanzo's plate was filled. The first taste made a pleasant feeling inside him, and it grew and grew, while he ate and ate and ate. He ate till he could eat no more, and he felt very good inside. For a while he slowly nibbled bits from his second piece of fruitcake. Then he put the fruity slice in his pocket and went out to play.

*From* Farmer Boy *by Laura Ingalls Wilder*

Why did Almanzo have to wait till last to be served his Christmas dinner? How did he feel as he waited?

# Jamaica market

Honey, pepper, leaf-green limes,
Pagan fruit whose names are
   rhymes,
Mangoes, breadfruit, ginger-roots,
Granadillas, bamboo-shoots,
Cho-cho, ackees, tangerines,
Lemons, purple congo-beans,
Sugar, akras, kola-nuts,
Citrons, hairy coconuts,
Fish, tobacco, native hats,
Gold bananas, woven mats,
Plantains, wild-thyme, pallid
   leeks,
Pigeons with their scarlet beaks,
Oranges and saffron yams,
Baskets, ruby guava jams,
Turtles, goat skins,
Allspice, conch-shells, golden
   rum.
Black skins, babel – and the sun
That burns all colours into one.

*Agnes Maxwell-Hall*

# School Dinners

If you stay to school dinners
Better throw them aside:
A lot of kids didn't,
A lot of kids died.

The meat is made of iron,
The spuds are made of steel,
And if that don't get you
The afters will!

*Anonymous*

# The guest

Keeping warm in winter:

Owl was at home. "How good it feels to be sitting by this fire," said Owl. "It is so cold and snowy outside."

Owl was eating buttered toast and hot pea soup for supper. Owl heard a loud sound at the front door. "Who is there, banging and pounding at my door on a night like this?" he said.

Owl opened the door. No one was there. Only the snow and the wind. Owl sat near the fire again. There was another loud noise at the door. "Who can it be," said Owl, "knocking and thumping at my door on a night like this?" Owl opened the door. No one was there. Only the snow and the cold. "The poor old winter is knocking at my door," said Owl. "Perhaps it wants to sit by the fire. Well, I will be kind and let the winter come in."

Owl opened his door very wide. "Come in, Winter," said Owl. "Come in and warm yourself for a while."

Winter came into the house. It came in very fast. A cold wind pushed Owl against the wall. Winter ran around the room. It blew out the fire in the fire-place. The snow whirled up the stairs and whooshed down the hallway.

"Winter!" cried Owl. "You are my guest. This is no way to behave!"

But Winter did not listen. It made the curtains flap and shiver. It turned the pea soup into hard, green ice. Winter went into all the rooms of Owl's house. Soon everything was covered with snow. "You must go, Winter!" shouted Owl. "Go away, right now!"

The wind blew round and round. Then Winter rushed out and slammed the front door. "Good-bye," called Owl, "and do not come back!"

Owl made a new fire in the fire-place. The room became warm again. The snow melted away. The hard, green ice turned back into soft pea soup. Owl sat down in his chair and quietly finished his supper.

*Arnold Lobel*

Why did Owl enjoy being at home?
What happened when he invited winter in?
What would have happened to Owl if he had had no house to live in in winter?

## Classroom activities

**Language** *food*

☆ Design a menu for a pet, baby, robot, or dinosaur. Try to obtain a menu to show the children first. Make a large book for each menu and let the children choose one item for each page and illustrate it.

☆ Ask the children to describe their favourite foods and make a menu for themselves – let them choose any combinations they like.

**Art** *food*

☆ Make individual collage pictures of food for hot weather and food for cold weather. Use tissue paper, paper plates, cups, card etc to get a good 3D effect. Use a strong glue.

**Projects** *food*

☆ Choose one of the basic foods (eggs, flour, rice, yams) and find out about all the different ways it can be prepared.

☆ Make a class or school recipe book including recipes for special occasions and festivals. Try to get as many children as possible to contribute recipes. Encourage them to find out how each is made, cook it if possible, and paint a picture of it to include in the book.

**Language** *shelter*

☆ Discuss and write about how to keep warm in cold weather and how to keep cool in hot weather. What would you eat, drink, wear? Would you do a lot of exercise or stay still? Each child can make their own survival booklet.

☆ Get the children to imagine themselves stranded on an uninhabited island, in a forest, or in a desert. After discussion ask them to design a shelter suited to the surroundings, write about it and draw it. You could invite an expert on outdoor survival to talk to the children and offer them advice on their designs.

**Language** *exercise*

☆ Make a class book of favourite playground games. Explain to the children that they need to make the instructions clear enough for someone, who doesn't know the game, to learn it. Arrange a games swop with another school.

**Mathematics** *exercise*

☆ Mapping: choose a number of exercises and find out which children like them best. Map the results:

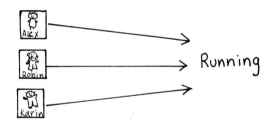

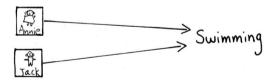

## Onito's hat

*Towards the end of winter in Japan the father of the family, or his son, throws beans into every room to chase away any demons that may be there. And all the while he calls, "Go out demons, come in happiness."*

One winter evening a little boy called Mako was scattering beans into every room, even the attic, and calling, "Go out demons, come in happiness."

Now for a long time a little demon called Onito had lived in Mako's attic – but Onito was a kind demon. Once he found a ball that Mako had lost and put it back without being seen. Another time he had brought in the washing from the line before the rain started.

He often polished Mako's shoes, and his father's, and did many kind things. But nobody knew it was Onito who did these things, because he was shy and always hid so that no one noticed him. So when Onito heard Mako scattering beans all over the house the little demon thought how strange people were. "Why do people think all demons are wicked? Don't they know that just like people, there are good demons and bad demons?"

Quickly he pulled an old hat on his head to hide his horns and crept out of the attic without a sound.

Outside the snow was falling fast and everything was covered in a crust of white. Onito's little bare feet sank into the snow, making tracks as he looked for a house where he would be welcome. But on this evening all the houses were decorated with holly, and holly has prickles which prick demons' eyes.

Suddenly Onito's nose began to twitch as he noticed a little house just in front of him. "It doesn't smell of beans and I can't see any holly," he said. And he looked around for a place to get in.

Just as he was peeping through a window the door opened and a little girl came out and scooped up some fresh snow into a basin. She blew on her fingers which were cold from the frozen snow, and Onito thought, "Now is the time to creep into the house and hide away as quick as a mouse." And this

Onito did, climbing on to the highest beam to be out of sight.

On a bed in the middle of the room the little girl's mother was sleeping. The little girl filled a handkerchief full of snow and laid it on her mother's hot forehead. This woke her and she opened her eyes.

"Are you hungry, darling?" she asked. The little girl shook her head. "No," she said, "I'm not hungry, I had something to eat when you were asleep."

"But where did you get food from, now that I'm ill?" asked her mother.

"Well," said the little girl, "A boy I didn't know knocked on the door and brought me a bowl of hot rice and peas. He said that this was a festival day and there was a lot of food left over, and as you were ill the neighbours thought of me."

"How kind," said her mother, and closed her eyes again.

But Onito thought, "I bet that little girl isn't telling the truth," and he ran along the beam and down the wall into the kitchen. And there the plates and bowls were empty – not a grain of rice anywhere.

"Just as I thought," said Onito. "She hasn't eaten anything at all." And he crept out through a broken window and dropped down on to the frozen snow.

A little while later there was a knock on the door of the house. The little girl opened the door and saw a strange little boy standing there with a straw hat pushed down over his ears. He held a bowl in his hand and he said, "This is a festival day and there is a lot of food left over, and as your mother is ill the neighbours thought you would like some." And Onito repeated as carefully as he could what the little girl had said to her mother.

Very surprised, the little girl hesitated. Then she took off the cloth and found a bowl of hot rice and some peas. Her face lit up with pleasure and she smiled at her visitor. While she was eating the little girl became thoughtful. "What is the matter?" asked Onito.

"I was wondering if I should throw beans to drive out demons and bring in happiness. Then mother might get well quickly."

Onito shivered. "But don't you think there may be kind demons too?" he asked. And then he disappeared. He disappeared as if by magic, leaving behind him nothing but his old straw hat.

"That's very strange," said the little girl, "He forgot his hat." And underneath lay a pile of little black beans. "Now I can throw beans to send out demons and bring in happiness."

So she started to scatter the beans until she suddenly remembered the strange little boy who had brought her food, and how he had disappeared so suddenly.

"Perhaps he was a good demon who came because mother is ill and I was hungry. In our house tonight it has been 'Come in demons and come in happiness'."

So she stopped scattering beans and waited hopefully for Onito to come back. And maybe one day he will.

*Kimiko Aman and Peggy Blakeley*

Why did the little girl and her mother need help?
How did Onito help them?
How do you think Onito's bare feet felt in the snow?
What do we all need in winter to keep us safe and warm?
Why did the mother especially need shelter? What happens to you when you are ill?

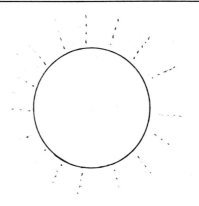

Keeping cool in summer:

## THE HARDEST THING TO DO IN THE WORLD

is stand in the hot sun
at the end of a long queue for ice
    creams
watching all the people who've just
    bought theirs
coming away from the queue
giving their ice creams their very
    first lick.

*Michael Rosen*

Why was it difficult to wait for the ice cream? What would happen to an ice cream if it was left in hot sun? Why do *we* need shelter from the sun? What things shelter us from the sun? (Sun shades, hats, trees, buildings.)

**Language** *rest*
☆ Ask the children to describe their bedrooms. What is their bed like? What other furniture is there in the room? Do they share their bedroom with other brothers or sisters? What do they use the room for apart from sleeping? – reading, playing.

☆ Ask the children to think of three reasons why they think their bedtime should be half an hour later, and three reasons why it should be earlier.

**Mathematics** *rest*
☆ Make a block graph of bedtimes and getting up times.

**Art** *rest*
☆ Being awake during the day and asleep at night is not a normal pattern for some animals and people. Find out about the people and animals who work at night. Make a collage of day and night and include the people and animals who are awake in each.

Needing exercise:

I was sitting in the sitting room
toying with some toys
when from a door marked: 'GRUESOME'
there came a GRUESOME noise.

Cautiously I opened it
and there to my surprise
a little GRUE lay sitting
with tears in its eyes

"Oh little GRUE please tell me
what is it ails thee so?"
"Well I'm so small," he sobbed,
"GRUESSES don't want to know."

"Exercises are the answer,
Each morning you must DO SOME"
He thanked me, smiled,
and do you know what?
The very next day he . . .

*Roger McGough*

Why didn't the little GRUE grow?
What helped him to grow from that day on?
How do you feel if you have to stay inside all day?
Why do you think you have playtimes instead of staying at
your desk all day?

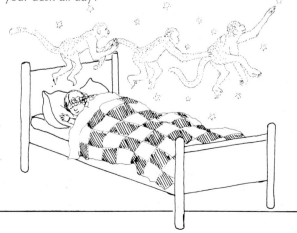

Needing rest:

## Bedtime

Five minutes, five minutes more, please!
  Let me stay five minutes more!
Can't I just finish the castle
  I'm building here on the floor?
Can't I just finish the story
  I'm reading here in my book?
Can't I just finish this bead-chain –
  It *almost* is finished, look!
Can't I just finish this game, please?
  When a game's once begun
It's a pity never to find out
  Whether you've lost or won.
Can't I just stay five minutes?
  Well, can't I stay just four?
Three minutes, then? two minutes?
  Can't I stay *one* minute more?

*Eleanor Farjeon*

Why do you need to sleep at night?
Do you try to stay up after bed time?
Do you think adults should allow you to stay up?

## Sweet Dreams

I wonder as into bed I creep
What it feels like to fall asleep.
I've told myself stories, I've counted sheep,
But I'm always asleep when I fall asleep.
Tonight my eyes I will open keep,
And I'll stay awake till I fall asleep,
Then I'll know what it feels like to fall asleep,
Asleep,
Asleeep,
Asleeeep . . .

*Ogden Nash*

**Songs**
*Tinder-box:* 12 When a dinosaur's feeling hungry,
13 A house is a house for me, 14 Jennifer's rabbit,
15 Everybody says
*Subject index:* Clothes, Food, Houses, Shelter,
Sleeping and dreaming

**Stories**
*Bedtime for Frances* R. Hoban (Faber)
*The Child Who Cried in the Night* (Basil Blackwell
    *Rights of Children* series)
*Eat and Be Eaten* I. Mari (Dent)
*Good-Night, Owl!* P. Hutchins (Bodley Head)
*A House is a House for Me* M. A. Hoberman (Penguin)
*Maisie Middleton* N. Sowter (Black)
"The Soup Stone" from *Folk Tales* L. Berg
    (Brockhampton/Piccolo)
*Things in the Kitchen* D. Hay (Collins)
*Wide Awake Jake* H. Young (Fontana)

**Information books**
*Bakery* V. Peet (Black)
*Come Over to My House* T. Le Sieg (Collins)
*Feeling Awful* L. Newson (Black)
*Johnny Gets Some Glasses* N. Snell (Hamish Hamilton)
*Lucy Loses Her Tonsils* N. Snell (Hamish Hamilton)
*Peter Gets a Hearing Aid* N. Snell (Hamish Hamilton)
*Sleep is for everyone* P. Showers (Black)
*Tom Visits the Dentist* N. Snell (Hamish Hamilton)
Also see books listed in *Home*

**Filmstrips**
*Bread* and *Protection* (Philip Green Educational Ltd)

# Needing others

**Objectives**
- [ ] To explore the need for love and care
- [ ] To think why we need friends
- [ ] To consider the need to feel accepted

Young children have a particular need to feel that they are loved and cared for. They also need friends and to feel accepted by others. Through recognising these needs in themselves they learn to recognise them in others.

**Starting points**

○ Play a recording of "The Streets of London". Discuss the meaning of the words.

○ Ask a group of children to prepare a mime about rejection and acceptance (see classroom activities).

○ With the children's help list some of the things that other people (adults, friends, sisters, brothers) do for them – prepare meals, make or buy clothes, play with them, teach them how to do things, care for them when they are ill, love them.

○ Who are the people who give us special care and attention? – nurses, doctors, dentists, crossing patrol. Prepare a project in class on people who help us and put on a special display of it for assembly (see classroom activities). Invite one or two of the people chosen for the project to come into assembly to talk to the children or be interviewed.

---

## The stone doll of Sister Brute

Sister Brute finds out what it feels like to love her family and to be loved by them:

Once upon a time, before the Brute family changed their name to Nice, Sister Brute had nothing to love. She had a mama and a papa. She had a big brother and a baby brother.

"But I have nothing to love," said Sister Brute to her papa. May I have a doll?"

Papa growled and walked away.

"May I have a doll?" Sister Brute asked her mama.

Mama gave her a stone. Sister Brute drew a face on the stone. Sister Brute made a dress for the stone. She gave it tea parties in the woods. She picked flowers for it, and she named it Alice Brute Stone. It was hard when she hugged it, and it was heavy to carry, but Sister Brute loved Alice Brute Stone.

One day Sister Brute took Alice Brute Stone for a walk, and met an ugly dog. His hair was matted and dirty. His hob-nailed boots were shabby and worn.

"Love me," said the dog to Sister Brute.

"No," said Sister Brute. "I have my stone doll to love. Go away."

"Love me," said the dog, "or I will kick you very hard."

"Then I will kick you back," said Sister Brute.

He kicked her and she kicked him, but the dog kicked harder with his hob-nailed boots.

"Go away," said Sister Brute, and she hurled her stone doll at the ugly dog.

"Nobody ever played dolls with me before," said the dog. "Now I know you love me."

So he followed her home with Alice Brute Stone in his mouth, and he kicked Sister Brute lovingly all the way.

Now Sister Brute had a doll to love, and she had the ugly dog with the hob-nailed boots too. But the doll was hard and heavy, and the dog kept kicking.

One day Sister Brute said to her mama, "All I have is tiredness and kicks and bruises."

"Maybe that is because you have been loving only a hard stone and a kicking dog," said Mama Brute.

"What else is there to love?" said Sister Brute.

"I don't know," said Mama Brute.

Then she looked at Alice Brute Stone's face. It was just like hers.

"You could love me," said Mama Brute, "and I will give you soft hugs and sing you lullabies."

"What will papa give me if I love him?" said Sister Brute.

"Maybe kisses and knee rides," said Mama.

"What about Big Brother and Baby Brother?" said Sister Brute.

"Smiles and string," said Mama. "Rusty bolts and coloured glass and turtles."

"Then I will try loving the whole family," said Sister Brute, "and I will keep on loving Alice Brute Stone and my ugly kicking dog too."

So she did.

Sister Brute loved them all, and they loved her back, and she had hugs and lullabies, kisses and knee rides, smiles, string, coloured glass and turtles and kicks and bruises.

*Russell Hoban*

How did the Brute family change after they started to love one another?
What do you do for people you love?
There are good and bad things about loving people. What are the good things? (Hugs, care, attention.)
What are the bad things? (Parents getting angry, fights with sisters and brothers.)

Sometimes I'm afraid that my mum and dad don't love me any more.

When I've done something I'm not supposed to, my parents tell me off and I don't think they love me at all.

Do you think the parents get cross because they don't love the child anymore?
Do you think they can be cross while still loving the child?

## Classroom activities

### Language

☆ Talk about the need for love and care with the children. Ask them to think further about and perhaps record the ways adults and others show their love and care for them. Talk to them about the times you have seen them being helpful – helping new children, being polite to dinner staff, and so on. Discuss how they could be more caring – help parents when they are busy, spend more time with older people who may be lonely, be more patient with younger children, consider whether they might be annoying someone by their behaviour.

### Dance and mime

☆ Ask the children to devise a dance or mime about a child's rejection from a group followed by his/her acceptance back into it. Discuss how the child and group might feel and behave in each situation. Divide the class into four or five groups and suggest a structure such as the following:

child is rejected by group→alone and friendless→another child comforts him and persuades the others to let him in again→group agrees and all play together

Use the children's ideas to improve this.

## A boy and his robot

The need for care and attention:

There was once a small boy who had no mother and father. He lived with his uncle, a kind old man who invented wonderful machines. One day the uncle made a robot. Some time later the old man became very ill. He told the robot to look after the boy as well as he possibly could. The uncle died and the robot was very sad. "Don't worry," he said to the boy. "I will look after you."

Every day, the robot made delicious, healthy meals. Every night, he told the boy wonderful bedtime stories. The robot showed him lots of interesting and exciting things. They went everywhere together. They often played together. The robot was a good horse and he also played chess and card games.

In return, the child looked after the robot. He plugged him in to charge his batteries and he oiled his joints. The two of them were very happy together. But one day two nosey women passed the house. They peered through the window. "What is that?" said one.

"It looks like a robot," said the other.

"How awful," they said together. "We must report this to the judge."

They hurried off and found the judge. "The boy is living with a monster," they told him. The very next day the police came and took the boy away. The robot and the boy were both very unhappy. The police took the boy to a home for children who had no parents and the robot was only allowed to see him once a week. They talked to each other through the fence, but nosey people always listened.

Each day the children had lessons together. The teachers were very friendly, but the boy still missed his robot. He used to tell the other children about his wonderful friend. Once a teacher heard his stories. "You were lucky to have such a good friend," she said.

The children asked, "Can the robot look after us for a while?"

"No," said the kind teacher sadly, "only people are allowed to do that."

That night the children decided to meet the robot. When the robot came, they told him that they had made a secret plan. They whispered it to him. The next day a strange looking man arrived at the home. He clanked as he walked and his nose and beard were not quite straight. The teacher pretended not to recognise the robot.

"I would like to take some children for a holiday," said the strange man. "I will look after them in my home."

The teacher smiled, "That is a wonderful idea," she said.

All the children were very excited as they set off with the robot. The robot looked after the children and played with them. They climbed all over him and he swung them through the air with his big hands. They were so happy together that even the nosey people stayed away.

Why did the boy and the robot need each other?
What did the robot do for the boy that no one else did? (Cared for him as an individual.)
What did the teacher do that was very kind?
Why did she do it? (She realised the boy needed the robot and that the robot was good with children.)

My Mum is a nurse She looks after old People and new People Christopher Bane. 6.

## A sad song about Greenwich Village

She lives in a garret
   Up a haunted stair,
And even when she's frightened
   There's nobody to care.

She cooks so small a dinner
   She dines on the smell,
And even if she's hungry
   There's nobody to tell.

She sweeps her musty lodging
   As the dawn steals near,
And even if she's dead
   There's nobody to hear.

I haven't seen my neighbour
   Since a long time ago,
And even if she's dead.
   There's nobody to know.

*Frances Park*

How old do you think the person in the poem is? Why? Why do you think she is alone? Do you know anyone like this?

Why did the dragon grow and grow? How would you feel if people pretended you weren't there?
Have you ever behaved badly when people ignored you/didn't understand what you were really like/thought you had been naughty when you hadn't?
How would you like people to behave when they meet you for the first time? (Be friendly, get to know you.)

## There's no such thing as a dragon *(extract)*

The need to be noticed, recognised and accepted for what we are:

*Billy Bixbee woke up one morning to find a tiny dragon in his room. He told his mother about it but she said "There's no such thing as a dragon". From that moment on the dragon grew and grew and grew. It ate up all Billy's breakfast and then went to sleep in the hall. Billy went upstairs to brush his teeth:*

By the time Billy came back downstairs the dragon had grown so much he filled the hall.

"I didn't know dragons grew so fast!" said Billy.

"There's no such thing as a dragon!" said Mother firmly.

Cleaning the downstairs took Mother all morning, what with the dragon in the way . . . and having to climb in and out of windows to get from room to room.

By mid-day the dragon filled the house. Its head hung out of the front door, its tail hung out of the back door, and there wasn't a room in the house that didn't have some part of the dragon in it.

When the dragon awoke from his nap he was hungry. A bakery van went by. The smell of fresh bread was more than the dragon could resist. The dragon ran down the street after the bakery van. The house went too, of course, like the shell on a snail.

When Mr Bixbee came home for lunch, the first thing he noticed was that the house was gone. Luckily, one of the neighbours was able to tell him which way it went. Mr Bixbee got in his car and went looking for the house. He studied all the houses as he drove along. Finally he saw one that looked familiar. Billy and Mrs Bixbee were waving from an upstairs window. Mr Bixbee climbed over the dragon's head, onto the porch roof, and through the upstairs window.

"How did this happen?" Mr Bixbee asked.

"It was the dragon," said Billy.

"There's no such thing . . ." Mother started to say.

"There IS a dragon!" Billy insisted. "A very BIG dragon!" And Billy patted the dragon on the head.

The dragon wagged its tail happily. Then, even faster than it had grown, the dragon started getting smaller. Soon it was kitten-size again.

"I don't mind dragons THIS size," said Mother. "Why did it have to grow so BIG?"

"I'm not sure," said Billy, "I think it just wanted to be noticed."

*Jack Kent*

### Project

☆ *People who help us.* Younger children can choose a person who helps them in school (nurse, doctor, dinner staff, caretaker, teacher), write about them and paint a portrait of them. Some of the children can read out and display their work in assembly while others dress up as the helper they have chosen.

Older children can divide into groups and choose a person to interview. Get them to prepare a questionnaire covering what the person does, what hours they work, whether they wear special clothes, what skills and training they need, why they chose the job, what they like or dislike about it, what other jobs they have done in the past, and so on. Send each group, with a tape recorder if possible, to different helpers at times convenient to *them*. Each group can choose to be reporters for a real or imaginary newspaper and write up the information they collect into articles for their newspaper. Make special reporters' hats, badges and identity papers. Collect all the articles together into a class newspaper or magazine. Choose a name for it and illustrate it.

### Songs

*Tinder-box:* 16 Love somebody, 27 Helping Grandma Jones, 31 Thank you for my friends, 51 I've just moved into a new house, 52 Talking, 55 You and I

*Subject index:* Friends, Needing others, Relatives and family

### Stories

*Annie, the Invisible Girl* (Basil Blackwell *Rights of Children* series)
*Being Alone, Being Together* T. Berger (Macdonald)
*The Dancer, the Bear and the Nobody Boy* D. Bour (Black)
*Doctor Sean* P. Breinburg (Bodley Head)
*A Friend Can Help* T. Berger (Macdonald)
*Frisk the Unfriendly Foal* E. de Fossard (E. J. Arnold)
*Not Now, Bernard* D. McKee (Andersen Press)
*The Rabbits' Wedding* G. Williams (Collins)

### Information books

*The Hospital* F. Peacock (Franklin Watts)
*How We Live* A. Harper (Kestrel)
*Linda Goes to Hospital* B. Wade (Black)

# Needing to be alone

**Objectives**
☐ To think about times when we need to be alone
☐ To think about the things we can do when we are alone

By the time children have reached the age of seven or eight, many are becoming more independent and need times to be alone. Some children always need more privacy than others.

**Starting points**
○ Discuss with the children what sort of things they like to do on their own, e.g. a hobby like model making or reading. Do they have a place where they can be alone? Do they ever feel they'd like to be alone but can't because of brothers and sisters perhaps?

○ Play a recording of *The sound of silence* (Simon and Garfunkel). Is there such a thing as complete silence? Even deep in the country there is noise. What sounds do you hear in the country, in the city? How are they different? Can you ever really be alone?

○ What is it like being an only child? What is good about it? What is bad about it?

○ Explore the difference between being alone and being lonely. What are the causes of loneliness. Ask the children if they like to be alone. When? Are they ever lonely?

**Songs**
*Tinder-box:* 17 All alone in my quiet head

**Stories**
*Being Alone, Being Together* T. Berger (Macdonald)
*Sally's Secret* S. Hughes (Bodley Head)

---

Having a special place where you can be alone:

## I know a place

I know a place
That nobody knows
Deep in the hollows of the branching wood,
Where nobody goes,
Where nobody goes.

Far from the path
That climbs to the hill,
Lost in the shadows of a lonely glade,
All silent and still,
All silent and still.

There I can hide
Whenever I please,
Safe as the linnet and the nightingale
That nest in the trees,
That nest in the trees.

Daily I pray
No stranger shall find,
Deep in the hollows of my secret wood,
The place that is mine,
The place that is mine.

What is the child's secret way of waking?
Can other people tell what you are thinking just by looking at you?
Think about the sort of things that you like to keep secret from other people.

---

Do you have a place where you can be alone?
What do you do there?
Why do you think people like to be alone? (Need to be quiet, have time to think, work out problems, work, imagine, day dream.)

Being alone inside your head:

## Waking

My secret way of waking
is like a place
to hide.
I'm very still,
my eyes are shut.
They all think I am sleeping
but
I'm wide awake inside.

They all think I am sleeping
but
I'm wiggling my toes.
I feel sun-fingers
on my cheek.
I hear voices whisper-speak.
I squeeze my eyes
to keep them shut
so they will think I'm sleeping
BUT
I'm really wide awake inside
– and no one knows!

*Lilian Moore*

# Behaviour

## Objectives
☐ To investigate different ways of behaving
☐ To consider the effect of our behaviour on others
☐ To think about the most effective behaviour we can use in different situations

Encourage the children to think of behaviour in a very broad sense, not just in terms of what is good or bad. Try to explore what makes us behave differently in different situations, and what form our behaviour takes.

## Starting points
○ Explore the words we use as greetings (hello, hi, good morning, and so on). You could find out the words for hello or welcome in different languages and make a display of them. Explore customary greetings (kissing on alternate cheeks, hand-shaking, bowing). As an introduction play a recording of *Hello, Goodbye* (Lennon and McCartney).

○ With the children, make a list of the people they have met or parted from that day. What did they say? How did they behave? Were they happy, sad, friendly? Did they smile, speak, wave?

○ Ask the children to think about their behaviour at the moment – sitting still being quiet, listening politely, being interested, day dreaming, whispering, talking or wriggling about. Ask them to think about the way their behaviour may be affecting *you*.

---

## Good morning when it's morning

Good morning when it's morning
Good night when it is night
Good evening when it's dark out
Good day when it is light
Good morning to the sunshine
Good evening to the sky
And when it's time to go away
Good-bye
Good-bye
Good-bye

*Mary Ann Hoberman*

What do you talk about when you meet your friends in the morning? What do you say when you leave them at night?

## Hello's a handy word

Hello's a handy word to say
At least a hundred times a day.
Without Hello what would I do
Whenever I bumped into you?
Without Hello where would you be
Whenever you bumped into me?
Hello's a handy word to know.
Hello Hello Hello Hello.

*Mary Ann Hoberman*

What other words do you use to say hello?
What else do you do when you meet someone? (Smile, shake hands, hug each other.)

## The bad-tempered ladybird *(extract)*

At five o'clock in the morning the sun came up. A friendly ladybird flew in from the left. It saw a leaf with many aphids on it, and decided to have them for breakfast. But just then a bad-tempered ladybird flew in from the right. It too saw the aphids and wanted them for breakfast.

"Good morning," said the friendly ladybird.

"Go away!" shouted the bad-tempered ladybird. "I want those aphids."

"We can share them," suggested the friendly ladybird.

"No. They're mine, all mine," screamed the bad-tempered ladybird. "Or do you want to fight me for them?"

"If you insist," answered the friendly ladybird sweetly. It looked the other ladybird straight in the eye. The bad-tempered ladybird stepped back. It looked less sure of itself.

"Oh, you're not big enough for me to fight," it said.

"Then why don't you pick on somebody bigger?"

"I'll do that!" screeched the bad-tempered ladybird. "I'll show you!" It puffed itself up and flew off.

*Eric Carle*

What do you think of the way the bad-tempered ladybird behaved?
What sort of words would you use to describe his behaviour? (Mean, bullying, impatient, selfish.)
What happened as a result of his behaviour?
What would you do if someone was as rude as that to you?

## Classroom activities

### Language

☆ List as many different words as the children can think of to describe types of behaviour – angry words, sad words, happy words and so on.

☆ After class discussion ask the children to write and illustrate examples of what they consider to be good and bad behaviour. Alternatively ask them to select a certain type of behaviour which is acceptable in some places but not in others, e.g.

| I can shout | I cannot shout |
|---|---|
| in the playground | in the classroom |
| in the garden | in the cinema |
| in the woods | in Assembly |

| I can read | I cannot read |
|---|---|
| in bed | in the sea |
| in school | on the swings |
| on the train | climbing a mountain |

☆ Choose examples of different types of behaviour and ask the children to describe how other people usually react to them. Discuss the reactions and the reasons why they might be different, e.g.

When I shout very loudly, my parents . . .
my teacher . . .
my friends . . .

## Cross-Patch

A door, a chimney, a pan and a chair decide to teach their owner how to behave politely and pleasantly:

There was once a little woman and her name was Betsy Cross-Patch. She was so very bad-tempered that she could not shut the door without slamming it, nor put a cup and saucer on the table without making them rattle; and she never spoke without scolding and complaining.

At last the door grew tired of being slammed. "It's not fair," he said to the chimney. "I'm a well-made, well-behaved door, but she's always grumbling about me. She shall have some reason for grumbling in future – I am going to stick!"

The chimney, the pan and the chair all agreed with the door that they too had had enough of the woman's complaints and they were not going to put up with it any longer.

Now the little woman had been to market that day, and all the way there she grumbled that the sun was too hot and the wind was too cold and the road was too dusty. All the time she was at the market she was grumbling that there was nothing worth buying, and that everything cost too much; and she never once stopped for a chat with any of the people who said "Good day" to her.

When she reached home she jerked the string that pulled up the latch and tried to push the door open.

But the door stuck!

"What can be the matter with it?" she cried. "It has always been a very good door before."

"Then why did you grumble about me?" asked the door, and opened so suddenly that the little old woman nearly fell over the sill.

She put her basket down with a thump and snatched up the bellows to blow the fire, for she was very hungry after her walk and wanted to cook her dinner. But no sooner had the flames begun to curl up the chimney, than the chimney began to smoke. It smoked and it smoked till the little woman thought her head would waggle off with sneezing and coughing.

"What can be the matter with it?" she gasped. "It was always a very good chimney before?"

"Then why did you grumble about me?" asked the chimney. The little woman tried to make her supper next but the pan boiled over. She tried to sit down but the chair overturned and tumbled her onto the floor.

"Good gracious!" cried the little woman. "It has been such a steady, comfortable chair. Why should it play tricks like this! I must be bewitched!"

"Not a bit of it," said the chair; "but as you always grumbled whatever we did, we thought we might as well deserve the unkind things you said about us. I'm sure I don't like overbalancing, and if you'll treat me fairly I'll never do it again."

"It's no pleasure to *me* to boil over," said the pan.

"I *hate* smoking," said the chimney.

"And I can't *bear* sticking," said the door, "but you can't get the best, even out of a door, if you're always finding fault, you know."

The little woman was so surprised that she could not think of a word to say for a long time. Then she got to her feet. First she picked up the chair and put it in its place; then she set the pan carefully on the hob, poked the fire gently, and shut the door without slamming it.

"Fair is fair," she said. "If I want treating pleasantly I'll have to behave pleasantly myself."

So the little woman stopped grumbling, and after that the door never stuck, and the chimney never smoked, and the pan never boiled over, and the chair never overbalanced, and they all lived comfortably together for always and always.

*Margaret Baker (slightly abridged)*

How did Betsy behave at the beginning of the story? What happened when she stopped grumbling?

# The two guinea pigs

Behold the hopeless guinea pig.
He's neither beautiful nor big.
Nor bright, nor brave, nor swift,
   nor strong.
He says that everything is wrong.
Ever whinier and wailier
He feels he is a dismal failure.

But wait! Don't go! Here comes
   another,
And just alike! It is his brother.
He has the same faults, everyone,
Yet somehow he is full of fun.
He tends his hutch, eats
   artichokes,
Sings hymns, sunbathes, makes
   little jokes.

I'm fond of both, but guarantee,
The second's better company.
MAKE THE MOST OF
   WHAT YOU'VE GOT,
YOU MAY FIND A
   SURPRISING LOT.

*Charlotte Hough*

How were the two guinea pigs alike?
How were they different?
Which guinea pig would you like to be
like? Why?

# Such a stubborn mule!

Nasreddin Hodja, a semi-historical, semi-legendary character, is one of the most celebrated personalities of the Middle East. *Hodja* was an honorary title denoting a scholar – in particular one learned in the Qoran and religious law. The stories about Nasreddin Hodja are countless. They stem from everyday events, and through their humour and wit point to some of life's deepest paradoxes and questions.

One day the Hodja decided he was tired of feeding his donkey, and asked his wife to go and feed it instead. She refused, however, saying that that was his work. In the end they agreed that whichever one of them spoke first should go and feed the donkey.

The Hodja retired to a corner and sat in it without saying a word. His wife became fed up with the tense atmosphere in the house, and went out to visit a neighbour. Once there, of course, she could not keep silent, and she told what had happened.

"He is such a stubborn mule!" she said. "He'll die of hunger rather than speak."

"I will send him some soup," said her friend, and she poured some out in a plate and sent her son to take it to the Hodja.

In the meantime, however, a thief, hearing no sound from inside the Hodja's house, entered quietly and began to stuff everything of value into his sack. Eventually he walked into the room where the Hodja was sitting, and was almost frightened out of his life. As the Hodja made no sound or move, however, he came to the conclusion that he was paralysed, and added to his collection of valuable objects under the very eyes of their owner. The Hodja was furious, but thought that if he moved, he would be bound to say something. The thief, as thorough as he was cheeky, thought it would be a pity to leave the Hodja's *kavuk* (hat) behind, and carefully removed it from his head. Then he left.

Five minutes afterwards, the boy arrived with the plate of soup. The Hodja was still determined not to speak but he felt he *had* to do something to try and catch the thief. He started to mime what had happened in the hope that the boy would run and fetch the police. The boy understood nothing. When the Hodja tried to describe how the thief had taken his hat from his very head, he waved his hand three times round his head and then pointed to it. The boy thought he had understood what the Hodja wanted, and making three circular movements with the plate of soup over the Hodja's head, he tipped the hot contents on to his skull.

Whatever the Hodja thought, he still said nothing!

The boy went back home, and told his mother and the Hodja's wife everything he had seen – how the cupboards and trunks were wide open, vases overturned, and how the place seemed to contain much less than when he last went there with his mother. He also told them how the Hodja tried to eat his soup through the top of his head.

"There must be something wrong!" said the Hodja's wife, and she hurried home as fast as her legs would take her. When she entered the house, she was for a moment, really speechless. Then,

"Merciful God! What has happened?" she cried.

"I've won! I've won!" rejoiced the Hodja. "You feed the donkey!"

Then he remembered the thief.

"But just look what trouble your obstinacy has caused!" he said.

*From* Tales of the Hodja *retold by Charles Downing*

Who do *you* think was more stubborn – the Hodja or his wife? Why?
What happened because of the contest to keep silent?
Who won the contest? Do you think it was worth winning considering what happened?

# A dreadful sight

We saw him so naughty and scratching and hitting,
And when he sat down, then he wouldn't stop sitting,
Right on the sidewalk with everyone staring,
But he didn't care – oh, he LIKED it not caring.

*Dorothy Aldis*

Grown ups and children sometimes behave badly. Can you think of a time when you behaved very badly?
How did you feel?
What happened?

# The people upstairs

The people upstairs all practice ballet.
Their living room is a bowling alley.
Their bedroom is full of conducted tours.
Their radio is louder than yours.
They celebrate week-ends all the week.
When they take a shower, your ceilings leak.
They try to get their parties to mix
By supplying their guests with Pogo sticks,
And when their orgy at last abates,
They go to the bathroom on roller skates.
I might love the people upstairs wondrous
If instead of above us, they just lived under us.

*Ogden Nash*

(To get the best from this poem discuss words like ballet, pogo, and orgy, first.)
Do you live in a flat or a house where you can hear the people next door?
Does the noise worry your family? Do people complain about the noise *you* make?
Is it possible to be absolutely quiet?
What can you do to avoid disturbing people?
How can families who live near each other get on well?
(Be considerate, give and take.)

# Sneaky Bill

I'm Sneaky Bill, I'm terrible mean and vicious,
I steal all the cashews from the mixed-nuts dishes,
I eat all the icing but I won't touch the cake,
And what you won't give me, I'll go ahead and take.
I gobble up the cherries from everyone's drinks,
And if there's sausages I grab a dozen links;
I take both drumsticks if there's turkey or chicken,
And the biggest strawberries are what I'm pickin';
I make sure I get the finest chop on the plate,
And I'll eat the portions of anyone who's late!

I'm always on the spot before the dinner bell –
I guess I'm pretty awful,
                    but
                     I
                      do
                       eat
                        well!

*William Cole*

What do you think about Sneaky Bill's behaviour? What would it be like to have Bill for a friend? What would happen to you if you were so selfish?

# Growing

When I grow up I'll be so kind,
Not yelling "Now" or "Do you MIND!"
    Or making what is called a scene,
    Like "So you're back" or "Where've you BEEN?"
Or "Goodness, child, what is it NOW?"
Or saying "STOP . . . that awful row",
    Or "There's a time and place to eat"
    And "Wipe your nose" or "Wipe your feet".
I'll just let people go their way
And have an extra hour for play.
    No angry shouting "NOW what's wrong?"
    It's just that growing takes so long.

*Max Fatchen*

## Drama

☆ Ask the children to mime contrasting types of behaviour using their faces and bodies.

☆ Sit the children in a circle and ask them in turn to say their names in a sad/angry/brave/shy voice. Join in yourself when your turn comes. Extend this work into a game. Let the children take turns to mime an action such as knocking at a door in a particular manner e.g. in an angry, timid, or happy way. The others have to guess how the person is feeling.

## Songs

*Tinder-box*: 20 Dipidu, 21 Mama don't 'low, 22 Mr Nobody, 26 Don't you push me down, 27 Helping Grandma Jones, 29 My dog's bigger than your dog

## Stories

*Alfred Herbert Hawkins, the Naughtiest Boy in the World* F. Dickens (Piccolo)
*Annie the Invisible Child* (Basil Blackwell *Rights of Children* series)
*Awful Jack* H. Cresswell (Hodder)
*The Bossing of Josie* R. and D. Armitage (Deutsch)
*The Elephant and the Bad Baby* E. Vipont (Hamish Hamilton/Puffin)
*Emma Quite Contrary* G. Wolde and A. Winn (Hodder)
*A Flower for Ambrose* A. and E. Standon (Longman)
*Frances Face Maker* W. Cole (Magnet)
*The Greedy Cat and the Parrot* S. C. Bryant (Methuen)
*Here are the Brick Street Boys* A. Ahlberg (Lions)
*In the bin* R. Jennings (Kestrel)
*Jasper and the Hero Business* B. Horvath (Franklin Watts)
*The Lady Who Saw the Good Side of Everything* Tapio and P. Decker (World's Work)
*Little Nippers* series: *Go on then* and *Growlings* J. McNeill (Macmillan)
*Little Red Monkey* J. Astrop (Hutchinson)
*Mahagiri* Hemelata (The Children's Book Trust of New Delhi)
"My Naughty Little Sister Shows Off" and "The Cross Photograph" from *All About My Naughty Little Sister* D. Edwards (Methuen)
*Nippers* series: *The boy in the park, Kickerdonkey, The Play, Robert's Story, Susan's Story* (Macmillan)
*The Selfish Giant* O. Wilde (Evans)

# Adults

## Objectives
☐ To consider how adults and children relate to each other
☐ To think of all the ways that adults care for children
☐ To think of the jobs and responsibilities adults cope with

Children's dependence on adults can produce strong positive and negative feelings – they may feel love and gratitude for the care and protection they receive and antagonism and frustration at being told what to do and how to behave. In giving children the chance to explore some of these feelings and investigate the responsibilities adults cope with, they may be helped to understand the adult point of view a little better.

## Starting points
○ Discuss some of the things adults provide for children e.g. care, food and clothes, comfort.

○ Explore the things which children enjoy which adults don't, and vice versa. What things do both enjoy?

○ Make a display of photographs and paintings of the jobs adults do. The children could paint a mural of people working. Discuss what different jobs involve, and encourage them to ask their parents about the work they do.

○ *What's my line?* A group of children mime various jobs – shop keeper, lorry driver, bus conductor, teacher. Can the other children guess what the jobs are?

### I woke up this morning

I woke up this morning
at quarter past seven.
I kicked up the covers
and stuck out my toe.
And ever since then
(That's a quarter past seven)
They haven't said anything
Other than "no".

They haven't said anything
Other than "Please, dear,
Don't do what you're doing,"
Or "Lower your voice."
Whatever I've done
And however I've chosen,
I've done the wrong thing
And I've made the wrong choice.
I didn't wash well
And I didn't say thank you.
I didn't shake hands
And I didn't say please.
I didn't say sorry
When, passing the candy,
I banged the box into
Miss Witelson's knees.
I didn't say sorry.
I didn't stand straighter.
I didn't speak louder
When asked what I'd said.
Well, I said
That tomorrow
At quarter past seven,
They can
Come in and get me
I'M STAYING IN BED.

*Karla Kuskin*

Can you remember a day when everything and everybody seemed to be against you? What happened?
(Try to get the children to think about what is reasonable and justifiable in parents telling them off or giving them advice – and what is not.)
What kind of people other than parents have a right to tell you to do things? (Park keepers, librarians, teachers). Why do they have these rights?

Father says
Never
let
me
see
you
doing
that
again
father says
tell you once
tell you a thousand times
come hell or high water
his finger drills my shoulder
never let me see you doing that again

My brother knows all his phrases off by heart
so we practise them in bed at night.

*Michael Rosen*

How do *you* feel when adults lecture you or get cross for no real reason that you can see?
Do you think adults are unfair sometimes? When? How do you feel about it? What do you do about it? What would you like to do about it?

### Know-alls

I hate know-alls
And show-alls.
    I get wild
When people say,
    "Look child!"
And nag
And finger-wag.
I'd like a gag
Or a bag
    To put over their heads,
    Especially,
When all along,
I *know* jolly well,
They're wrong!

*Max Fatchen*

## Grownups

1  In The Park
Grownups wear hard heels
And stay on the concrete.
I would rather feel the grass
For my own two feet.

2  At The Table
Grownups hold napkins in their laps,
And rarely use them for kites or caps
Or magic tricks or boats or slaps.

3  Asking Questions
Grownups seldom listen
When they ask, "How old are you?"
All they want to do is say,
"Why, it seems like yesterday
That you were only two!"
The next one who asks me,
I'll tell "I'm ninety-three."

*Eve Merriam*

Why do you think the adults prefer to
stay on the concrete/use napkins? Why
do you think they don't listen?
What things do you like doing which
adults don't?
What things do adults and children
both enjoy doing?

## As I was sitting

As I was sitting
And the breeze was blowing
I was knowing
That when I grow up,
There will be a lot of tough stuff.
I'll have to run to work
And catch the bus,
Work all day long
And get a cheque that isn't strong.
Have to pay the bills for heating every week.
Well, let me tell you something:
*I'd rather freeze to death ! ! !*

*From* Come with us: children speak for themselves

Are you looking forward to being grown up? What would be
good about it? What would be bad about it?

## My mum

My mum is a very hard worker. If I didn't have my mum I wouldn't
know what to do – she helps me when I cannot do anything.
Sometimes I moan and grumble about my mum, but she isn't that
bad. If my mum was ill, I reckon my family would be in a mess. I
sometimes think I do too much, but my mum does more than me.
When I am unhappy my mum comforts me, when I am ill in bed my
mum cares for me. She does what is good for me. When there is a
school trip my mum fusses around me to make sure everything is all
right. She lets me take a packed lunch when I don't like the school
dinners. My mum washes all my clothes and makes sure I'm clean.
All these things are like being at work in a mixed shop – my mum is
everything! She's a cleaner, a bed-maker, a chef or cook, a banker, a
caterer, a tour organiser, a laundress, a worker in the house, and a
dietician. When I have to talk to someone I can talk to my mum and
she will understand me and try to make it better for me.

*Angela Lowett, aged 9*

Who does these jobs in your home? Do you help?
Can you think of any more things that need to be done?

My Mum teaches woodwork
at my sisters nushrey
school she is there to make
sure the children do not
hammer their fingers and thumbs.
I espeshily like her when she
kisses me and cuddles me.

Katy Cosh 7yrs.

Stop the cuts

when my Daddy
forgets to make the
breakfast
I make It

Christopher Palmer 6

## My dad's work

My dad works at 3.00 in the morning. He delivers breads and pies, cakes and buns and doughnuts to stores. He brings me some home. He comes home at 2.00 in the afternoon. When he comes home, he watches TV, and then he eats, and then he goes to bed in the middle of the afternoon.

At breakfast the next morning, my mother makes me and my two brothers and my sister breakfast. When we eat, my dad ain't home. He goes to work before we're up.

my mum is an architect
her job is to design gardens
She helps me when I get hurt
and plays with me when
I'm bored and buys me
things

Do you know what your mum or dad does at work?
Do they have to work very hard? Do they like the job they do? Would you like to do their job?

## My mother repairs radios

My mother repairs radios. She works on an assembly line and only makes a part of the radios. When my mother is done her first radio, she gives it to the woman next to her who puts it in a box. Another woman takes radios from boxes and puts them on the assembly line for parts to be put in. Other women get radios that have been already made and put them in radio boxes and the truck brings them to the stores.

## Very odd jobs

If plumbers plumb and bankers bank
And sailors have to sail,
Do ironmongers mong their iron?
Do tailors really tail?

If brewers brew and farmers farm
And currant-pickers pick,
Then do fishmongers mong their fish?
Do vicars really vic?

*Elizabeth Hogg*

What sort of work would you do if you were a plumber? a banker? tailor? . . .

Tristram Hunt 6

○ Use *My mum* as the starting point for some written work which can be read out by the children. Display their paintings of parents working in the home (see classroom activities).

### Classroom activities
#### Language
☆ Discuss further the children's relationships with the adults who care for them and allow them to express the love and admiration they feel for adults and the frustration and guilt they may also experience as a result of adult control if they wish.

☆ Ask the children to describe how they think they will be when they are adults. This could cover some or all of the following points:

What they might look like, wear, eat
How they might walk, talk
Where they might live
Whether they will get married, have children
How they will look after their children
Whether their home will be the same or different
What kind of things they will do in their spare time
What job they will do

☆ Read *My mum* and ask the children to describe the work their mums or dads do in looking after the home. Get them to write about it and illustrate it.

☆ Use the following as the starting point for an alphabet poem of words or phrases the children hear their parents use frequently:

A is for ask your mother
B is for blow your nose
C is for come here at once

#### Art
☆ Read *Daddy fell into the pond*. Ask the children about funny incidents that have happened in their families then ask them to draw comic strips of them.

☆ Make a collage or paint a picture of a favourite adult doing something interesting, funny or clever.

## Bad news

Billy finds out that his dad is going to lose his job:

One night Billy came home from his tea and saw his dad sitting by the fire, staring into the flames.

"How do, Dad," said Billy.

His dad didn't reply.

Billy went through into the back-kitchen. His mother was using the new-fangled potato peeler they'd bought at Bishop Auckland market. The man who had demonstrated it had made it look easy as wink to use: but when Billy's mam had first tried it she had nearly lost her thumb.

"Mam?"

"What is it, Billy?"

"What's up with me dad?"

"There's nothing up with your dad."

"Is he in a bad temper or something?"

"Don't be daft, Our Billy. And stop dabbling your fingers in my tatie water – it's mucky enough already, isn't it!"

His mother finished the potatoes now. She washed the peeler under the tap and wiped it clean.

"Do you like the new peeler now, Mam?"

"It's all right," she said. "It's just a matter of getting used to it, that's all."

"Mam?"

"What is it now, Billy?"

She had just picked up the oven-glove and was about to open the oven-door. She didn't want to be interrupted.

"There is something up with me dad, isn't there?"

She took a swift breath of annoyance. But then the look on her face softened.

She bent down to him and whispered quietly: "They're going to close down the pit, Our Billy. It's definite now. Your dad will lose his job."

*Dick Cate*

Why might life be difficult for Billy's family with his dad out of work? (Might be difficult to find another job in that area, family might have to move, less money available for paying bills and buying food, very depressing for his father.)

Have any of your family had difficulties finding a job?

Do you think you will be able to find a job when you grow up? What could you do instead?

## Daddy fell into the pond

Everyone grumbled. The sky was grey.
We had nothing to do and nothing to say.
We were nearing the end of a dismal day,
And there seemed to be nothing beyond,
                THEN
*Daddy fell into the pond!*

And everyone's face grew merry and bright,
And Timothy danced for sheer delight.
"Give me the camera, quick, oh quick!
He's crawling out of the duckweed." *Click!*

Then the gardener suddenly slapped his knee,
And doubled up, shaking silently,
And the ducks all quacked as if they were daft
And it sounded as if the old drake laughed.

O, there wasn't a thing that didn't respond
                WHEN
*Daddy fell into the pond!*

*Alfred Noyes*

### Songs

*Tinder-box:* 21 Mama don't 'low, 24 Supermum!
25 Let's pretend
*Subject index:* Jobs

### Stories

*The Big Green Book* R. Graves (Kestrel/Puffin)
*Come Away from the Water, Shirley* J. Burningham (Cape)
*The Jackson Family* series: *Mum and Dad, Uncle George and Auntie Mary* Ulises Wensell (Evans)
*Just for You* Mercer Mayer (Dent)
*Little Nippers* series: *The Doctor, Put the Kettle On, When Dad Felt Bad* (Macmillan)
*Look Who's Here* J. McNeill (Macmillan)
*Me and Mr Stenner* E. Hunter (Hamish Hamilton)
*Monty the Runaway Mouse* E. de Fossard (Arnold)
*Mother is Mother* Shankar (The Children's Book Trust of New Delhi)
*Ramona and her Father* B. Cleary (Hamish Hamilton)
*Time to get out of the Bath, Shirley* J. Burningham (Cape)
*Tony's Hard Work Day* A. Arkin (Deutsch)

### Information books

*Beans* series: *Carpenter, Bakery, Fishing boat, Garage, Pottery* (Black)
*How We Live* and *How We Work* A. Harper (Kestrel)

# Brothers and sisters

## Objectives

☐ To consider how brothers and sisters feel about one another
☐ To think about how they influence and behave towards one another
☐ To think of ways they can take responsibility for each other and help and care for one another

## Starting points

○ A class can paint pictures of themselves with their brothers and sisters, (or of themselves on their own if they are only children). Mount them attractively and display them (see classroom activities).

○ Ask the children how many of them have a brother or sister. Who has more than one brother or sister? Who has no brothers and sisters? Choose a few children to describe their brothers and sisters or ask them to choose one thing they like or dislike about them.

○ Choose a brother and sister from the audience and ask them about their relationship. What games do they play together? When do they get angry with one another? What would happen if there was only one chocolate biscuit left – would they share it, quarrel over it? What happens at bedtime – do they go at the same time or one before the other? What would happen if one was upset? Compare the two points of view.

## Classroom activities

### Language

☆ Ask the children to write an account of their brother or sister, or what it is like to be an only child. Those writing about their brothers and sisters could think about the following questions:

What does their brother/sister look like?
How old is he/she?
When do they argue and what about?
When do they look after one another?
How do they help each other?

Ask them to illustrate their work with pictures of themselves with their brothers and sisters showing their relative sizes and writing underneath their name and age.

## The very first story *(extract)*

And there in a cot that used to be my old cot, was my new cross little sister crying and crying!

My mother said, "Sh-sh, baby, here is your big sister come to see you." My mother lifted my naughty little baby sister out of the cot, and my little sister stopped crying at once.

My mother said, "Come and look."

My little sister was wrapped up in a big, woolly, white shawl, and my mother undid the shawl and there was my little sister! When my mother put her down on the bed, my little sister began to cry again.

She was a little, little red baby, crying and crying. "Waah-waah, waah-waah," – like that. Isn't it a nasty noise?

My little sister had tiny hands and tiny little feet. She went on crying and crying, and curling up her toes, and beating with her arms in a very cross way.

I looked at her little red face and her little screwed up eyes and her little crying mouth and then I said,

"Don't cry, baby, don't cry, baby."

And, do you know, when I said, "Don't cry, baby," my little sister *stopped crying*, really stopped crying at once. For me! Because *I* told her to. She opened her eyes and she looked and looked and she didn't cry any more.

My mother said, "Just fancy! She must know you are her big sister! She has stopped crying."

I was pleased to think that my little sister had stopped crying because she knew I was her big sister, and I put my finger on my sister's tiny, tiny hand and my little sister caught hold of my finger tight with her little curly fingers.

My mother said I could hold my little sister on my lap if I was careful. So I sat down on a chair, and my god-mother-aunt put my little sister on to my lap, and I held her very carefully; and my little sister didn't cry at all. She went to sleep like a good baby.

And do you know, she was so small and so sweet and she held my finger so tightly with her curly little fingers that I loved her and loved her, and although she often cried after that I never minded it a bit, because I knew how nice and cuddly she could be when she was good!

*Dorothy Edwards*

Being too young to understand:

## My brother

Today I went to market with my mother.
I always help her buy the things we eat.
Not sitting in the pushcart like my brother
Who gets our dinner piled around his feet.
I know where jam is. Coffee. Bread and butter.
Each thing I bring she says to Davy: "No!
Don't touch that, Sweetie!" Mostly Davy doesn't.
This morning Davy did some touching though –
He spread his hair with cottage cheese all over.
Bit through paper. Gave our ham a chew.
Liked the butter. "DAVY!" cried my mother.
She started to scold my little brother.
Couldn't.
Burst out laughing.
I did too.

*Dorothy Aldis*

Do you look after a little brother or sister?
When do they make you cross? When do they make you laugh?
What sort of things can you do that babies can't?
What kind of things can you do to help look after babies and smaller children?
Do you think it is right to get cross when they don't understand they are doing something wrong? How do you feel when a little brother or sister does something really annoying – like breaking one of your favourite toys or spoiling a game you are playing? What do you do? What do you think you should do when this happens?

## David and his sister Carol *(extract)*

*David's parents have decided to adopt another baby. Miss Evans, a social worker, has started to make the arrangements and one day she comes and says:*

"I think we have just the right baby for you. She is only six weeks old.

"Her mother and father love her very much, but they are very young and they have nowhere to live together and bring up their baby. They want me to find a family for her where she will be happy and have lots of love. I've told them about you and they think you would be the right family to have their baby."

Mummy and Daddy and I were very excited. We all hugged each other.

"When can we see her?" I asked.

"Please come to my office tomorrow morning," said Miss Evans.

We cleaned the room again that evening and made everything tidy. I put the rattle in the cot. We decided to call my new sister Carol. I was so excited I thought I would never be able to sleep. The next morning we all got up early. I put on my best clothes. We had breakfast but we were all so happy we couldn't eat very much. Daddy drove us into town, and we parked the car.

We went to Miss Evans' office, but we were too early so we had to sit and wait in another room. There were some comics and toys but I was so excited that I just held Mummy's hand.

At last Miss Evans came in and said, "You can come in and see her now." We went in. The baby was just waking up. Her eyes were very big and dark. My Mummy didn't say anything. She looked a bit as if she was crying. She hugged Daddy and me.

"Isn't she lovely," I said. "Yes, she's wonderful," said Mummy.          *Althea*

How did David and his parents prepare for the new baby? How did they feel as they waited to see her? Why were Carol's parents unable to look after her themselves?

## Little

I am the sister of him
And he is my brother.
He is too little for us
To talk to each other.

So every morning I show him
My doll and my book;
But every morning he still is
Too little to look.

*Dorothy Aldis*

Do you have a baby brother or sister? Are they too little to play with you yet?

I'm the youngest in our house
so it goes like this:

My brother comes in and says:
"Tell him to clear the fluff
out from under his bed."
Mum says,
"Clear the fluff
out from under your bed."
Father says,
"You heard what your mother
said."
"What?" I say.
"The fluff," he says.
"Clear the fluff
out from under your bed."
So I say,
"There's fluff under his bed, too,
you know."
So father says,

## Sometimes

Sometimes I share things,
And everyone says
"Isn't it lovely? Isn't it fine?"

I give my little brother
Half my ice cream cone
And let him play
With toys that are mine.

But today
I don't feel like sharing.
Today
I want to be alone
Today

I don't want to give my
little brother
A single thing except
A shove.

*Eve Merriam*

Have you ever felt like getting rid of a sister or brother? If so why? What sort of things make you really angry with them?
What sort of things do you share? What don't you like sharing? Why?

"But we're talking about the fluff
under *your* bed."
"You will clear it up
won't you?" mum says.
So now my brother – all puffed up –
says,
"Clear the fluff
out from under your bed,
clear the fluff
out from under your bed."
Now I'm angry. I am angry.
So I say – what shall I say?
I say,
"Shuttup stinks
YOU CAN'T RULE MY LIFE."

*Michael Rosen*

Are you the youngest in your house? What do you like about it? What's bad about it?

## For sale

One sister for sale
One sister for sale
One crying and spying young sister for sale;
I'm really not kidding
So who'll start the bidding?
Do I hear a dollar?
A nickel?
A quarter?
Isn't there, isn't there, isn't there any
One kid who will buy this old sister for sale?

*Shel Silverstein*

## Big sister and little sister

*Once there was a big sister and a little sister. The big sister took great care of her little sister – kept her off the road, played with her, made sure she didn't get lost, and when she was upset big sister would comfort her by holding out her handkerchief and saying "Here, blow."*

Big sister knew everything. "Don't do it like that," she'd say. "Do it this way." And little sister did.

But one day little sister wanted to be alone. She was tired of big sister saying, "Sit down." "Go there." "Do it this way." "Come along." And while big sister was getting lemonade and biscuits for them, little sister slipped away, out of the house, out of the garden, down the road, and into the meadow where daisies and grass hid her.

Very soon she heard her sister calling, calling, and calling her. But she didn't answer. No one told little sister anything now. The daisies bent back and forth in the sun. A bumble bee bumbled by. Suddenly big sister was so near, little sister could have touched her.

My Scarey feelings
Monsters hide under the pillow
My brother cries
I Sing to my brother
My brother cries til mid night
I give up
I Stop singing
My brother goes to sleep
I do too

Roger Linington 5.

Big sister sat down in the daisies. She stopped calling. And she began to cry. She cried and cried just the way little sister often did. Little sister stood up but big sister didn't even see her, she was crying so much. Little sister went over and put her arm around big sister. She took out her handkerchief and said kindly, "Here, blow." Big sister did. Then little sister hugged her.

And from that day little sister and big sister both took care of each other because little sister had learned from big sister and now they both knew how.

*Charlotte Zolotow*

Why do you think the big sister did all those things for her little sister? What kind of person do you think the big sister was?
Why did the little sister run away?
Would you have run away from the big sister? Why?
Does your older brother or sister ever annoy you? How?
How do you behave with your younger brother or sister?
Does he/she copy you? How?
How do you and your brother/sister help each other?

☆ After discussion get the children to write a description of the kind of brother or sister they would *like* to have – their appearance, age, behaviour. What would they like to do together? What would they like their imaginary brother or sister to do for them?

**Mathematics**
☆ Record the number of brothers and sisters the children each have on a block graph. Draw a graph showing relative ages.

**Songs**
*Tinder-box:* 19 How many people live in your house?
26 Don't you push me down

**Stories**
*A Baby Sister for Frances* R. Hoban (Faber)
*Big Sister, Little Brother* T. Berger (Macdonald)
*Dogger* S. Hughes (Bodley Head/Lions)
*Emily's a Guzzleguts* J. J. Strong (Evans)
*Go and Hush the Baby Crying* B. Byars (Bodley Head)
*Jenny and Steve* Ulises Wensell (Evans)
*Little Nippers* series: *My Brother* and *That Baby* (Macmillan)
*Mog and the Baby* J. Kerr (Collins)
*My Baby Brother, Bernard* S. Ellentuck (Abelard-Schuman)
*My Brother, Ned* Sumiko (Heinemann)
*My Naughty Little Sister* D. Edwards (Methuen/Puffin)
*A New Baby* T. Berger (Macdonald)
*One-Eighth of a Muffin* R. Orbach (Lions)
*Peter's Chair* E. J. Keats (Bodley Head)
*Stevie* J. Steptoe (Longman)
*Titch* P. Hutchins (Bodley Head)
*The Trouble with Jack* S. Hughes (Bodley Head)

**Information books**
*Wayne is Adopted* S. Wagstaff (Black)

# Older people

## Objectives

☐ To consider how people change as they get older
☐ To think about what it is like to be older
☐ To consider old people's special needs and how we can help them
☐ To recognise old people's abilities and knowledge and think of the ways they help us

It will be helpful for the children to start by defining what we mean by "old", since to young children, old can mean over twenty. Encourage the children to think about some of the difficulties for old people in our society and how we can help them, but also stress that old people have a great deal to offer us in return.

## Starting points

○ Ask a few children to describe what they think being old is like. How old is old?

○ Ask some children to read out some of their written work and display paintings of old people (see classroom activities). Ask the other children about the old people they know – grandparents or neighbours. What are they like? What do they do? When do the children visit them? What happens when they visit? What do they talk about?

○ What happens to old people as they grow older? Make the point that many old people are very fit and independent while others have to cope with failing health which may call for special care and attention. Who provides special care? (old people's homes, grown up children, home helps, neighbours).

○ Play a recording of *Fings ain't wot they used to be* (Lionel Bart) and discuss the words.

○ Invite an old person into the school to talk to the children about their childhood. What was different about it? What was the same?

---

Old people were children once too:

### The little old lady

That little grey-haired lady
Is as old as old can be
Yet once she was a little girl
A little girl like me.

She liked to skip instead of walk,
She wore her hair in curls,
She went to school at nine and played
With other little girls.

I wonder if, in years and years,
Some little girl at play,
Who's very like what I am now
Will stop to look my way.

And think; 'That grey-haired lady
Is as old as old can be,
Yet once she was a little girl,
A little girl like me.

*Rodney Bennett*

In what ways is the old lady different from the little girl?
What sort of things can you do that old people can't?
What things can they do which you can't?

---

## The Japanese Headman

An old person's wisdom and experience help him to save the lives of his neighbours:

In a little village of Japan, near to the sea, lived an old Japanese gentleman. He was the chief man of the village, and owned many fine rice-fields; to him in their difficulties came all the villagers to obtain advice and comfort when they needed it; he helped them with rice and money if they needed help, and settled their disputes when they arose.

One day after the rice harvest there was a festival in the village, and all the villagers were busy merry-making. The headman had not gone down with the rest, but sat at home with his little grandson. Suddenly there was an earthquake; they are not at all uncommon in Japan, and nobody took much notice of it; the houses rocked to and fro, and then all was still again. But the old headman, watching from his doorway, saw the sea rushing back from the land, quite a long way out; he was old, and had seen it happen before and knew what it meant. The villagers all shouted in surprise, and ran down to the beach to watch the curious sight. There was no time to send a messenger to warn them, and this noble, loyal, old Japanese gentleman did the only thing possible. He caught up a lighted torch and set fire to his new rice-stacks, one after the other, and they flared up into the sky, making a blaze of light.

The people on the beach caught sight of the great fire, and the alarm bell of the temple rang out. Back they all streamed as fast as they could run, and up the hill to the burning rice-stacks. Those who arrived first began to extinguish the flames; but the old man said "No, no, let it burn. I want all the people to gather here."

When the villagers heard that, and found that he had himself set fire to the rice, they said, "Poor old man, he is mad."

"Are they all here?" asked the old headman; and they answered, "Yes, we are all here; but what does it all mean?"

"Look at the sea," he cried, and when they looked they saw that the sea was rolling back to the land again in a great wave that seemed as high as a mountain. It dashed in over the village and spread roaring over the fields, then it rolled back to its old bed, having swept all the village away. But the villagers were safe, for they were on the higher ground where the headman's house was: and the old man stood there, poor as the poorest of them, because, by his loyalty to his friends and comrades, he had burned all his crops to warn them of the danger.

*Traditional Japanese*

Why did the old man know there was danger when no one else did?
How did he save everyone?
How else did he help the villagers?
(Gave them advice and comfort, settled disputes.)

# The very old birthday party

Long ago, when my sister was a naughty little girl, we had a very old, old great-Auntie who lived in a big house with lots of other very old ladies and gentlemen. Our mother said, "She is going to have a birthday party next week, and I think it would be very nice if you little girls could come to it. You see it is a very special party because old Auntie will be one hundred years old."

Well now, when the birthday came we were very excited. We wore our best Sunday dresses and looked very smart girls. I bought our Dear Old Auntie a nice little white handkerchief with blue flowers on the corner.

It took me a long time to think what to buy. But my little sister didn't think at all. She knew just what she wanted. She said, "I'm going to buy one of those glassy-looking things with the little houses inside that make it snow when you shake them."

I thought it was a silly thing to give to such a very old lady, but my naughty little sister said, "It isn't silly. I would like one of the glassy things for *my* birthday."

My sister and I had never been to an old people's Home before, so we were very quiet and staring when we got there. There were so many old people. Dear old ladies and dear old gentlemen all with white hair and smiling faces, and they all talked to us and shook hands with us in a very friendly way. And we smiled too. The lady who looked after the old people was called Miss Simmons and she was very kind. "We are all very glad to see such young people," she said to my sister, "Do you know I don't think we've ever had anyone quite as young as you before?"

What a very little old wrinkly pretty lady our old Auntie was! She had a tiny soft little voice and twinkly little eyes and she took a great fancy to my naughty sister at once. She asked her to sit next to her.

The old Auntie was very pleased with her presents. But when she saw what my sister had brought she clapped her hands together in a funny old-lady way and she said: "Well-well-well. What a lovely treat! I haven't seen one of these since I was a little girl. I saw one in another little girl's house and I always wanted one. Now I've got one at last!"

Miss Simmons said, "I see you have a box of sweeties too. But I don't think you had better eat them yet. We have a birthday cake with one hundred candles for you to cut and a very nice birthday tea. It would be a pity to eat sweeties and spoil your appetite."

Now my sister had heard Mother say that sort of thing to her but she was surprised to think that people had to say such things to old ladies.

And what do you think? When kind Miss Simmons went off to see about the birthday tea, old Auntie opened her box of sweeties and gave one to me and one to my sister and then she ate one herself! And she laughed and my sister laughed.

When Miss Simmons came back and saw what old Auntie had done she shook her finger at her. "You are a very naughty old lady," Miss Simmons said.

Then Miss Simmons looked at the hundred-years-old lady, and my bad little sister, both laughing together and she said, "Goodness me, you can see you are relations. You both look alike!"

And do you know, when I looked, and Mother looked, at the naughty old lady and my naughty little sister, we saw that they did!

*Dorothy Edwards (abridged)*

## Classroom activities

### Language

☆ The children can write an account of an old person they know well. Ask them to structure it round the following questions:

What does s/he look like?
What does s/he enjoy doing?
What does s/he find difficulty doing?
In what ways could you be helpful?
What does s/he do for you?

☆ Discuss the good and bad things about being old in our society. Here are some ideas:

Enjoying retirement
Being able to work part time
Helping with grandchildren
Having more leisure

Being alone and lonely
Being ill
Being isolated from family
Finding it difficult to adjust to retirement after an active working life

Discuss how difficulties for old people can be made easier. What does society provide for old people? – meals on wheels, home helps, old people's social clubs. How do families provide for their older members? How could both improve on what they do for old people?

### Art

☆ Group the children in pairs and ask them to use their imaginations to paint portraits of each other as they think they will look when they are old.

### Project

☆ Ask an old person to talk to the children about their childhood and use this as the starting point for a project on life for the children of fifty years ago.

## Much nicer people

Old, old lady,
      Why have you bolted your door?
We don't want people tracking our carpets
With dust and dirt any more.

Old, old lady,
      Why have you drawn your blinds?
My sister and I make much nicer people
Entirely in our minds.

*Elizabeth Coatsworth*

Some old people find it very difficult to cope with change.
Why do you think they don't like the way things are now?
Do you think many people visit these old ladies? Why? Why
not?
Do you think it would help the old ladies if they saw more
people? Why? Why not?

## A special person

I like my grandad. He is really nice. He lives in
Lancashire and he has got a poodle. He has got grey
hair and blue eyes. When I go to their house they
always spoil me. They get me clothes and toys and
when my grandad picks me up at the station he tells
me to feel in his pocket and find lots of sweets. He
says to me, "What's in there?"
   "Sweets," I say, and he says they are for me.
   Last time I was there I went to a party and my
nan bought me a long dress. Now you know my nan
and grandad are kind to me.

*Rachel, aged 8*

Do you like visiting grandparents? Why?
Do you have a grandparent who has an interesting hobby or
special skill?

I like going to visit Gran and Granpa My Granpa is a brilliant inventor If you have a greenhouse you have to water it every day. EVERY DAY! Well my Granpa has invented a machine and you turn the handle and it waters plants automatically and automatic windows open when it is hot and fans come on and lots of other things too It is very useful when he goes away on holiday I like inventing things too.

Charles Hartill 7

# Friends

**Objectives**
- ☐ To consider how we make friends
- ☐ To think why we like particular friends
- ☐ To examine what kind of behaviour makes a good friend

As well as examining relationships with friends some consideration can be given to isolated children and how other children could help them.

**Starting points**
- ○ Make a display of classroom work – children's writing, models of imaginary friends, paintings (see classroom activities).
- ○ Discuss qualities of friendship (see classroom activities).

**Classroom activities**

**Language**

☆ Talk to the children about the way they make friends – by asking the other person about themselves, suggesting interesting things to do together, sharing things. How do they know if someone wants to be their friend? – they smile, say hello, ask them to play, show an interest in them.

☆ Write about an adventure with an imaginary friend. The friend could be a person, animal, object, mythical creature, someone or something very big or very small, someone with magic powers. Discuss the children's ideas as well. Ask them to write about an adventure they had together in a space capsule, in a cave, on an island, or on top of a high tower.

☆ Ask each member of the class to think of and suggest a quality of friendship:

A friend is someone who . . .

Ask the children to write each suggestion out in felt-tip pen, to display with a drawing of their favourite friend.

## The boy who went looking for a friend
*(extract)*

Friends are very important. We need them to play with and to share our experiences. Good friends like us the way we are and enjoy doing things with us.

*Sam was a lonely little boy who had no friends so his mother suggested he went to look for one. He found a tiger to play with in the meadow and they played some very exciting games together but then the tiger got bored and went away. He made friends with the monkeys playing in the trees at the bottom of the garden, but they climbed too high and he couldn't play with them anymore. He had an exciting time with some people from the circus who stopped at the gate and showed him a lot of tricks but then they had to move on to the next town and he was left alone again.*

*He was so miserable the next day that he thought he would never find a friend who would stay and play with him and he went down to the river.*

Then round a bend in the river came a little boat with a blue sail. It came past Sam. Then it stopped by the watercress and a boy got out. He was just Sam's size of boy, with an ordinary brown face and brown hair.

"Hello!" he said, "I didn't know you lived here. My name is Philip. What's your name?"

"Sam!" said Sam.

"Get in my boat and we will sail some more," said Philip. They sailed all afternoon. Up and down the river bank they went, watching the fish in the clear green water. They saw wild ducks swimming and cows coming down to drink. They saw a wild, bright pheasant in the long grass. All the time they talked and made up stories. It was the best day of all. When it was sunset Philip said, "We must go home now or our mothers will come calling us. May I come and play with you tomorrow, Sam? You are a good sort of friend to share my boat with me."

"Of course," said Sam, very pleased.

Sam went home and said to his mother, "I've got a friend and I didn't have to ask him to come and play tomorrow. He asked *me*."

"He sounds the best sort of friend then," said Sam's mother.

And this story is called, "The Boy Who Went Looking for a Friend", and here is an end to it.

*Margaret Mahy*

All the people that Sam played with at first were very exciting but they weren't the best friends. Why was Philip a good friend? (Sam and he liked the same things, they had a lot to talk about and were interested in each other.)

Have you ever felt lonely? We need friends when we are lonely.

What do you do with your friends?

What do they do for you?

Why does Batman collect worms? To feed Robin!

Why do elephants never forget? Because no one ever tells them anything!

What do you get if you cross an elephant with a kangaroo? Big holes in Australia!

## Friends

I fear it's very wrong of me,
And yet I must admit,
When someone offers friendship
I want the *whole* of it.
I don't want everybody else
To share my friends with me.
At least, I want *one* special one,
Who, indisputably,

Likes me much more than all the rest,
Who's always on my side,
Who never cares what others say,
Who lets me come and hide
Within his shadow, in his house –
It doesn't matter where –
Who lets me simply be myself,
Who's always, *always* there.

*Elizabeth Jennings*


## Just me, just me

Sweet Marie, she loves just me
(She also loves Maurice McGhee).
No she don't, she loves just me
(She also loves Louise Dupree).
No she don't, she loves just me
(She also loves the willow tree).
No she don't, she loves just me!
(Poor, poor fool, why can't you see
She can love others and still love thee.)

*Shel Silverstein*


Do you think it is wrong for the child to want his friend all to himself? Why? Why not?

How do you feel when your best friend plays with someone else? Would your best friend get angry if you played with someone else? Do you think best friends should only play with each other?


## Jethro makes friends with a jumbie

*Jethro, a little boy who lives in the Caribbean, was seven when his big brother Thomas promised to take him fishing to Anegada on his eighth birthday. Now it was nearly Jethro's birthday and Thomas was refusing to take him fishing because he was still too small. Jethro was furious. In a temper he stamped out of the village along a jumbie trail. Everyone warned him about the jumbie but Jethro was too angry to listen:*

"*Mean* old brother!" he said, and stamped – and hurt his foot.

Then he saw the jumbie. Under a big grey curly-branched loblolly tree lived the jumbie. It is not easy to describe what a jumbie looks like. He is a spirit of the dead, and he has been one for so long that he has forgotten whose spirit he was in the first place. As a result he has no shape – he is just a fuzzy ball of light.

Jethro glared at the jumbie. He was much too cross to be frightened.

The jumbie looked at Jethro in surprise. He made a long, low, blood-curdling noise, his favourite, which never failed to make human beings turn and run away, screaming.

"Owoooooo-ooooo," said the jumbie.

"Oh stop it," Jethro said impatiently. "You is just a figment of the imagination, and I got no time for you. I don' believe in jumbies."

"What?" said the jumbie, outraged.

"You not real," Jethro said.

"Not real, eh?" said the jumbie. "I show you!"

And the fuzzy ball of light flashed with a glare like an exploding star, and hovering over Jethro's head was an enormous mosquito, the size of a helicopter. Roaring and whirring, it came down,

nearer and nearer, great long legs towering above Jethro, huge terrible eyes staring at him, long snout aimed at him like a cannon barrel.

Jethro glared right back at the big round eyes.

"You don' scare me none," he said crossly. "You not real."

And suddenly there was no mosquito, but only the fuzzy ball of light that was the jumbie.

"Hah!" Jethro said.

"You not raised right, chile," the jumbie said severely. "You don' have respect."

And in an instant the ball of light flashed into nothing again, and standing over Jethro was a gigantic scorpion.

The scorpion was tall as a tree, covered in brown armour plate that glittered like polished bronze in the sun. Its great curved sting rose high in the air and pointed down over its back, needle-sharp, quivering.

Jethro took a step back, looking nervously up at that sting, and he stepped on a sharp stone with one of his sore feet. It hurt. At once a new wave of bad temper washed over him, and he shouted angrily at the scorpion, "Go 'way, you big ol' bug! You can't sting me with that stinger, 'cause I don' *believe* in you!"

And the scorpion vanished as if it had never been, and the fuzzy ball of light was there, whirling, instead. The jumbie was growing very irritated with Jethro; he was making a low ominous humming sound. All at once with no warning he vanished again, and behind him Jethro heard a fearsome clanking, crashing sound. He turned around. He gasped.

Coming toward him through the bush like a great long-legged machine was a tremendous land crab. Its flat body reared higher than a house, and its one huge attacking claw was held high and dreadful, blotting out the sun. Even when it is twenty inches high, the land crab is the ugliest beast in the Caribbean. At twenty feet high, it was terrible. Jethro shuddered.

But the sight of a crab made him think of the sea. And the sea made him think of fishing. And at once he remembered Thomas, his back-sliding brother who had promised to take him fishing and had broken his word. And Jethro was cross with the whole world again.

He yelled at the land crab, "Go 'way! You great pot of gundi! I keep tellin' you, I don' believe in jumbies!"

This time a funny thing happened.

The land crab did not suddenly vanish. It grew smaller and smaller, until it was the size of an ordinary land crab, which is about the same as a cat, though spindlier. And then it seemed to collapse in on itself, and once more it was the fuzzy ball of light that was the jumbie.

But the ball of light did not seem so bright as before. The jumbie made one last effort at a terrifying noise, but it came out very small. "Ow . . . . ooooo . . . . oo . . . .'"

And the noise turned to sniffles and snuffles, and to his great surprise Jethro realized that the jumbie was crying.

"You breakin' all the rules!" the jumbie sobbed. "People *always* scared of jumbies. That what keeps us goin'. If you just stand there refusin' to believe in we, what goin' happen?"

"Well," said Jethro. "What goin' happen?"

"I goin' vanish, that's what. That be the end of me. Look, I gettin' dimmer all the time. Ooooo . . . hoooo . . ." He sobbed harder than ever, and Jethro saw that it was true: the fuzzy ball of light was indeed getting smaller and smaller, very fast.

He said uncertainly, "Oh dear." Then he said, "Well, maybe I does believe in you just a little bit."

The sobbing stopped. The ball of light grew a little brighter. "You does?" the jumbie said, sniffing.

"Sure I does," Jethro said heartily. "And that was one impressive land crab, man."

The light gave a happy little bounce, like a glowing football. "I feelin' more like myself every minute," the jumbie said happily. "Hey my son, what you name?"

"Jethro Penn," said Jethro.

"You is a friend of mine, Jethro Penn. What I can do for you?"

*Susan Cooper*

Why wasn't Jethro scared of the jumbie?
What happened to the jumbie when Jethro said for the third time that he didn't believe in him?
How did they become friends?
Why do you think they liked each other?
The friendship between Jethro and the jumbie got off to a very bad start. Have you ever made friends with someone after disliking them at first? How did you become friends?

## Don't go, Miranda

Here comes Miranda with riddles and jokes.
    Here comes Miranda again,
With a bagful of sweets and a couple of cokes
    To show her superior brain.

Miranda asks questions that certainly drag.
    She puts us to shame when at school.
But she's bringing the cokes and a jellybean bag
    So we're playing it friendly and cool.

The answers to riddles we simply don't know
    For somehow our brain-box grows numb.
We try very hard not to tell her to go
    When she's calling us "stupid" and "dumb".

Miranda's a know-all and gives herself airs.
    She's terribly old in her ways.
But she's buying us chips and some chocolate eclairs,
    So isn't it better she stays?

*Max Fatchen*

Do the children like Miranda? What do they like about her? What don't they like about her?
Why does Miranda have to give the children coke and sweets? Do you have friends who are only friendly when you have some sweets? Are you like this sometimes?

☆ Write a poem about how it feels to have no one to play with. You could give the younger children a format to work on:

| First line | 1 word | Sad |
|---|---|---|
| Second line | 2 words | I feel |
| Third line | 3 words | lonely, miserable, afraid |
| Fourth line | 4 words | So I run home |
| Fifth line | 1 word | Alone |

☆ Have a joke telling session or competition – some are given on page 57. Results can be judged by the response – either groans or laughter. Ask some children to talk about other things they enjoy doing with friends.

**Art**
☆ Paint or draw a friendly face. Get the children to smile at one another and observe the results closely before they begin.

☆ Make a model or a collage of one of the imaginary friends the children have written about.

## Ranjit and the tiger *(extract)*

*One day a little boy named Ranjit met a tiger in the jungle near his village. The tiger was hurt – he had caught his foot in some creepers. Ranjit helped him to get free and the two became friends. The tiger took the boy back to his cave deep in the jungle and there he made friends with the tiger's mate and their cubs:*

Ranjit was happy staying with the tigers. He played with the cubs who kept running into each other and falling over, and he explored the cave which went deep into the mountain and once he had a ride on the tigress's back.

But he couldn't stay there for ever. He had to get back home. His mother would worry about him if he was out after dark.

"Goodbye, tigers," he said. He knew they could not understand him but he felt he had to say something to them. He stroked each one of them in turn and patted their heads which they seemed to like. Then he waved goodbye and set off home.

But he didn't feel so safe in the jungle as he did when he was with the tiger. There were strange moving shapes of animals. He knew that there were creatures lurking in the dark places of the forest. He hurried on. Sometimes he saw the swift movement of the cobras in the bushes and he ran, cutting his arms on sharp branches. He was beginning to wish he had stayed with the tigers. But now he had to keep on to his village.

He heard a sound behind him and, turning, he tripped and fell. He was soon on his feet again but when he looked up there in a tree just above him was the long and powerful body of a leopard. It was staring straight at Ranjit and its mouth was curled up in an ugly snarl. Ranjit knew that it was getting ready to leap. If he ran it would soon catch up with him. If he stayed there it would leap out onto him. What could he do? If only he could call his tiger friends.

It was his only chance. He put his hands to his mouth and shouted in a loud voice: "GOODBYE TIGERS." He hoped the tigers would hear him and recognise his voice.

The leopard was surprised by the call and stopped for a minute. He didn't know what to make of the call.

Ranjit stood his ground and stared at the leopard. The leopard stared at him. The leopard wasn't sure what to do. He crouched ready to spring and with a snarl on his face, but he didn't spring. And then Ranjit heard it.

The sound of the tiger. So his friend had heard him.

The tiger came bounding up, huge and fierce. It leapt up at the leopard who drew back spitting and snarling. The tiger lashed out with his terrible claws. The leopard shrank back and then turned tail and bounded away into another tree and into the jungle.

Ranjit turned to his friend.

"Thank you, tiger," he said. "I did you a good turn, and now you have done one for me."

*Paddy Kinsale*

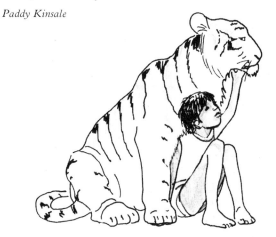

# Other living things

## Objectives

☐ To think about pets and how we can care for them best

☐ To think about the variety of life around us – wild birds, animals, insects, plants, flowers and trees

☐ To encourage a respect for the living things that share our world

Young children are often fascinated by animals and pets, but they need to learn how best to look after them and when to leave well alone. Try to encourage a respect for all living things.

## Starting points

○ Display the children's pet paintings and get them to read pet stories (see classroom activities).

○ Bring a dog or other pet into assembly and demonstrate proper grooming and care. Make sure the animal is used to children.

○ Invite the local vet, RSPCA or PDSA education officer into school to talk to the children about the proper care of their pets.

○ Ask a police-dog handler or guide-dog handler to come and show the children their dog's special abilities and explain how they are trained.

○ Play a recording of *The Ugly Bug Ball* for fun. Perhaps some children could make bug costumes and invent a dance.

○ Each class can grow a variety of trees from seed. When they are big enough, take assembly out of doors and plant the trees in the school grounds. The children can record their tree's growth and note the changes which happen to it during the year.

Horse chestnut branches
The buds are sticky
The Leaves are like umbrellas
The stems are covered in snow
hands are coming out
Light green cups

Marcus Freeman 6

## Whose garden?

It's just a little garden, about so wide. The peas and carrots and tomatoes grow in slightly crooked rows but the petunias around the edge have plenty of room to bloom pink and the marigolds marching down the middle almost make it look like two gardens.

Whose garden is it?

The wriggly brown earthworm thinks it's his garden because he lives there. He wriggles his way through the rich black earth, leaving it richer and softer. The robin thinks it's her garden. She sings her morning song there and has her breakfast of bugs there, too. The yellow butterfly spends hours flirting among the marigolds. Sometimes it's hard to tell which is flower and which is butterfly. He is sure the garden belongs to him.

The ladybird decided this was the perfect garden in which to raise her family. Now she has lots of little ladybird babies and she teaches them to look after the garden. The fuzzy bumblebee comes to the garden on business. She is so busy gathering sweetness from the flowers that she scarcely has time to see how pretty they are. So much to do! If bees could talk, this one would surely insist the garden is hers.

Whose garden is it?

You'd almost think the big bright sun owned the garden. The garden couldn't grow without the sun's warm golden smile and the garden seems to smile right back up at him. But the garden needs rain, too. The rain makes it stand tall and smell fresh. The others leave when the rain visits the garden as if the garden belonged only to the rain.

Whose garden is it?

A small freckle-faced girl planted the seeds. She pulls the weeds and waters it when the rain doesn't have time. If you'd ask her, she would say it was her garden.

Whose garden is it?

*Marilyn Kratz (slightly abridged)*

The garden belongs to everyone and everyone is important in it. How do the worm, ladybird, robin, girl help the garden grow?

Do you think the girl could make the garden grow on her own?

How do the sun and the rain help the garden?

The Peach tree Stands Still all Day Long At the end of the garden Standing all alone a Peach fell off

Victoria Williams 7.

## Classroom activities

### Language

☆ Ask the children to write about a real or funny pet (e.g. My camel, Georgina). They could describe their adventures together in written work and paintings. They should try to cover their pet's name, appearance, food, home, and any unusual adventure they have had together.

☆ With the children make a collection of all the words they can think of to describe animal skins or sounds. Display them on the walls:

☆ Make pet-care booklets including instructions, illustrations, and a design for an ideal home. You could stimulate the children's ideas by discussing the care of school pets and ways of improving their environment.

☆ Discuss *Dildrum, King of the Cats.* In stories we often give animals human abilities or characters. Many of our sayings reflect this, e.g. crafty as a fox, hungry as a wolf. Do the children think that animals do have the same sort of feelings that we have? Are they able to talk? How are animals different from us? In what ways are they similar?

### Mathematics

☆ Make a survey of the children's pets using the relationship arrow.

### Science

☆ Make a study of four mammals choosing those for which you have suitable reference books. Divide the children into groups, one to study each animal. Find out about and compare their habitat, size, appearance, food, ways of moving, noises. Visit a local wood if possible to look for signs of them – droppings, burrows, prints, fur, chewed nuts. Record the findings in paintings, drawings and written work.

GUINEA PIGS

Cuddly warm no fleas.

Have GUINEA PIGS

They're sweet

little things to hold

And their eyes

keep wide open

Joanna Fabian 7.

## Dildrum, King of the Cats

One evening an old gentleman who lived in the middle of Lancashire sat reading in his parlour. Outside the wind was beginning to growl like a dog that smells strangers, and every now and then the rain was dashed against the windows like a handful of gravel; but the curtains were drawn, the wet night was shut out, and inside all was cosy. Spectacles on nose, the old man sat back in his winged chair, and rested his slippered feet on a little footstool. He was reading, and the room round him was quiet.

Suddenly upon the wide hearth there began to fall a little rain of soot drops, and as they pattered down, the old gentleman put down his book and adjusted his spectacles. The fire dimmed strangely and went down, the candle flames began to flicker and to shake – and then from out of the mouth of the chimney there sprang a great grey cat. He was a wild outlandish cat, with fur matted with the rain, a long lean body, one green eye and one brown one, and a quick eager look on his face. Resting his paws on the footstool, he looked up searchingly into the old man's face, opened his mouth and then, in a perfectly clear voice said, "Tell Dildrum that Doldrum's dead!" – and then, leaping back into the chimney, he kicked down more soot, and vanished.

The old man could scarce believe his eyes. Surely the cat had been real. There could be little doubt of that for there on the hearth were the patches of fallen soot, and there on the footstool were the marks of two sooty paws! But had the cat really spoken? Had he really uttered those strange words about Dildrum and Doldrum? The old man blinked with confusion and wondered if he could trust his senses.

Just then the door opened. In came the old man's wife and after her, Julius, their own cat. Julius was no ragamuffin of a cat. He was handsome from top to toe. His fur was a lovely quaker grey, except for his nose and the tips of his ears which were a rich dark plum colour. His whiskers were long and silky; his eyes were of a blueness never seen in a cat; and his walk was slow and majestic. He walked sedately into the room, stretched himself on the hearth-rug, and looked into the fire with calm philosophic eyes.

"Here's your tea, Matthew," said the old woman. "I've brought you a dish of your favourite China tea, and two little ... Why, Matthew, I declare that you aren't listening to a word that I'm saying. What has happened to you? You look as if you'd had a shock."

"Not a shock, my dear – but something has happened tonight that has made me wonder if I can trust my senses any more."

"Then first take your tea," said his wife, "and tell me all about it as quietly as you can."

"Well, my dear," began the old gentleman, "I don't know that I can expect you to believe me, but this – I take my oath on it – this is what happened tonight in this very room. Just as I was reading, down that chimney, believe it or not, came a cat, a great grey creature, with one green eye and one brown eye, and a body as lean as a rake . . ."

The old man paused for as he came to the description of the grey cat, Julius pricked up his ears, got up, and turned so that he sat facing the old man. Then he fixed upon his master's face so intent and human a look that the old gentleman could not go on with his tale.

"Just look at old Julius! What's the matter, old pussy? Do you want to hear, eh? Well, I'll tell you."

So, half-forgetting his wife, the old man began to talk to the cat.

"Yes, down the chimney came this great grey messenger. He leapt out on to the hearth, put his two feet upon my footstool, opened his mouth and said 'Tell Dildrum . . .'

At this Julius opened his wide blue eyes and he looked more intently than ever.

"'Tell Dildrum,' he said," went on the old man, "'that Doldrum is dead.' Well, I never heard anything so funny in all my life! Dildrum and Doldrum! 'Tell Dildrum,' he said – why, what's the matter, Julius?"

Julius had leapt with all four feet now on to the footstool. In his eyes there was a queer look, half of sorrow, half of excitement and triumph. Then, suddenly, he too opened his mouth, and in a rich and princely voice, he said "Alas! Is Doldrum dead? Why, that makes me the King of the Cats!"

Thereupon the flames of the candles began to flicker again. The fire sank and dimmed. Julius – or Dildrum – leapt on to the hearth, and with one spring vanished up the chimney. When they had recovered from their shock, the two old people ran out and looked up; but there was nothing unusual to be seen. The great sagging clouds were passing over the sky. The fringes of the trees were scratching at the roof of the house; but no Julius was to be seen. He had gone to his kingdom, and was already sitting in state with a golden crown on his princely head.

*Traditional Lancashire folk tale, retold by Fred Grice (slightly abridged)*

## Hurt no living thing

Hurt no living thing;
Ladybird, nor butterfly,
Nor moth with dusty wing.
Nor cricket chirping cheerily,
Nor grasshopper so light of leap,
Nor dancing gnat, nor beetle fat,
Nor harmless worms that creep.

*Christina Rossetti*

Do you think it is possible *not* to hurt other living things? Why? Why not? Do you think it is wrong to hurt them? What can we do to avoid hurting other living things unnecessarily?

## The seed

How does it know,
this little seed,
if it is to grow
to a flower or weed,
if it is to be
a vine or shoot,
or grow to a tree
with a long deep root?
A seed is so small
where do you suppose
it stores up all
of the things it knows?

*Aileen Fisher*

☆ Keep small creatures for observation for a short time. You will need:

for worms – a large glass container, layers of earth, sand, peat, and leaf mould kept slightly damp
for caterpillars – an ice cream carton covered with gauze and containing plenty of the correct kind of leaves for them to feed on
for snails – a glass container, pebbles, rocks, and a little earth and leaves kept moist.

Get the children to observe and make detailed drawings of the way they move, breathe, and feed. Stress the importance of caring properly for all living creatures and return your guests to their proper habitat as soon as possible.

☆ Go pond-dipping. Investigate your findings with the aid of a microscope.

### Art
☆ Ask the children to paint a picture of an animal from life if possible. Use school pets as models if you can. Encourage them to observe carefully the animal's size, shape, colour, type of skin, movements. Mount the paintings and ask the children for one sentence each describing the animal.

☆ Make butterflies with stuffed felt bodies, tarletan or net wings. Decorate with appliqué, sequins and embroidery. You could make other insects using the same techniques – bees, ladybirds and so on.

☆ Make a chart of leaf outlines and ask the children to match actual leaves to the shapes.

### Music
☆ Choose a poem about an animal, bird, fish or insect. Discuss the words of the poem with the children and the character of the creature it describes. Experiment with voices and instruments to make a short piece of music to accompany a reading of the poem.

## Projects

☆ Visit a zoo to stimulate discussion, written work and paintings. How do the children feel about keeping animals in zoos? What are the advantages – gives us the opportunity to learn about and respect other creatures. What are the disadvantages from the animals point of view?

☆ Bird watches. Set up a bird-table near a suitable window. Cover the window with dark paper with slits cut into it for the children to look through. (You could prepare the children by visiting a local reserve if possible. Ask the warden to talk to the children about the birds and show them a real hide.) Find out about suitable bird food. Put small groups of children on five-minute bird watches and get them to record the variety of birds which visit the table. Don't be discouraged in cities. There are plenty of interesting birds but you may have to have patience and wait for quite a while for them to arrive. Make a count of the number of sightings of different species and their food preferences.

| | | | | | | |
|---|---|---|---|---|---|---|
| cheese | ▣ | \|\| | | | \|\| | \| |
| sultanas | ⚅ | | \|\|\| | \|\| | | |
| BACON RINDS | ▨ | | | \|\|\| | \| | |
| bread | ▢ | \| | \|\|\|\| | | \|\|\|\| | \|\| |
| | | ROBIN | Thrush | Sparrow | Starling | BLUE TIT |

☆ Find out about growing plants and trees from seeds and pips. Oranges, lemons, lychees, avocados, peanuts all grow well though the children will have to experiment carefully with growing conditions and give their pips regular attention.

## Songs

*Tinder-box:* 34 Place to be, 35 Gardens, 45 I would like to be, 46 I went to the cabbages, 48 Let it be
*Subject index:* Animals, Birds, Caring for our surroundings, Flowers, Gardens, Nature, Trees

## Stories

*Animal Disguises* A. Fisher (Nelson)
*Animal Jackets* A. Fisher (Nelson)
*Bird Clock* I. Lucht (Blackie)
*Birth of a Duckling* Koenig and Isenbart (Dent)
*A Dog So Small* P. Pearce (Puffin)

## Carlo the crocodile makes his escape

The surroundings which suit people best are not always the best for animals:

*Miss O loved animals and believed that nature was very cruel to them. She spent her life travelling round the world rescuing fish from cold wet ponds and putting them in fish tanks, putting the birds in nice warm cages for the winter, and covering the desert sands with carpets so the lions wouldn't burn their paws. On her travels one day, she found a baby crocodile lying in the sun by a riverbank doing nothing but eat flies. She decided to rescue him from his boring life and took him home to the city with her. She named him Carlo:*

Carlo had a television, a swimming pool in the bathroom, a fridge full of the best sardines and five big toothbrushes, all different colours. But he had no friends. He was very lonely. He spent all day looking out of the window and never went out. He watched the cars and people go by. Sometimes he saw animals too, birds, cats and dogs. But he never saw anybody who looked like him.

One evening Carlo was watching a programme about a faraway country with great deserts and a wide river. Somehow it seemed familiar. Suddenly he saw something else. It took his breath away. Crocodiles! "So that's what I am," cried Carlo, "a crocodile, and there are others like me."

He decided even before the programme had ended to go to this beautiful river and meet the other crocodiles. But how was he going to get the money for his journey? Then he had an idea. He put on Miss O's coat and hat and went out. The streets were dark, quiet and empty. Carlo walked fast. At the far end of the street, something glittered. It was the fountain he was looking for. He knew from Miss O that many tourists came to see the fountain and each of them threw a coin into it for good luck.

Carlo pulled off the coat and hat, and jumped into the water. He began to pick up the coins and put them into a handbag. Suddenly he heard a

scream. A man was at the edge of the fountain. He was pointing at Miss O's coat and screaming at the top of his voice, "Help, help, a monster has pulled a woman into the fountain." With one giant leap, Carlo was out of the water and running as fast as he could.

Next morning Carlo took the handbag, and went to the airport. The town was in a panic. The newspapers were full of it.

THE SECRET OF THE FOUNTAIN! Who is the person kidnapped last night by a MYSTERIOUS MONSTER ...? Grey coat and hat found by Mr K, only witness to horrific mystery!

In all the confusion nobody took any notice of Carlo. He boarded the plane just in time. After the landing, Carlo knew immediately where to go. He could smell the river. When he got there, it was more beautiful than anything he had ever seen. As he stood there, gazing around, he saw someone in the distance. It was Miss O. Miss O was approaching her favourite spot on the river. It was here, many years ago, that she had found a small green crocodile. Then the water splashed and she heard a voice: "Goodbye, Miss O!"

Miss O looked up and saw a crocodile, swimming away from her. Her Carlo? But why would he want to leave her? Wasn't he happy with his swimming pool, television, sardines and five toothbrushes all of different colours? Then a strange thought crossed Miss O's mind. Perhaps Carlo didn't like living in a flat. Perhaps crocodiles prefer to swim in a river. And perhaps lions like to run on hot sand, and seals to swim in cold water, and ...

"Good luck, Carlo!" she called to him, "And goodbye!" – but I don't know whether he heard.

*Anna Fodorova*

Why didn't Carlo like the city?
Why did he prefer the river?
Miss O liked animals very much but was she really being kind to put the birds in cages/fish in tanks/Carlo in her flat?

## A pigeon

As it lifted up off the ground
Its wings spread like leaves
Its tail opened like a fan
Its feet curled up tight.
It sees a spot of white on the grass
It swoops round and dives at the
    bread
It comes to the grassy ground
It comes to the piece of bread
It swoops it to its beak and eats it.
Then it walks around for more
    bread,
Its feet go up and down
Its wings are like cobwebs
Its feathers are scruffy
Its colours are like a butterfly's
Its patterns are like an artist's.

*Marion Sheen*

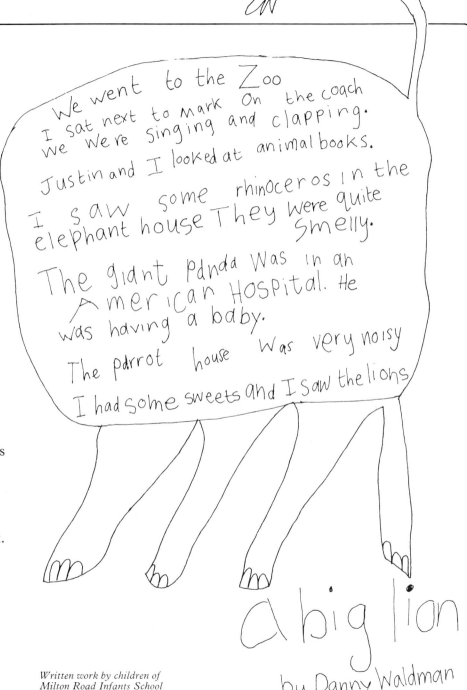

We went to the Zoo
I sat next to Mark on the coach
We were singing and clapping.
Justin and I looked at animal books.

I saw some rhinoceros in the
elephant house They were quite
    smelly.

The giant panda was in an
American Hospital. He
was having a baby.

The parrot house was very noisy

I had some sweets and I saw the lions

a big lion
by Danny Waldman

*Written work by children of
Milton Road Infants School*

*Harry's Bee* P. Campbell (Puffin)
*How the Whale Began and Other Stories* T. Hughes
    (Puffin)
*Joe and the Gladiator* C. Cookson (Puffin)
"Leaf Magic" from *The Second Margaret Mahy
    Story Book* (Dent)
*Let's Grow a Garden* G. Fujikawa (Zokeisha
    Publications)
*Mog the Forgetful Cat* J. Kerr (Collins)
*Mole* L. Murschetz (Methuen)
*My Cat* N. Gray (Macmillan)
"My Naughty Little Sister Makes a Bottle Tree" from
    *All About My Naughty Little Sister* D. Edwards
    (Methuen)
*Nippers* series: *Arthur Small, Ginger* (Macmillan)
*Old Macdonald Had Some Flats* J. Barrett (Kestrel)
*Partouche Plants a Seed* B. Shecter (Piccolo)
*Some Swell Pup* M. Sendak and M. Margolis (Bodley
    Head/Puffin)
"The Strange Egg" from *The First Margaret Mahy Story
    Book* (Dent)
*Titch* P. Hutchins (Puffin)
*Trouble With Animals* J. Strong (Black)
*Web in the Grass* B. Freschet (World's Work)
*What Horrible Creatures* C. Opperman (Dent)
*What Shall I Choose* (Church Information Office
    Benjamin Books)

**Information books**
*Animals in Winter* V. Luff (Black)
*The Cornfield* V. Luff (Black)
*Funny Facts* series: J. L. G. Sanchez and M. A. Pacheo
    (Evans)
*The Garden Year* C. Spangenberg (Black)
*It's Easy to Have a Caterpillar to Stay, It's Easy to Have a
    Snail to Stay, It's Easy to Have a Worm to Stay* ed. C.
    O'Hagan (Chatto)
*Let's Read and Find Out* series: *Bees and beelines,
    Birds at night, How a seed grows, Ladybird ladybird
    fly away home, Watch honeybees with me, Where
    does your garden grow* (Black)
*Look It Up* series: *Cold-Blooded Animals, Warm-
    Blooded Animals* (Macmillan)
*Nature in Close-Up* series (Black)
*The Pip Book* K. Mossman (Penguin)
*Tree Calendar* I. Lucht (Black)
*Who Wants Pets?* A. Prince (Methuen)
*The Young Pet Owner's Handbook* J. Pope (Purnell)

# Home

## Objectives
☐ To think why we need homes
☐ To think about the variety of homes there are
☐ To think about the people who live with us
☐ To consider the activities that take place in the home

Homes give us shelter, a gathering place for the family, and a centre for many different activities. Encourage the children to consider their homes carefully and to think about what they enjoy or dislike about them.

## Starting points
○ Ask the children about where they live and how many people live with them. This could lead into a discussion of the variety of family structures – families with one adult or many, one child or many, adopted children, no children, extended families and so on.

○ Make a housing display using photographs or children's paintings. Estate agents will often supply photographs, or get a class to paint different kinds of housing – flats, bungalows, castles, house-boats, and so on. Compare the advantages of leading a travelling life with those of staying in one place. Compare the advantages of living in a castle with those of living in a bungalow, and so on.

○ Make an interior plan of one of the homes above, or the home in *Wanted*. Display it in assembly and discuss what we use different rooms for.

○ Discuss the times when everyone in the family is at home together, and the things they do together. Talk about the things which we do inside rather than out (eat, sleep, read, etc).

○ Base an assembly on *Boxes* (see classroom activities).

## Classroom activities
### Language
☆ Ask the children to describe their favourite time of day at home. Who is there? What are they doing? Why do they enjoy it?

## Folks

I've heard so much about other folks' folks,
How somebody's Uncle told such jokes
The cat split laughing and had to be stitched,
How somebody's Aunt got so bewitched
She fried the kettle and washed the water
And spanked a letter and posted her daughter.
Other folks' folks get so well known,
And nobody knows about my own.

*Ted Hughes*

How many people live in your house?
Are any of them special in any way?

## Wanted

I'm looking for a house
Said the little brown mouse,
            with
One room for breakfast,
One room for tea,
One room for supper,
And that makes three.

One room to dance in,
When I give a ball,
A kitchen and a bedroom,
Six rooms in all.

*Rose Fyleman*

What rooms would you have in your home if you could choose?
What do you use the rooms for in the place you live now?
Most homes have bathrooms, kitchens, living rooms and bedrooms but do you know what a lounge is? A study? A conservatory? Can you think of any other kinds of rooms?

## Boxes

My street is a row of boxes, all the same.
The same gardens, the same doors,
The same firm four sides and lid.
The same blank windows stare out
Like cold impersonal eyes.
But open up the boxes
And you might get a surprise.

There's the man at twenty-seven
Plays the trombone in the bath
And rides his bike around the kitchen
To give the kids a laugh.
While at twenty-eight the lady
Wraps her telly up in chintz
And roars old fashioned love songs
In a voice that makes you wince.
Then she knocks the wall to tell them
To keep quiet at twenty-nine
Where they're busy filling bottles
With home made spaghetti wine.

And so on and so on
In every box the street has got.
The outsides are identical
But the contents – they are not.

*George Moore*

Do you live in a row of houses or block of flats which look the same from the outside? What makes them all different inside? (People, furniture, decoration, activities.)

## Chitra makes a curry

Making a meal for a family is hard work and takes practice to do well. In this story, a little girl from an Indian family finds out about the difficulties involved when she offers to cook subzi (a vegetable curry) and chapattis (a kind of bread) for the evening meal:

When I started to think about it on the way home from school I wondered whether I would really be able to manage on my own, so I asked my friend Lata to come home with me and help me. She's Indian too, and I secretly hoped that she would know more about it than I did. It would be more fun to do it together anyway.

Mum had left a big paper bag full of peas on the table, some onions and a few potatoes. I started to scrape the potatoes while Lata shelled the peas. It took rather a long time, and rather a lot of pea-pods got on the floor, but we thought that we would have time to clear them up later. I didn't want to cut the onion up because it always makes your eyes water and sting. But Lata didn't want to do it either and we had quite an argument about it, so I did it in the end. In two minutes the tears were streaming down my face and I could hardly see what I was doing.

Next we had to fry the onion and it smelt lovely now, all sizzling and golden. Then we had to add the spices – chillies and turmeric – but while we were rummaging in the cupboard looking for them we forgot all about the onion . . . I'm afraid it wasn't nice and golden any more when we went over to look at it, but just nasty bits of black stuff floating about in the fat.

So we started again with another onion and Lata chopped it this time. Now we got it right and sprinkled in the spices before the onion was too cooked. This was the bit I enjoyed doing most, because the spices are lovely colours, the chillies bright scarlet and the turmeric deep yellow. We put in the vegetables and some water to make a nice gravy, put a lid on the saucepan and left it to cook. I was not sure how long we should leave it as I never noticed how long it took Mum to cook the subzi when she made supper. But I thought that we could keep on having a look and poking the potatoes to see if they were done.

Now we had finished that subzi we wondered whether we should start making some chapattis. I felt rather doubtful as I thought they would be too difficult to make. Mum always says that it takes a lot of practice to make good chapattis. But Lata pointed out that at least we could get the dough ready so that when Mum got home she would only have to roll it out and cook it. So we got the brown flour out of the bin and started mixing it with water in the big plastic bowl.

"How are you getting on?" asked Dad, looking around the kitchen door. "Something smells good. Will it be ready soon?"

"Dad," I said, "I think there's something wrong with this dough. It's all sticky."

Dad thumped and pounded the dough and it started to look a bit more like Mum's dough. He was enjoying himself showing us what to do, and now he had flour all over his trousers and his shirt too.

"You see if I don't cook the best chapattis you've ever tasted," he said.

But he didn't have a chance to show us how clever he was, because just then Mum came in. We all stopped talking and looked rather guilty because we thought she was going to be really cross to see all the mess. We just stood there among all the potato peelings and pea-pods, with flour all over our fronts and up to our elbows. But she wasn't cross at all, she just laughed and laughed.

She took off her coat and rolled her sleeves up, and put on an apron over her sari.

"Come along, you leave the chapattis to me. Get the plates on the table and call the boys, then come and eat."

Everybody had to agree that the subzi tasted very good – even Raju, my brother – and I was very proud and pleased.

*Ursula Sharma (abridged)*

Who does the cooking in your home? Do all the family help to prepare the meal? Do you help?
What is your family's favourite meal?
Do you always eat together or only sometimes?
What sort of meal do you have on special occasions?

☆ Younger children can make small books shaped like houses or flats, and colour in the details of the exterior. Get them to write about their homes inside, illustrating each page:

> my home has a kitchen
> > a bedroom . . .

or

> at home I play
> > I eat . . .

☆ Older children might enjoy writing about and painting an imaginary home either in an unusual place – top of a mountain, under the sea, on Mars – or for an unusual person or animal – a giant, gnome, monster, creature from outer-space. Discussion beforehand will produce more varied and interesting results. Make sure they can justify their design with regard to their choice of place or person.

**Mathematics**
☆ Make a block graph or do a mapping exercise of the kinds of homes the children live in.

**Science**
☆ Make a collection of building materials – bricks, cement, straw, tiles, slate, wood, tin, stone, mud. Compare for strength and durability. Which would make the warmest building? How would you construct a house from each of the different materials? What else would you need? Find pictures or slides of houses made of the different kinds of materials. Look at the school and houses close by and examine the building materials used.

☆ Investigate the homes of four different animals e.g. rabbit, squirrel, crow, otter. Where do they make their homes? Why do they make them there? What do they use to make them? – earth, twigs, feathers. How do they make them? – with beaks, front or back legs.

☆ Spread out some newspaper and carefully take a nest to pieces. *Only take nests in autumn and winter.* How many different types of building material are there? How has the nest been built? Stick examples of the different materials used on a big sheet of sugar paper and label them.

## A traditional Japanese house

*Kiku lives in a big city in Japan. Her home is in a block of flats much the same as flats anywhere in the world. But once a year she goes to the country to visit Obaa-san her grandmother. Obaa-san lives in a traditional Japanese house, built specially to suit its surroundings:*

Obaa-san lives in an unpainted wooden house. The floors are covered with padded, shiny straw mats, called *tatami*, all the same size. The rooms are divided by sliding doors, made of wood and thick paper or cloth. Some of the doors leading to the garden are made entirely of wood (these are closed at night) but others have panes of glass or paper which is semi-transparent. When the sun shines, Obaa-san shows Kiku how to move her fingers so that her hands throw shadows shaped like butterflies and rabbits and horses' heads on the sunlit paper panes.

There is scarcely any furniture in Obaa-san's old-fashioned house, and no chairs at all. Everyone sits on cushions on the floor. Kiku and Ichiro find it difficult to keep still for long, sitting on their feet, so Ichiro often sits cross-legged.

Obaa-san has no beds in her house either. The family sleeps on thick padded quilts on the floor, with thinner quilts to cover them. In the daytime, the quilts are put away in built-in cupboards.

One night there is an earthquake – luckily, a small one. Kiku hears the wooden shutters rattling before she wakes up enough to realise that the house is swaying. The tremor stops as the children roll out of bed, so there is no need for them to run to the front door and stand under the lintel. That is the safest place in an earthquake.

*Juliet Piggott*

Homes all over the world are specially designed to suit the weather and local conditions? What sort of weather do you think this house is suited for? What sort of special conditions might it have to stand up to? (Earthquakes – explain what a lintel is and why it is the safest place.) How is this house different from your home?

It is nearly spring. Carla and Zoe took a nest to bits last week. They found lots of things. Birds must be very clever to make nests with their beaks and feet. They found some mud and rope and a stone and some straw and leaves and leave skeletons and twigs and moss and a snail shell and the nest felt a bit prickly     Dan Hawthorn 6.

Auntie Alice
Lives in a palace.

Uncle Fred
Lives in a shed.

Cousin Louise
Has a house in the trees.

Uncle Boris
Has a house in the forest.

Baby Mabel
Sleeps in her cradle.

Sister Joanna
Sits under the piano.

*Janet Smith*

What do you think it would be like to live in each of these places?
How would you like the inside of your palace to be?
How would you arrange the inside of your shed?

### Art

☆ Paint a picture or make a collage of the family enjoying their favourite meal.

☆ Read *Boxes* and discuss the things which make every home different. Make a wall display of identical boxes which can be opened to show a wide variety of family life inside. Ask the children to make contrasting collages of family activities, put them into boxes with flaps on the front for the children to open, and pin them to the wall in a row.

☆ Design the interior plan of the house in *Wanted*, or of a caravan, houseboat, or castle. Give careful consideration to the needs of the occupants in your designs.

### Songs

*Tinder-box:* 13 A house is a house for me, 19 How many people live in your house? 36 Skyscraper wean

*Subject index:* Home, Houses, Relatives and family

### Stories

*The Bears Who Stayed Indoors* S. Gretz (Benn)
*Come Over To My House* T. Le Sieg (Collins)
*A Funny Sort of Christmas* D. Cate (Hamish Hamilton)
*A House is a House for Me* M. A. Hoberman (Kestrel)
*The House of Four Seasons* R. Duvoisin (Hodder)
*The House Where Jack Lives* M. Crompton (Bodley Head)
*The Jackson Family* series: *Everyday Life*, and *Our Home*, Ulises Wensell (Evans)
*My Family* F. Sen (Bodley Head)
*Our Home* C. Larsson (Methuen)
*A Roof Over Your Head* B. Naughton (Blackie)
*Tilly's House* F. Jaques (Heinemann)

### Information books

*At Home in 1900* S. Purkis (Longman)
*Building a House* B. Barton (Julia MacRae Books)
*Houses and Homes* C. Cocke (Macdonald)
*How They Live Now* series: *Dimitra of the Greek Islands* Matthews, *Kiku of Japan* J. Piggott, *Rashid of Saudi Arabia* Freeth, *Ravi of India* Hardy and Aruna (Lutterworth)
*How We Live* A. Harper (Kestrel/Puffin)
*People Around Us: Families* (Black)
*Strands* series (Black)
*The World of Homes* series (Macmillan)

# School

## Objectives

☐ To consider what schools are for and what kinds of activities take place there

☐ To think about the different kinds of people who work in school

☐ To compare the school with the home

☐ To think about the school buildings, situation and surroundings

## Starting points

○ Discuss with the children what school is for. Why do they come to school? What do they expect to happen at school? Discuss the variety of activities which take place there.

○ Each class might be invited to talk about or demonstrate a project they are currently working on.

○ Make a collage of the people who work at the school – children, teachers, administrative staff, cooks, caretakers, pets. Interview some of these people in assembly or ask them to give a short talk about their work and answer the children's questions. (See *Needing others* for interviewing.)

○ With the children's help make a large plan of the school for display in assembly. Include the playground and immediate surroundings. Make the plan as detailed as possible including the layout of classrooms, hall, playground, grass, trees, entrances.

○ Invite some of the children to read out accounts of their first day at school (see classroom activities). Discuss and compare their experiences with those of the other children.

○ A class which has been on an outing recently could share their experiences with the other children through displays of art and written work (see *We went to the zoo*).

○ Some children may be attending classes outside school in dance, music, athletics and so on. Others may be attending special schools where they learn about their religion, language or culture – Sunday school, Sikh school, etc. A group of children might be invited to talk about or demonstrate what they learn there.

## Starting school *(extract)*

It was the summertime and Dawn was nearly five. She lived in a house in Chapel Street and there was a school at the end of the road. Her brother Leroy and her sister Heather went there and Dawn knew that she would soon be going there as well. So she asked Leroy what it was like.

"It's all right," he said. "There's lots of things to do. You have milk in the morning, and when it's playtime, you go out in the playground with your friends. Everybody goes out so I can see you then."

At last, the big moment came. It was Dawn's first day at school. Mum had the morning off work so that she could take Dawn along. They all walked down the road together. Dawn held Mum's hand, and Leroy and Heather kept just a bit in front.

When they got to the school gate, Leroy said, "See you at playtime," and then he and Heather ran off. Dawn and Mum went into the school together. Mum had to see so many people. There was such a lot to talk about. Dawn got bored just standing and waiting. But at last, Mum took her into a big, sunny room. Dawn saw a lady with children all around her.

"That's your teacher," whispered Mum.

When she saw them the lady smiled and came over.

"This is Dawn," said Mum.

"Hello, Dawn," said the teacher.

Dawn said "hello", and then the teacher told her to look around the classroom and choose something to do. There was a sand tray and a water tray. There were lots of paint pots with brushes in them and there was a special little house to play in. There were building bricks and boxes of Lego and a doll's pram with two dolls in it. Dawn was surprised to see so many toys in school. Then she saw some crayons and a lot of paper, and the teacher said,

"Would you like to do some drawing, Dawn?"

"Yes, please," said Dawn, and she sat down at a table.

It took her a long time to draw her picture because she kept looking around at all the other children in the room. Dawn didn't know any of them and she began to feel a bit lonely.

After a while, the teacher said it was playtime. All the children ran out to play and Dawn ran out as well. She wanted to see Leroy. The playground was very big and noisy and there were so many children. They were all running about and playing, but Dawn didn't have anyone to play with. She looked everywhere for Leroy, but she couldn't see him. She looked and looked. She didn't know what else to do. Where could he be?

She began to cry, and Jenny and Meena, two girls from her class, came over.

"Don't cry," said Meena.

"I want to go home," said Dawn, and she cried even louder.

Jenny put her arm around Dawn. "Are you a new girl?" she asked.

"Yes," sobbed Dawn, "and I want Leroy."

"We'll find him for you," said the girls. "What's your name?"

So Dawn told them her name, and as they all walked together across the playground, Dawn began to feel a bit better.

Why did Dawn begin to feel lonely? What made her feel better? What did you like about your first day at school? What didn't you like about it?

## Classroom activities

### Language

☆ Ask the children to describe how they felt on their first day at school. Make a collection of words describing their feelings – strange, excited, happy, frightened, lonely, interested, proud.

☆ Get the children to write an account of their first day. What happened? Who did they meet? What did they do? What did they like or dislike?

☆ Read *Out of School* then ask the children to write a description of how they *come* to school.

☆ Write descriptions of the things the children like best and like least about school. Ask them to give their reasons.

☆ Write sports reports of recent matches the children have been involved in or watched.

☆ Talk to the children about the PTA (especially just before a meeting is about to take place). Explain the reasons for it and what happens at the meetings.

### Mathematics

☆ Make a chart of the different ways the children travel to school – by car, bus, bicycle, on foot, train.

### Art

☆ Paint a picture or make a collage of a favourite activity.

☆ Paint or draw the school from the outside or draw an interior plan of the classroom.

☆ For fun the children could make a "rogues gallery" of paintings of the teachers in the school.

☆ Design an ideal classroom. Get the children to explain in a written account what they have included. Allow them to include anything they like.

## Look out!

The witches mumble horrid chants,
You're scolded by five thousand aunts,
  A Martian pulls a fearsome face
  And hurls you into Outer Space,
You're tied in front of whistling trains,
A tomahawk has sliced your brains,
  The tigers snarl, the giants roar,
  You're sat on by a dinosaur.
In vain you're shouting "Help" and "Stop",
The walls are spinning like a top,
  The earth is melting in the sun
  And all the horror's just begun.
And, oh, the screams, the thumping hearts –
That awful night before school starts.

*Max Fatchen*

Is this how you felt on the last day of your holiday? Why? Why not?

## Speaking English

When I came to Canada, I didn't know how to speak English. When I went to school, I saw so many kids that I never had seen before. I felt like a mouse being surrounded by cats. Now that I know a little English, I don't feel like that no more.

*From* Come with us: children speak for themselves

Why might life be difficult for someone who has come from abroad and is learning a new language? (Would find it difficult to speak to people and make new friends, would have difficulty understanding lessons in school.)
Have any of you felt like this?
How could you help someone learning your language? (Help them to learn, speak to them a lot, be patient if they get things wrong at first.)
What could they teach you? (Words in their language, things about the country they have come from.)

## An interview with the school caretaker

**Interviewer:** How long have you been a caretaker?
**Peter:** I have been a caretaker for three years.
**I:** Do you like being a caretaker?
**P:** Yes, most of the time I enjoy it, but sometimes it is boring.
**I:** How many schools have you worked in?
**P:** Two schools as permanent school keeper and about 7 different schools as a relief school keeper.
**I:** Which school did you like best?
**P:** So far I like this school the best.
**I:** Why did you become a school keeper?
**P:** Well, school keeping has run through my family.
**I:** How many hours do you work?
**P:** Most days I work 7 am–12 noon and 2 pm–10.30 pm.
**I:** What type of work do you do as school keeper?
**P:** I have to make sure that the school is clean and safe for the children to come into. I do minor repairs and keep the grounds tidy.
**I:** Do you ever have a holiday?
**P:** I do have time off but only in the school holidays.
**I:** Do you have any pets?
**P:** Yes, I've two cats and a dog, one of the cats is called Angel and one is Bubble and my dog is called Mick.
**I:** Thank you very much for your cooperation, Peter.

Rodge said,
"Teachers – they want it all ways –
You're jumping up and down on a chair
or something
and they grab hold of you and say,
'Would you do that sort of thing in your own home?'

"So you say, 'No.'
And they say,
'Well don't do it here then.'

"But if you say, 'Yes, I do it at home.'
they say,
'Well, we don't want that sort of thing
going on here
thank you very much.'

"Teachers – they get you all ways."
Rodge said.

*Michael Rosen*

Do teachers get it all ways?
When do you think teachers are unfair? (Encourage the
children to discuss what they consider to be fair behaviour
and what they consider to be unreasonable, e.g. being sent
out of school lunch, or the whole class being punished
because one person behaved badly).

(Ask the children about some of the
terms used in the poem, e.g. rising hum,
hop-scotch hop, aviators wheeling off.)
How do you leave school? (Running and
shouting, dashing to the sweet shop.)
What do you like to do at school?
What do you like best about school?
What do you find the most boring?

## Out of school

Four o'clock strikes,
There's a rising hum,
Then the doors fly open,
The children come.

With a wild cat-call
And a hop-scotch hop
And a bouncing ball
And a whirling top,

Grazing of knees,
A hair-pull and a slap,
A hitched-up satchel,
A pulled down cap,

Bully boys reeling off,
Hurt ones squealing off,
Aviators wheeling off,
Mousy ones stealing off,

Woollen gloves for chilblains,
Cotton rags for snufflers,
Pigtails, coat-tails,
Tails of mufflers,

Machine gun cries,
A kennelful of snarlings
A hurricane of leaves,
A treeful of starlings,

Thinning away now
By some and some,
Thinning away, away,
All gone home.

*Hal Summers*

### Project

☆ Base a project on the history of the school. Use
old log books, education office records, memories of
former pupils, photographs. How did the school get
its name? How old is it? Compare present with past
statistics – number of children, staff, rooms. Has the
surrounding neighbourhood of the school changed –
new houses, factories. What was on the school site
before it was built? If yours is a very new school find
out about the planning and building process.

### Songs

*Tinder-box*: 23 Work calypso

### Stories

*All Sorts of Children Go To School* J. Marshall (Warne)
*City Kids* series: *And the teacher got mad, Cooking at
school, The day I lost my busfare, Hatching chickens
at school, Wet days at school, When Tony got lost
at the zoo* L. Wilson (Nelson)
*David's First Day at School* N. Snell (Hamish Hamilton)
*Darby the Donkey* E. de Fossard (E. J. Arnold)
*I Went to School One Morning* G. Waldman (Bodley
Head)
*My Brother Sean* P. Breinburg (Bodley Head)
*The New Teacher* M. Cohen (World's Work)
*Nursery School* H. Rockwell (Hamish Hamilton)
*Tim and Terry* J. R. Joseph and D. Knight (Constable)
*Tough Jim* M. Cohen (World's Work)
*Willy Bear* M. Kantrovitz (Bodley Head)

### Information books

*At School in 1900* S. Purkis (Longman)

# Neighbourhood

## Objectives
☐ To think about the variety of surroundings in which people live
☐ To think more carefully about the children's own neighbourhood.

## Starting points
○ A class could prepare a collage of their neighbourhood. Display this in assembly and use it as the starting point for discussion about the wide variety of places in which people live. List some of these with the children's help – in towns, villages, cities, beside rivers, beside the sea, on islands, in deserts, in lighthouses, in forests, on the tops of hills, in valleys, in boats on canals and so on. Show the children slides or photographs of as many of these environments as you can and discuss what it might be like to live there.

○ Discuss the neighbourhood in which the school is situated. What surrounds it? – buildings, countryside. Do many people live in the area or very few? Draw a map of the surrounding district. (See classroom activities.)

○ Ask some children to read out their accounts of what they pass on the way to school (see classroom activities). Ask the other children about the things they see, hear and smell on the way to school.

○ Display the *Country Code*. Discuss it with the children and ask them why they think the rules have been made.

○ Make a collage of *Vicary Square* for display (see classroom activities).

○ Play a recording of *Penny Lane* (Lennon and McCartney) and display the words. Discuss the song.

○ Play a recording of *Empire Road* (Fagan) and discuss the words.

## Underneath my feet

I'm standing here – no one around,
But beneath my feet and in the ground,
Hundreds of seeds sprout and grow,
Wriggly worms burrowing slow;
Moles and rabbits are deeper down,
Curled up in their homes beneath the ground.

When I'm walking down the street,
All sorts of things are beneath my feet,
Water pipes and electric wires,
Voices, too, on telephone wires,
Hundreds and thousands of bubbling drains,
Passing over the underground trains.

*Richard Greening*

## Summer morning

In the still summer morning
What do we hear?
Blackbirds' rich calling,
Wren shrill and clear,
Pigeon's soft cooing
High in the fir,
Far distant mooing
Where the cows are.

On a clear summer morning
What can you see?
Spiders' webs gleaming
On hedgerow and tree,
Bright poppies blowing,
Lark high and free
Greeting this morning
With song, joyously.

*Jennifer Andrews*

Where is the person standing in the first part of the poem? How do you know?
Where is the person in the second part of the poem?
Why is the underground of the city so different from that of the countryside?
◁ What do you think is under the floor you are sitting on now?

## All along the street

The stopping, starting traffic
And the tipper-tap of feet
Weave a tapestry of magic
All along the street.

Here a rich, brown smell of coffee,
There a bakery smell of bread,
Not for sale, but given free;
And they throw in for good measure
The stopping, starting traffic,
And the tipper-tap of feet,
That weave a tapestry of magic
All along the street.

*F. J. Teskey*

What sounds do you hear when you are on your way to school?
What colours do you notice around you?
Do you pass any bakery shops which smell good? What other things can you smell as you walk along a street?

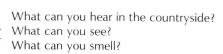

What can you hear in the countryside?
What can you see?
What can you smell?

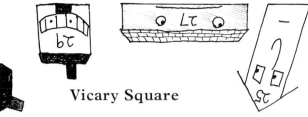

## Vicary Square

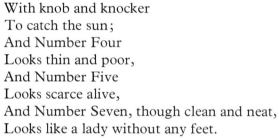

In Vicary Square at Tithe-on-Trent
The houses are all different,
As if they grew by accident.
For Number One
Is full of fun

With knob and knocker
To catch the sun;
And Number Four
Looks thin and poor,
And Number Five
Looks scarce alive,
And Number Seven, though clean and neat,
Looks like a lady without any feet.
But Number Eight
Is grand and great
With two fat lions
Beside the gate,
And Number Nine
Is deuced fine,
And Number Ten
Squats like a hen.
Number Twelve
Is by itself
Like a marble clock
Upon the shelf.

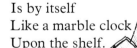

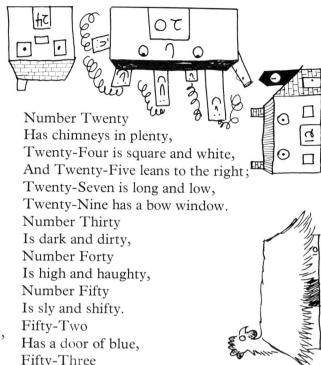

Number Twenty
Has chimneys in plenty,
Twenty-Four is square and white,
And Twenty-Five leans to the right;
Twenty-Seven is long and low,
Twenty-Nine has a bow window.
Number Thirty
Is dark and dirty,
Number Forty
Is high and haughty,
Number Fifty
Is sly and shifty.
Fifty-Two
Has a door of blue,
Fifty-Three

Has a walnut-tree
And a balcony on the second floor.

After Fifty-Four
There aren't any more.

*James Reeves*
What are people's homes like in your
neighbourhood?
Is your home in a street like the one in
the poem? Are the houses all different?
Do you ever imagine that houses have
personalities and look mean or friendly?

### Classroom activities

**Language**

☆ Write about the characters or homes which appear in *Auntie Alice*. Illustrate the descriptions.

☆ With the children list as many different names for roadways as possible – avenue, lane, drive, path, crescent, byway, street, bridlepath, motorway, ridgeway and so on. Explore the meanings of the words and the differences between them.

☆ Write a description of the local park. What does it have in it? What would the children like to have in it?

**Mathematics**

☆ Get the children to do a traffic census. Groups of children can each take a ten minute shift of tallying a particular type of vehicle – bicycle, bus, car, lorry, van, motor-cycle.

☆ Observe structural shapes in buildings or bridges – squares, rectangles, arches.

**Art**

☆ Make a collage of *Underneath my feet* showing the contrast between the underground life of the town and that of the country. Encourage the children to do some preliminary research.

☆ Get individual children or small groups to work on a painting of one of the houses in *Vicary Square*. Join them all together to make a collage.

☆ Visit a river then make a wall frieze of its course from source to estuary, including countryside, town, bridges, boats, people fishing.

**Music**

☆ Older children could try writing a song about their district (use the song *Penny Lane* as a starting point).

☆ Choose an environment – a city street, the sea bed, a wood – and experiment with sounds to create a descriptive piece of music.

## Ups and downs

If you live in the tallest block,
Towering up so high,
Through the window you can see
Right inside the sky,
Cloud and star and sunset red,
Starlings winging home to bed.

If you live in a basement flat
Just below the street,
Through the window you can count
All the pairs of feet.
Roller-skate and high-heeled shoe,
Guess which pair belongs to who.

*Elizabeth Hogg*

Where would you rather live – up in the sky or down below ground? What can you see from your windows?

## Brixton Market

A place with black and white faces
A big lovely market, people shouting
And happy sometimes
Children playing in the street
Lots of yam, bananas
Coconuts, mangoes and sweet potatoes
That is Brixton.

*Darren, Santley Junior Mixed School*

Is there a market near you? What is it like? What can you buy there?

## The park

In the middle of the city
Is an open space called a Park;
It is difficult for us to do what we like there
Even after dark.

In the middle of the Park there is a statue,
A huge man made of stone;
We are not allowed to climb his legs or scribble on his trousers,
He has to be left alone.

In the middle of the grass there is some water
Surrounded by an asphalt path;
We are forbidden to fish or throw stones into it
Or swim or take a bath.

In the middle of the water is an island
Full of mysterious things,
But none of us has ever set foot upon it
Because none of us has wings.

*Olive Dehn*

What do you think parks are for? Why is this park not much fun for children? What would you put in a park that was just for children?

## The park

I'm glad that I live near a park
for in winter, after dark,
The park lights shine
As bright and still as dandelions
On a hill.

*Rochelle Beman, Simon Marks Primary School*

# Sing a song of people

Sing a song, sing a song of people,
Sing a song, walking fast or slow;
Sing a song, sing a song of people,
People in the city, up and down they go.

People on the sidewalk, people on the bus,
People passing, passing in back and front of us;
People on the subway, underneath the ground;
People riding taxis round and round and round.

People with their hats on going in the doors,
People with umbrellas when it rains and pours;
People in tall buildings, and in stores below,
Riding elevators, up and down they go.

People walking singly, people in a crowd,
People saying nothing, people talking loud;
People laughing, smiling, grumpy people too,
People who just hurry and never look at you.

Sing a song, sing a song of people,
Sing of those who like to come and go.
Sing a song, sing of city people,
All the people that you see and never know!

*Lois Lenski*

Cities are very busy places. So many people live there that they can't all get to know one another. Who are the people they get to know? (People they work with, neighbours, shopkeepers, people who share their interests.)
Who are the people you know in your neighbourhood? Do you know everyone or just a few?
Do you like cities? Why?

# Things about my neighbourhood

In my neighbourhood the houses have beautiful colours. They are made of bricks and they have porches. The backyards are very big and most of them have grape or peach trees and green grass. Most of the houses also have big trees in front of them. The parks are around two blocks away from the neighbourhood. The stores are also near and there are a lot of them.

There are many different kinds of people that live in my neighbourhood. There are Black, English, Chinese, Pakistani, Italian, and many more. They are all very friendly and kind and also helpful. My next door neighbours are Italian and they are very helpful to us and we are helpful to them. We all get along very nice, most of us do.

I think my neighbourhood is beautiful and I love it, especially the people.

*From* Come with us: children speak for themselves

## Project

☆ Make a survey of the neighbourhood of the school. You could start by studying in detail a small part of the immediate school surroundings – street, stretch of river, beach, lane or field. Encourage careful observation noting the buildings, roads, gardens, trees, plants, road signs, shop signs and so on. What materials are used for fences, gates, road surfaces, pavements. Are the houses numbered or named. What colours are the doors and windows painted. Make a large detailed map including your findings where possible.

Find out about matters of local interest – famous people who have lived there, jubilee parties or festivals which have taken place, historical incidents and so on. Interview local residents about their feelings for the area. Find out about facilities for the community – library, community centre, Citizen's Advice Bureau, swimming pool, and so on.

Find out about the place names in the district. How did the school, town, village, streets get their names. How old are the names? The background to names can be very interesting.

## The pit heap

Billy's family may have to move house to another area in order to find work for his dad:

Billy looked up at the pit heap. It was big and black and ugly. But he knew he'd feel sorry when it had gone, when it had been reduced to a pale memory.

"I'm just going over to the heap, Our Sandra," he called.

"Mind you don't get mucky, then. Remember you've got your best shoes on!"

Billy was thinking that this might be the last time he crossed the colliery field. The other night his dad had said they might have to leave after all. There were no jobs in the area. "And we have to work to live, Billy," he said. "It's as simple as that."

It seemed to Billy that he knew every tussock of grass in this field. The trees that stood round it seemed like old friends. He knew where there were five nests down at the other end where the hawthorns were as plump and comfy as tea-cosies. And up in the far corner he knew a marshy bit where you could get tadpoles every year.

In a way, these things seemed to belong to him. Or perhaps that wasn't it. Perhaps it was that he belonged to them. Or was it that they belonged to one another?

He walked along the bank of the Stinky Beck until he reached the railway sleeper that acted as a footbridge. As he watched, a water-rat plumped into the water and began to swim across. Normally Billy didn't like rats, not even water-rats. They gave him the heeby-jeebies. Sometimes rats got into their hen-hut and pinched the eggs. Billy watched its nose forming a spreading vee as it pushed through the grey water. When it reached the other side it heaved itself onto a stone.

Billy didn't want to frighten it away. It occurred to him that this might be the last time he would ever see a water-rat in the Stinky Beck. So he sat very still, not moving a muscle.

*Dick Cate*

What did Billy see when he went for his walk?
Why did he look at everything so carefully?
How did he feel about the places and things he saw? Why?
Are you fond of the place where you live? Why?
How would you feel if you had to leave?

## Stepney

I think Stepney is a very smokey
    place
But I like it
People in Stepney do things
    wrong
But I like them
Everything in Stepney has its
    disadvantages
But I like it

It does not have clean air like the
    country
But I like it
The buildings are old and cold
But I like them
The summer is not very hot
But I like it.

*Rosemarie Dale*

**Songs**

*Tinder-box:* 18 Sing a song of people, 33 The world is big the world is small, 34 Place to be, 35 Gardens, 36 Skyscraper wean, 37 City beasts, 38 Until I saw the sea, 42 Coming down

*Subject index:* Colours, Houses, Nature, Neighbourhood, Places and countries, Rivers, Sea

**Stories**

*The Boy and the Kite* M. Velthiujs (Black)
*Bubu's Street* B. Gilroy (Macmillan)
*Burnie's Hill* E. Blegvad (Collins)
*A Day by the Sea* J. Solomon (Hamish Hamilton)
*The Elm Street Lot* P. Pearce (Kestrel/Puffin)
*Green is Beautiful* M. Rogers (Andersen Press)
*Green is for Growing* L. Parr (Methuen)
*Lesley's Story* L. Berg (Macmillan)
*Let's Be Friends* I. and L. Sandberg (Methuen)
*The Little House Omnibus* L. I. Wilder (Methuen)
*The Magnifying Glass* A. B. Sucksdorff (Black)
*Nini on Time* E. Lloyd (Bodley Head)
*Our Farm* C. Larsson (Methuen)
*Runaway Danny* C. Berridge (Deutsch)
*Samson the Sheepdog* D. Burt (E. J. Arnold)
*The Sun's Birthday* J. Pearson (Doubleday)
*There Aint No Angels No More* G. Goodwin (Collins)

**Information books**

*Beans* series (Black)
*Canal People* A. Pierce (Black)
*How They Live Now* series (Lutterworth)
*India* Z. Lindsay (Black)
*Into the Past* series: In the Street in 1900 S. Purkis and In the Country in 1900 E. Merson (Longman)
*Let's Read and Find out* series: The clean brook and Where the brook begins M. Farrington, Bottom of the Sea A. Goldin (Black)
*My World* M. Pollard (Macdonald)
*The River* V. Luff (Black)
*Sharing Nature With Children* J. Bharat Cornell (Exley and Interaction Inprint)
*Strands* series (Black)

# Water, rain and snow

## Objectives
☐ To investigate the nature of water
☐ To explain simply why it rains
☐ To think how rain looks, feels and sounds
☐ To consider the need for water
☐ To think why it snows and investigate its advantages and disadvantages

## Starting points
○ Discuss the necessity of water for all living things. Make a list of the forms water can take – a still pool, rushing stream, waterfall, rain, ice, snow, condensation, fountain, rainbow, tears, seas and oceans, geyser. Think of its properties. Think of all the uses we make of water.

○ Explain simply why it rains and discuss the need for rain.

○ Make a display of the children's paintings and written work on rain (see classroom activities). Invite some children to describe what they enjoy and dislike about it.

○ Explain snow in simple terms and discuss its advantages and disadvantages. Display paintings and models the children have made for *Winter morning* (see classroom activities).

## Classroom activities

### Language
☆ Discuss the effects of rain falling in puddles and collect a list of words which describe them – ripples, splashes, concentric circles, plops, shivers. How might the water feel when the wind blew across it?

☆ Ask the children to write a description of a rain storm followed by bright sunshine. Discuss the effects of raindrops collecting on grass, leaves and cobwebs, rushing down gutters and splashing onto pavements and into puddles. What is it like when the rain has stopped – reflections in puddles, glistening of sun on raindrops, rainbow, smell of freshness.

---

### What made Tiddalik laugh

In the Dreamtime, there lived a giant frog called Tiddalik. One morning, when he awoke, he said to himself: "I am s-ooo thirsty, I could drink a lake!" And that is what he did!

Then he drank a river. And then a billabong, and then a stream. But Tiddalik was still thirsty. All day long he searched for water. All day long he drank. Slurp, gurgle, slurp.

At last Tiddalik rested. He had to, for his whole body was swollen with water. "That's better," he said to himself, and fell fast asleep.

When the sun rose the next morning, there was not a drop of water to be seen. The rivers were dry. The lakes were dry. The streams were dry. Leaves withered on the trees. Flowers wilted in the heat.

"What are we going to do?" asked the birds and the animals. "Tiddalik has drunk all the water in the world."

"There is only one thing we can do," said a wise old wombat. "We must make Tiddalik laugh."

The animals were puzzled. "What does he mean?" they asked.

"When Tiddalik laughs," the wombat explained, "he will open his mouth, and all the water he has drunk will come spilling out."

So the animals decided to hold a Playabout. They all gathered round Tiddalik. "Let the Playabout begin!" said the wombat.

Some animals told jokes. But Tiddalik did not laugh. And pulled faces. But Tiddalik did not laugh. Some played nasty tricks. But Tiddalik did not laugh. And some did funny dances. But Tiddalik did not laugh. Some sang silly songs. But still Tiddalik did not laugh.

Deep down in a burrow under the earth, Platypus awoke with a start. "What is that noise?" Platypus had not joined in the Playabout, for she belonged to no animal tribe, and kept herself to herself. She had fur like a wombat, feet and beak like a duck. She swam underwater like a fish, and laid eggs like a snake. So she lived alone and rarely saw another creature. But now Platypus was cross. She marched up the tunnel into the daylight.

"Excuse me!" Platypus grumbled. "But I was trying to get some sleep!"

Tiddalik's eyes popped out of his head. He had never seen such a strange animal in all his life. He began to smile, and a few drops of water fell from his mouth. And then Tiddalik laughed. How he laughed! He roared and guffawed. He chuckled and chortled. Oh how he laughed! And from his mouth all the rivers and lakes and streams came swooshing out.

"Well done Platypus!" said the wombat.

"Thank you for making Tiddalik laugh," said all the animals.

The grass grew. The flowers grew. Everyone drank their fill, as the waters returned to the earth. After Tiddalik there were no more giant frogs in Australia, only small ones. But like him, they can fill themselves up with water, and save it for a dry day.

*Traditional Australian folk tale retold by Joanne Troughton*

What happened to the land when Tiddalik drank all the water? Why were the birds and animals so worried? Australia, where this story comes from, can be very hot. But even this country, which never gets so hot, needs water as much as Australia. Can you imagine what would happen if no more water came out of the taps? Where does the water in the taps come from?

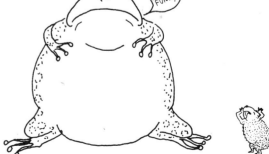

77

☆ With the children make a collection of words describing different types of rain – drizzle, downpour, torrent, raining cats and dogs. The children can write these on rain drop shapes cut out of card, and suspend them from an upturned umbrella to make a mobile. Make sure it is low enough for them to read and use in their writing.

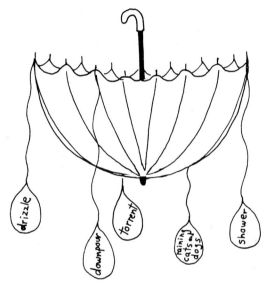

☆ Collect proverbs about rain and discuss their meaning. Why are there so many traditional sayings about rain? When do farmers want it to rain? When do they hope it won't?

☆ Write a snowman story or a description of playing in the snow.

**Science**
☆ Read Shel Silverstein's "Rain". Can rain really get inside your head? Why not? Discuss waterproofing. What makes our skin waterproof. How else do we keep dry? – waterproof clothes, umbrellas. What makes them waterproof. Discuss how other creatures stay dry – ducks have preening glands to oil their feathers, sheep's wool has an oily layer. How do insects survive a rain storm? Collect samples of material – wool, cotton, fur, brick, plastic, foil, wood, paper, fur. Drop water on to them or stand them in shallow trays of water. Try to measure as accurately as possible how much water each absorbs.

## Rain sizes

Rain comes in various sizes.
Some rain is as small as a mist.
It tickles your face with surprises,
And tingles as if you'd been kissed.

Some rain is the size of a sprinkle
And doesn't put out all the sun.
You can see the drops sparkle and twinkle,
And a rainbow comes out when it's done.

Some rain is as big as a nickel
And comes with a crash and a hiss.
It comes down too heavy to tickle.
It's more like a splash than a kiss.

When it rains the right size and you're wrapped in
Your rainclothes, it's fun out of doors.
But run home before you get trapped in
The big rain that rattles and roars.

*John Ciardi*

(When it rains again watch how the drops fall down the window. Go outside and look at the drops of rain falling in puddles.)
What sort of rain do you like best? (soft, misty rain, slow heavy rain or rain that "rattles and roars".)
What do you like about rain? (Lying in bed listening to it, walking through driving rain.)
What do you dislike about rain? (Playing football in a muddy field, getting soaked on the way to school.)

## Rain

I opened my eyes
And looked up at the rain
And it dripped in my head
And flowed into my brain
So pardon this wild crazy thing I just said
I'm just not the same since there's rain in my head.
I step very softly
I walk very slow
I can't do a hand-stand
Or I might overflow.
And all I can hear as I lie in my bed
Is the slishity-slosh of the rain in my head.

*Shel Silverstein*

How do you cure water on the brain?
Tap it!

## Winter morning

Winter is the king of showmen,
Turning tree stumps into snow men
And houses into birthday cakes
And spreading sugar over lakes.
Smooth and clean and frosty white,
The world looks good enough to bite.
That's the season to be young,
Catching snowflakes on your tongue.

Snow is snowy when it's snowing,
I'm sorry it's slushy when it's going.

*Ogden Nash*

What do you enjoy about the snow? What can you do when it snows? (Build snowmen, go sledging, ski-ing, ice skating.)

## Mr Marcus Able and the Birds

A gentleman called Marcus Able
Built the birds a feeding-table,
Filled it up with nuts and bread
And bacon-rind hung overhead,
And lumps of meat and lumps of fat
And bits of this and bits of that,
And water in a little dish
For them to drink if they should wish,
And scraps of grain and piles of seed –
Just everything that wild birds need.
Soon winter passed and then came spring,
And all the birds began to sing.
They sang to Mr Marcus Able
To thank him for the feeding table.

*Phyllis Flowerdew*

In winter we feed the birds we have to feed the birds because they can't peck the insects out of the hard ground. Michelle Nyangereka

Do you feed the birds in winter?
Why is it difficult for them to find food and water in the snow?
What happens to farm animals in winter? Where do the cows go? Why is it a disaster for sheep if it snows after Easter?
How do wild animals survive the winter? What does hibernation mean. What happens to animals' coats in winter?

☆ Make weather charts for the different days of the week.

☆ Fill a bowl with water, carefully measure its depth, and place it on a radiator or sunny window sill for a few days. Measure the depth of the water again. What has happened? Why?

☆ Floating and sinking. Fill a deep tray or sink with water then test a variety of objects (plasticene, cork, coins, polystyrene, wood, bottles) to see how and why they float or sink. Can some of the things which sink be made to float? (Plasticene can be made into a boat.)

☆ Discuss what happens to birds and animals in winter. How are farm animals cared for? How do wild animals and birds survive winter? – they hibernate, migrate, store food, feathers or coats turn white. What happens to insects in winter?

**Art**
☆ The children can run sheets of paper under water then paint or print a picture of a rainy day or a stormy sea. Use the edges of card to print slanting lines or to comb the paint into waves. Try out different effects. Make watery reflections by painting a picture on one side of the paper, brushing water on to the other then folding and pressing together.

☆ Ask the children to make individual collages of themselves in waterproof clothing using plastic bags and scraps of PVC.

Alternatively they can paint a picture of themselves with waterproofs and umbrellas on a rainy day. They can make themselves look happy or sad and write their reason for this underneath:

I like the rain because …

☆ Make a class collage or painting of the countryside in the story about *Tiddalik*. One half could show the land after Tiddalik had drunk all the water – yellow, brown and red with drooping trees and thirsty animals. The other half can show the same scene restored to life by the water.

☆ Discuss rainbows – when do we see them? How do the children feel when they see one? Why are rainbows beautiful? The children can paint a large rainbow in the correct colours and mount it on the wall. Label the colours. Make the sun and grey clouds out of tissue paper. Display individual pictures of the children in their rain clothes round the rainbow.

☆ Read *Winter morning* and use it to stimulate ideas for models and paintings of winter – "the king of showmen", "houses into birthday cakes" and so on.

**Music**
☆ Talk about the sounds which rain makes falling on different surfaces. Listen carefully when it rains and try imitating it with body sounds, voices and instruments.

**Songs**
*Tinder-box:* 41 Weather song, 42 Coming down, 38 Until I saw the sea
*Subject index:* Rain, Snow, Weather, Rivers, Sea

**Stories**
*Aio the Rainmaker* F. French (Oxford)
*A Day by the Sea* J. Solomon (Hamish Hamilton)
*Egrin and the Painted Wizard* A. Walsh (Puffin)
*Now the Days are Colder* A. Fisher (Nelson)
*Rain* P. Blakeley (Black)
*Sally-Ann in the Snow* P. Breinburg (Bodley Head)
*When the Rain Stopped* M. Sacré and C. Dernez (Lutterworth)

**Information books**
*The Clean Brook* M. Farrington (Black)
*The River* V. Luff (Black)
*Water* T. Jennings (Oxford)

**Filmstrip**
*Water* (Philip Green Educational Ltd)

# Sun and fire

## Objectives

☐ To explain simply what the sun is and why it is essential for life

☐ To think about the contrast between night and day

☐ To discuss what the children enjoy and dislike about the sun

☐ To think about the harmfulness of too much sun

☐ To consider fire – its usefulness and dangers

## Starting points

○ Make a display of the children's paintings and collages (see classroom activities).

○ Explain that the sun is a star just like those the children can see on a clear night except that this star is much closer to the earth. It is much bigger than the earth and so hot that it keeps the earth warm and light. All living things – people, animals, birds, fish, plants, insects – need the sun's warmth and light in order to live. Discuss what it would be like if the sun suddenly stopped shining.

○ Explain simply why we have night and day. Explain how the sun's beams of light are strong enough to give us daylight in spite of the thickest clouds. What is the sun like? What shape is it? What shape is the earth? What happens when our part of the earth is turned away from the sun? List some of the differences between day and night. What do we do during the day and during the night? What do birds and animals do during daytime? What happens to plants in the daytime? What happens to them at night. What is moonlight?

○ Discuss why we need warmth and fire. What do we use them for? What happens if fire gets out of control?

## Classroom activities

### Language

☆ Discuss and write about the theme of night and day. Compare the different activities which take place in each, the clothes we wear, the appearance of houses, gardens and streets, and the feelings the children have about night and day.

## The boy who trapped the sun

*Little Wolf and his sister Yakara lived in a forest by a lake. One day Little Wolf killed a white swan and ordered his sister to make him a fine new coat from its feathers so that he could visit his friends on the other side of the lake. When it was done he set out on his journey but by the time he reached the lake the sun was high in the sky and very hot. He felt sleepy and lay down to rest. When he awoke he found that the sun's heat had shrivelled his beautiful new coat:*

"Horrible sun," shouted Little Wolf. "My beautiful coat – you have burnt it. Spoilt it. I shall punish you for this."

The boy ran home. His little sister was surprised to see him and said, "Why have you come back so soon?"

"I went to sleep," explained Little Wolf, "and while I slept that wicked old sun burnt hot as fire and spoilt my fine white coat. I shall punish the sun for that."

"But how can you punish it, Little Wolf?" asked Yakara.

"I shall catch it. Trap it," said Little Wolf. "Trap it in a net so it can't come up and then it will be sorry."

"If you stop the sun from coming up to light up the world what will happen?" said Yakara. "Little Wolf I think it is you who will be sorry."

"I shan't," shouted Little Wolf. "Make me a net, a magic net from your hair."

So Yakara had to make a net from some of her long black hair and early next morning the boy took the magic net and spread it by the side of the lake at the place where he knew the sun would rise. Slowly, slowly, the sun came up. Then snap the net caught it and held it fast!

"Ha ha," shouted Little Wolf. "Silly old sun. Caught you. Now you can't come up. Serves you right."

The boy ran home to his sister feeling pleased.

But soon he did not feel quite so happy. The sun did not rise so the day did not come. The boy and the girl shivered and were frightened in the gloomy grey light. They hid in their house. The birds hid away in the trees and bushes trembling with fear instead of singing. The things that grew in the earth stopped growing. The trees, the corn, the vegetables. The rabbits hid away in their burrows. Every creature great and small hid away and shivered with fear. The fish hid away in the water weeds. Nothing grew, or swam, or ran, or flew, or sang all over the world.

"Little Wolf, Little Wolf. What have you done?" cried Yakara.

"I didn't know that without the sun the world would shiver," said Little Wolf.

"You must go and break the net and set the sun free," said his sister. But Little Wolf said, "I can't get near it. The sun burns too hot."

"Then who will break the net?" said Yakara.

Beside the lake lived the woodpecker bird. He was brave and his beak was strong. He flew from his tree across the lake. As he came near the sun it burned his feathers but he pecked and pecked at the net. The sun burnt a mark as red as blood on his head among his green but the woodpecker pecked and pecked again until suddenly "Snap" the net was broken.

Slowly the sun began to rise lighting the sky and warming the earth. The birds flew about in the forest and sang. The flowers opened their coloured petals, red and yellow and blue in the sunshine. The trees in the forest, the corn in the field, the vegetables, all began to grow. The rabbits and all the other creatures came out of their hiding places. The fish came out of the gloomy weeds and swam and darted and leapt in the water.

Everything grew or swam or ran or flew or sang all over the world. Then the boy and his sister came out of their house. Yakara heard the birds singing and said, "Everything's all right again now Little

Wolf."

"I'm sorry Sun," said Little Wolf, "I didn't know – but now I know – the world can't live without sunshine."

*Traditional South American myth retold by Anita Hewett*

## Trog and the fire

"My feet are cold," Mother said.
"My hands are cold," Father said.
"My nose is cold," Trog said.
"My feet *and* my hands *and* my nose are cold," said Grandpa Gripe.

Father, Mother, Trog and Grandpa were sitting in the hut. They had no fire and it was very cold.

"The Quickerwits are never cold," Mother said. "They have fires. Go and see how they make them."

"I will," Trog said.

Trog went over the hills to the land of the Quickerwits. They were sitting by a big fire.

"How do you make fire?" Trog asked. "We are very cold in our huts."

"It's easy," the Quickerwits said. "It's very easy! We make a hole in a block of wood. Then we put the sharp end of a stick in the hole. We roll the stick between our hands, round and round in the hole. Round the stick we put dry grass and dry moss. The rolling makes the stick hot. The stick sets fire to the grass. The grass sets fire to the moss. The moss sets fire to big twigs – and we have a fire."

Trog went back to Father, Mother and Grandpa Gripe. "It's easy to make fire," he said. "Watch me." And Trog made a fire.

*Ben Butterworth*

How is your home heated in winter?
Long, long ago, before people had discovered how to make fire, there were many things they could not do. Can you think of some of the things we need fire or heat for? Think of as many different things as you can.

◁ What happened when the sun didn't rise?
What happened to the woodpecker who flew right up to the sun to free it? What happens to things which are kept in hot sun too long? What happens to us if we stay in hot sun too long?
What happened when the sun was freed?
What do you think of the way Little Wolf behaved?
What do you think of the way Yakara behaved? Should she have done what Little Wolf told her?

## The Men of Lorbottle

One evening when the men of Lorbottle were sitting outside enjoying their mugs of beer, one of them spoke up and said, "Neighbours, I would like to talk to you about something that has been on my mind for long. Of all the times in the year, there is none I like better than when the moon is shining. So long as she is sitting in the sky and smiling at me, I do not care how far I have to travel; and in harvest time, I can work all night if only she is up to shine me a light."

"If I had spoken that speech myself, John," replied another villager, "I could not have expressed my feelings as well as you have done. Many a time when I have been stumbling home at night time, or hitting my poor shins against the milking stools in the dark mornings, I have thought, 'Ah, if only the moon was shining, I would do my work with a good heart.'"

"I am glad you agree with me," said John, "for I have a plan. Our moon runs about like a badger, →

☆ Make lists of hot and cold words – scorching, scalding, sweltering, fiery/freezing, chilly, icy.

☆ Discuss warmth with the children. When do they feel warm? What things are warm? What do they think "warm feelings" are? Make a list of things which finish the sentence "As warm as ..."

As warm as a sunny day
As warm as a cuddle
As warm as my cat's fur

In contrast make a list of things which make us feel cold:

As cold as a glass of iced squash
As cold as blizzard

Write out the warm sentences on circles of card painted in warm colours – reds, yellows, oranges. The cold sentences can be written on snowflake shapes or zigzags painted in blues, greens and greys. Display these on the walls or hang them up.

☆ Make a collection of words for light and darkness with the children's help, e.g.

| | |
|---|---|
| bright | shadow |
| radiant | gloom |
| glistening | dim |
| sunbeam | dusk |

Ask them to make up a poem about the sun or a dark night using the words.

☆ Discuss and write about how to keep warm in cold weather and cool in hot weather – eat warm food, have a hot bath, dress warmly/have a cold shower, sit still in the shade, drink cold drinks.

☆ Use *The boy who trapped the sun* as the starting point for finding out about sun legends – the Greek legend of Phaeton driving the horses of the sun, the story of Icarus, The Egyptian sun god Ra sailing in his golden boat across the sky, the sun-woman of the Australian Aborigines lighting her fire of sticks to cook her mid-day meal and covering up the red ashes with clouds at night, the god Indra in his sun chariot.

sometimes out of his hole but most times in it; and I think we should catch her, and put her in those trees over there, so that she can shine for us every night without fail."

"Yes, but how can you do that?" asked a third neighbour.

"Nothing so easy," said John. "Last night I watched where she came up. If we go there tonight, we can pick her up like a big cheese and bring her home on my big sled."

All the villagers thought that John's plan was an excellent one, so they took out the sled and pulled it to the top of the bank where he had seen the moon rise. But alas, the moon was not there. Instead they saw her coming up behind the next hill.

"We have missed her to-night, but to-morrow night we will catch her just as she comes up," said John.

So the next night they all went in good time to the far hill; but alas, she was not there either. She crept up quietly from behind another hill, even farther off. The men were disappointed but not dismayed. The next night, and the next night, they pulled their sled over hill after hill, until at last they were forced to give up the chase.

"It is a pity that we cannot carry out your plan, John," they said, "for it was a noble one and did you great credit. But the moon is as shy as a curlew."

"Good neighbours," said John, "if only we were as spry and strong as young men we could have taken her. But such distances are not for such as us." So they gave up the idea of catching the moon, and did as well as they could without her.

*Traditional North Country folk tale retold by Fred Grice*

Why did the Men of Lorbottle want to catch the moon?
Why couldn't they?
What is moonlight?
Why have people been able to land on the moon but not on the sun?

## Science

☆ Ask the children to give reasons why the sun is essential for life. Then ask them why it might be dangerous – sunburn, sunstroke, drought, forest fires, and so on.

☆ Experiment with growing seeds in different conditions – some in direct sunlight, others in a cupboard or in the shade. Record the effects of too much or not enough light and warmth.

☆ Choose four nocturnal animals – badger, owl, bat, fox – and divide the children into four groups one for each animal. Ask each group to find out about what makes their animal different from those that come out in the daytime – their appearance, habitat, abilities, activities. Record the findings in writing, paintings and collage.

☆ Discuss what a shadow is. Go outside and measure shadows at different times of day. Make a sundial. Why doesn't it work at night? What is night? – one side of the earth in shadow. Why does the moon change shape? (demonstrate this using a globe and torches in a darkened room). What happens when the sun is eclipsed?

## Art

☆ Make a mosaic of the sun. Use pieces of gold, orange and yellow paper, tin foil, sequins. It could radiate beams of light. Mount it on the wall and on the facing wall make a smaller mosaic of the earth in greens, blues, browns. Show the children some photographs of the earth taken from space. Use gauze or net to make cloud layers.

☆ Think of different ways of depicting the sun then cut the shapes out of card and paint them. The children could write on them their reasons for liking the sun. Hang them up as mobiles.

☆ Make a collage of a place in daylight and at night. On one side you could have a dark sky and stars, night animals and birds, flowers closed, people asleep. On the other side paint the sun in the sky with birds flying, animals feeding, flowers wide open and turned towards the sun, children playing.

☆ Make individual collage pictures of clothes for hot and cold weather.

☆ The children could paint a series of pictures telling the story of *The boy who trapped the sun*. Write sentences under each giving a summary of the story and mount them on the wall in sequence.

## Music

☆ Ask the children to say out loud the words for darkness and light which they listed (see above). Do the dark words sound different from the light words? In what way? Ask them to find ways of making bright shining sounds and soft dark sounds using instruments.

## Drama

☆ Dramatise the story of *Trog and the fire*.

**Songs**
*Tinder-box*: 41 Weather song, 43 Sun Arise
*Subject index*: Space, Sun, Weather

**Stories**
*The Bluebird's Shadow* P. Curry (World's Work)
*Children of the Sun* J. Carew (Little Brown & Co)
*How the Sun was brought back to the Sky* M. Ginsburg (Hamish Hamilton)
*The Little Donkey and the Stars* P. Curry (World's Work)

**Information books**
*Heat* T. Jennings (Oxford)

# Air, wind and storms

## Objectives

☐ To think about air, why we need it, and how we use it

☐ To think about the wind – what it is, what it can do, how we use it

☐ To think why we enjoy or dislike the wind

☐ To think of the dangers of high winds and storms

## Starting points

○ Ask the children what it is that is all around them but which they can't see, touch, feel, hear or smell. How do they know the air is there? What would happen if there was no air? How long can they hold their breath? Why do we need to breath? How do people breathe? How do fish breathe?

○ Tell the children that you are going to ask them a riddle then read *The wind* by James Reeves. Who or what is the poem about? What is the wind made of? We can't see it so how do we know it is there? Discuss the effects of the wind, the sounds it makes, and what it feels like.

○ Make a display of kites, hand windmills, wind chimes, mobiles, weather vanes. Demonstrate how they are made and how they work. What is a real windmill used for? What is a sand yacht? Etc.

## Classroom activities

### Language

☆ Discuss the noises the wind makes. The children can draw large leaf shapes, paint or crayon them in leafy colours and write one of the words on each in felt tip pen. Stick these or tie them to a large tree shape or a dead branch. They can refer to the "wind-tree" in descriptive writing about the wind.

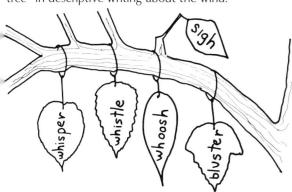

## Hanuman

Hanuman, the monkey god, was a joy to his mother and father. When he was born, his father the god of the winds, said proudly: "My son will be great and strong."

One day, when Hanuman was playing, he saw the morning sun peeping through the trees. "What a bright beautiful thing that is," he thought. He couldn't take his eyes off the sun or think of anything else. He wanted to get nearer the sun, so that he could have a better look. He decided to climb up a tree. As he gazed, the morning sun grew bigger and brighter.

"Oh I must have this wonderful thing to play with," Hanuman said to himself.

With one giant leap, Hanuman flung himself high above the ground, like his father the wind, and he rushed at the sun.

The sun was terrified. Hurriedly he called back all his bright rays. His face became dark with fear as he hid himself behind a cloud. This didn't stop Hanuman. After all, he was the son of the wind god. He flew through the clouds at great speed. He was determined to catch the sun. The sun ran this way and that in terror. "Help! Help!" cried the sun.

Indra, the thousand-eyed king of the gods, was passing by on his elephant. When Indra saw what was happening to the sun, he was very upset.

"The sun must be saved," he thought. Without wasting any time, he lifted his arm and angrily threw a thunderbolt at Hanuman. Hanuman was hit. He fell headlong to earth. The clouds and birds sadly watched him falling and wept at the fate of little Hanuman.

As the wind god swept across the earth, suddenly he saw the body of his son lying on the ground. He left his business and rushed straight to Hanuman's side. Lifting up his son's limp body, he carried it in great sorrow away from the earth. As he passed, stormy winds blew across the land, uprooting trees and scattering leaves and flowers.

When the wind god left the earth, life itself came to an end. Because there was no air, no one could breathe. Men and animals died. So did birds, insects and all living things. The trees dried up, the leaves drooped, the flowers faded. There was no movement on earth and no sound.

When Indra saw this, he realised what a terrible mistake he had made. "I killed the son of the wind god, so now he has left the earth in anger," he sighed. "I must find him and make him happy again. Otherwise the earth will remain a dead place for ever."

Riding on his elephant, Indra set out in search of the wind god. He looked in every corner of the three worlds – heaven, earth and hell. At last Indra found him in the world below sitting in a dark cave, full of grief. The body of Hanuman lay in his lap.

Indra said "Forgive me, O Wind God. I hurt Hanuman only to save the sun. Please don't be angry. Your son is not really dead. He will live as long as he likes. Death will come to him only when he wishes. When he grows up, he will be more powerful than anyone on earth."

The wind god's sorrow turned to joy when he heard this. Hanuman came back to life. His father agreed to come back to the earth, along with Hanuman.

Once again fresh, life-giving breezes blew over the earth. The whole world woke up, as if from a deep sleep. Men and women, animals and birds, plants and trees, began to stir and go about their work as before. Slowly the earth became as it had always been.

*Traditional Indian myth retold by A. Ramachandran*

## The wind

I can get through a doorway without any key,
And strip the leaves from the great oak tree.

I can drive storm-clouds and shake tall towers,
Or steal through a garden and not wake the flowers.

Seas I can move and ships I can sink;
I can carry a house-top or the scent of a pink.

When I am angry I can rave and riot;
And when I am spent, I lie quiet as quiet.

*James Reeves*

What else have you seen the wind do? (Dry washing, turn windmills, bang doors and dustbin lids, blow leaves, paper, hair across face, make waves on a pond or the sea.)
What do you like about windy days?
How does a tumble drier dry clothes? (Hot air blowing through.)
What do we use to dry wet hair?
What are windmills used for? What other forms of nature do we use to work for us? (Solar energy, hydro-electricity.)
How did ships use wind? Are there still any boats that use wind?

## The wind

The wind stood up, and gave a shout;
He whistled on his fingers, and

Kicked the withered leaves about,
And thumped the branches with his hand,

And said he'll kill, and kill, and kill;
And so he will! And so he will!

*James Stephens*

We need air to breathe, the sun to keep us warm, rain for water to drink, the earth to live on and to grow food in. When can all these things be dangerous? (Hurricanes, floods, sun stroke and drought, earthquakes.)

☆ Ask the children to describe how they feel coming to school on a windy day – excited, happy, wild, angry, irritated, frightened. Why?

☆ Discuss the dangers of very strong winds – storms at sea, damage to buildings and crops, floods. What is a hurricane? a tornado? a whirlwind? Ask the children to write about an adventure on a very windy day and paint a picture of it.

### Science

☆ Discuss how seeds are dispersed by the wind. Make a collection of some different types of seed, e.g. sycamore and dandelion, and examine their shape and design.

☆ Put a tray upside down on the floor. Tear up some paper and scatter the paper around the tray. Lift up one end of the tray and let it fall. What makes the wind that blows away the paper? How must you drop the tray to make the wind blow softly? strongly?

☆ Crush a paper towel into the bottom of a glass tumbler. Hold the glass upside down over a bowl of water and push it all the way down to the bottom. Lift it out without tipping it. The paper towel will be dry. Why? You can't see air but it is there.

☆ Measure wind speed with an anenometer made out of crossed sticks and paper cups. Colour one of the cups as a marker. Work out how to measure the speed of the wind using it.

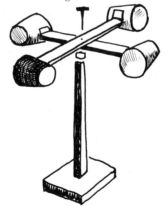

☆ Ask the children to list the ways they can tell which way the wind is blowing.

### Art

☆ Make kites, hand windmills, mobiles, wind chimes, weather vanes, and wind socks. Hang them where they can blow in the draughts from windows or set them up outdoors.

### Drama

☆ Mime the way people walk against a strong wind. Ask the children for other suggestions for mime – pegging out washing, flying a kite, chasing hat's and papers which have blown away.

### Songs

*Tinder-box:* 40 Mysteries, 41 Weather song, 44 Who has seen the wind?

*Subject index:* Shelter, Storms, Weather

### Stories

*The Boy and the Kite* M. Velthuijs (Black)
*Hurricane* A. Salkey (Puffin)
*I Don't Want To, Said Sara* H. Peterson (Burke)
*Mrs Mopple's Washing Line* A. Hewett (Bodley Head)
*The Wild Man of the Four Winds* J. Broughton (Hamish Hamilton)
*The Windmen are Coming* M. Koci (Lutterworth Press)

### Information books

*Air* T. Jennings (Oxford)
*Let's Read And Find Out* series: *Air is all around you* and *Flash, crash, rumble and roll* F. M. Branley (Black)

# Caring for our surroundings

## Objectives

☐ To explain to the children in simple terms how we depend on our surroundings for survival

☐ To think about the ways we spoil our surroundings

☐ To think about ways of improving them

## Starting points

○ Talk to the children about the importance of the air, water, sun and earth for all living things. What can make the air dirty or polluted? Why is it important for rivers, lakes and the sea to be kept clean? (for fish, our own supplies of water and so on). The earth in which we grow food needs careful farming in order to conserve its natural fertility. Delicate balances exist within and between the different kinds of habitat – you cannot destroy one habitat without affecting others.

○ Play or sing the song *This land is my land* (Woody Guthrie) and discuss the meaning of the words. Tell the children about the Indians of North America and how they believed that the land was free like the air and the sea. They could not understand why or how the white man thought he could own it and divide it up. What do the children think of this idea?

○ Make a display of classroom work on litter – rubbish monsters, anti-litter posters, etc. (See classroom activities.)

○ Make a litter collection in the school grounds and display the bags in assembly. The children could then perform a play devised around *The litter bug* or *Joachim the dustman* for a special parents' assembly (see classroom activities).

○ Base an assembly on art and written work the children have produced in their endangered species project (see classroom activities.)

### Joachim the dustman

There was once a town which was overflowing with rubbish. The townspeople kept buying new things and throwing away the old. Sometimes they even bought things they didn't really want. If one family bought a new television set, then everyone else had to have one too – just to keep in the fashion.

Unfortunately the fashion kept changing. So the houses were packed full of things which nobody really wanted, and the streets were piled high with rubbish.

The rivers and ponds were choked with old cartons, cases, coffee pots, cuckoo clocks and casseroles. In the streets, cars were stuck fast in the rubbish and people had to walk to work.

The town councillors were at their wits' end. They hung a big notice outside the town hall:
REFUSE COLLECTOR WANTED –
HIGH WAGES FOR THE RIGHT PERSON

But no one applied for the job. It was too dirty. Then one day, when the piles of rubbish were almost covering the windows, a man came to the town hall. His name was Joachim and the only thing he owned in the whole wide world was his beautiful red moustache. Every morning he brushed it and combed it with great care. He was a man who liked everything clean and tidy. The councillors couldn't have found a better person for the job but a few of them had to shilly-shally and ask questions. How on earth was one man going to clear away all that rubbish? And surely he'd be too expensive?

"Don't worry," said Joachim, "I don't want any wages. Just let me keep all the rubbish."

At once Joachim started to work. The first thing he did was to hunt through the piles of rubbish until he found a rusty old tractor. He oiled it and tinkered with it until the engine started then he chugged off to the harbour where he found some old steel cables. He used these to truss up a great bundle of rubbish. Then he towed it away to his rubbish tip.

As the streets grew cleaner and cleaner, the rubbish on Joachim's tip grew higher and higher. Every evening, when his work was done, Joachim climbed to the top of the pile and built the rubbish into towers and pinnacles and turrets. In no time at all a magnificent castle reigned over the rubbish tip. It even had a drawbridge which went up and down. The townspeople were delighted to have their town clean and tidy again.

But one day the town councillors paid a visit to Joachim to see what he was doing with all the rubbish. They were very surprised to see the castle and when Joachim invited them inside they were amazed at what they saw: all kinds of furniture, gaily patterned carpets and shining walls hammered out of copper, tin and aluminium.

When they left the councillors began to grumble amongst themselves: "His castle's much better than our town hall," said one. "We must keep an eye on him. He'll soon be getting too big for his boots," said another. "He must give us his castle. We'll tell him that we need it to protect our town."

They all agreed to this and sent the town herald to tell Joachim.

Joachim was very upset that the town council should think he wanted to hurt anyone. All he wanted was to make the world a pleasanter place. Sadly he climbed up to his castle to think it all out.

Down in the town, the councillors ordered the army to assemble. The townsmen struggled to button up their uniforms and hurried to the parade ground, then they marched off in a long column and sang rowdy army songs to keep their courage up. Hardly any of them knew what the trouble was about but it made a pleasant change from watching television.

While Joachim had been sitting thinking in his tower the rubbish in the streets had piled up again. →

## Classroom activities

### Language

☆ Discuss how and why human beings pollute the earth – rubbish, chemical pollution, oil spillage at sea, smoke, noise. Think about ways of remedying this now and in the future – making less waste, clearing up waste, more careful use of chemicals, smokeless zones.

☆ Get the children to imagine they are clearing-up-machines. What do they look like? What do they do? Where do they work? What kind of things do they clear up?

☆ Write limericks about a litter bug. Read some limericks to the children and explain the rhythm and rhyming scheme. Invite them to write their own about a person who pollutes and litters the world.

☆ Discuss how the children themselves can help conserve or improve their surroundings. In the countryside they could follow the *Country Code* (guard against fires, fasten gates, leave no litter, and so on). At home they could take care not to waste or pollute water (by using too much washing up liquid for instance), they could keep their own environment (home, garden, park, playground) clean. More ideas can be obtained by writing to a conservation organisation such as *Friends of the Earth*.

### Science

☆ Choose an insect – a ladybird or honey bee and investigate how it helps us and the environment.

86

---

It was quite impossible for the soldiers to march through it. They had to climb instead, and by the time they reached the edge of the town they were so tired that they settled down amongst the rubbish and went to sleep.

The next morning the councillors sent the herald off with a white flag. By the time he reached Joachim's castle his flag was black and grimy.

"The town council sends me to offer you terms of peace," he shouted, waving his grubby flag. "After careful consideration they have decided that you may keep everything, just as long as you keep the town clean."

But Joachim wasn't so sure. "Keep your town," he said. "I've shown you how to clean it – now you'd better learn how to do it for yourselves."

Off drove Joachim. The farther he got from the town the happier he grew. Soon a great flock of birds came flying up and settled on the tractor. You could hardly see what it was that was rattling through the countryside. But there in the middle was Joachim in a cloud of bright feathers, singing and waving his hat. And looking forward to cleaning up the next town.

*Kurt Baumann and David McKee (slightly abridged)*

Why did the townspeople have such problems with rubbish? How did Joachim solve their problems? What did he do with the rubbish?

---

## The litter bug

I know there is a litter bug
Living down our street.
He gathers all the bus-tickets
And swirls them round my feet.

And when he has a lollyice,
He *always* drops the stick.
He throws down crumpled paper bags;
He *really* makes me sick.

If I should ever see him,
He'll have no chance to hide.
I'll take him to the nearest bin
And *dump* him straight inside.

*Kit Patrickson*

## The singing bird

*The singing bird sang beautifully because it was free. When the king took its freedom it stopped singing:*

Under the palm tree sat the King whilst overhead the sun burned down. "My, my," said the King, "it is very hot today, and I am so thirsty." And he called his servant to fetch him a pitcher of water from the river-bank.

"Servant," he said, "do go and fetch me a pitcher of cool water." And off went the servant obedient to the King's command.

On the river-bank the servant was kneeling down to fill the pitcher, when suddenly, overhead, he heard some fluttering wings and some twittering and trilling.

And a beautiful bird hovered above him and began to sing.

The water quite forgotten, the servant listened and then began to sway and dance to the beautiful music. Meanwhile, back in the village the King was getting cross and longing more and more for his drink of cool water.

So he called for his wife, the Queen.

"Wife," he said, "do go and find out what has happened to my servant." And off she went, obedient to the King's command.

As she drew near the river-bank the Queen heard the beautiful singing and was soon joining in the swaying and dancing with the servant.

Meanwhile, back in the village the King was getting crosser and longing more and more for his drink of cool water. So he called for his son, the Prince.

"Son," he said, "do go and find out what has happened to the servant and your mother, the Queen."

And off went the Prince, obedient to the King's command.

As he drew near the river-bank he heard the beautiful music and was soon joining in the swaying and dancing with the servant and his mother, the Queen.

Back in the village, the King grew more and more impatient.

"Bother," he said. "I shall go myself and find out what has happened to my servant, my wife the Queen, my son the Prince and my pitcher of water."

And off he went.

As he drew near the river-bank, the King too heard the singing of the beautiful bird and saw his servant, his wife the Queen, and his son the Prince, swaying and dancing to the music. And soon he was moved to join in and as the bird sang his beautiful song, the King danced.

And as he danced, the King thought "I must have this bird for my own. No other King has anything like it and people will come from miles around to hear this wonder."

And the King stopped dancing to whisper to his servant to catch the bird. The servant reached out his hand and the bird was caught.

And immediately the singing stopped and all was silent on the river-bank.

The dancing stopped too and the King took the bird from the servant.

"Sing, bird, sing," pleaded the King. But the bird was silent.

"Sing, bird, sing," begged the servant. But the bird was silent.

"Why won't you sing?" asked the King's wife, the Queen. But the bird was silent still.

"You must sing for my father," said the Prince, his son, "for my father is a mighty King." But the bird still kept silent.

At last the King, his wife the Queen and his son the Prince started back to the village. The pitcher was full of water, the day was still hot and the King was still cross.

But the servant stayed behind on the river-bank, coaxing the bird to sing, but it would not.

Instead that beautiful bird gazed around at all the wild creatures who were free, the lion, the elephant, the fish in the river, the birds in the air. And he kept his beautiful song for himself.

The servant thought, "The bird does not sing because he's been captured. I must set him free." And he put the bird down gently on a green bush.

And the bird didn't pause, not even for a second. He lifted his wings and soared into the air and sang and sang and sang.

And he's singing still for all we know.

*Traditional African story retold by Barbara Resch*

Why did the bird stop singing?
What pets do we have in school?
Do you think we should keep them here? Why/Why not?

☆ Find out about and discuss the earth's natural resources. Some of these can only be used once and can never be replaced. Which? (coal, oil). Others can be replaced if care is taken – trees can be replanted, paper, glass and metals recycled. Other sources of power can be used over and over again – water, wind and sun.

**Art**

☆ Make a rubbish monster. Each child can make their own, or make one big one together. Create a character for your monster and give it a name. Is it male or female, nice or nasty? What does it like to eat? Where does it live? How does it move?

☆ Design anti-litter posters for the children's street, district or school.

☆ Make a class collage or individual collages using a theme from *Joachim the dustman*, e.g.

A town piled up with rubbish
A castle of rubbish

**Drama**

☆ With the children devise a play on *The litter bug*. One group could be litter bugs going for a picnic and leaving their rubbish behind them. Another group, the tidy-uppers and the litter bins, could come along after them and tidy up the mess. Make litter bug hats decorated with sweet wrappings, and tidy-upper hats decorated with flowers. The litter bins can be dressed up in black plastic bags with dustbin hats made out of corrugated paper. They could hold bags for the tidy-uppers to fill. Sing *The Tidy Song* (Tinder-box 47)

**Projects**

☆ *Endangered species*. With the children find out about one of the world's endangered species – e.g. the tiger, whale or giant panda. Find all the information you can about it. Why is it in danger of extinction? (e.g. because of pollution, over-hunting, the destruction of its natural habitat). What is being done to protect it? Record your findings in writing, paintings and wall displays. (*The World Wildlife Fund* can be approached to supply information and display material.)

☆ Organise a collection of litter in the school grounds. Perhaps a dust cart could be borrowed from the council. Make sure the children wear old gloves and clothes and supply them with brushes to sweep up any sharp pieces of litter.

Examine the litter they collect to see what kind of things are thrown away and make graphs or charts of the results.

Make a survey of the litter bins in the area of the school. Where are they? How many are there? Are there enough? If there aren't the children could ask the council to install more!

# Sarah Cynthia Sylvia Stout

Sarah Cynthia Sylvia Stout
would not put the garbage out!
She'd boil the water
and open the cans
and scrub the pots
and scour the pans
and grate the cheese
and shell the peas
and mash the yams
and spice the hams,
and make the jams.
But though her daddy
would scream and shout,
she would not take the garbage out.
And so it piled up to the ceilings:
Coffee grounds, potato peelings,
mouldy bread and withered greens,
olive pits and soggy beans,
cracker boxes, chicken bones,
clamshells, eggshells, stale scones,
sour milk and mushy plums,
crumbly cake and cookie crumbs.
At last the garbage piled so high
that finally it reached the sky.
And none of her friends
would come to play.
And all the neighbours moved away.
And finally Sarah Cynthia Stout
said, "I'll take the garbage out!"
But then, of course, it was too late.
The garbage reached beyond the state,
from Memphis to the Golden Gate.
And Sarah met an awful fate,
Which I cannot right now relate
because the hour is much too late.
But, children, think of Sarah Stout
and always take the garbage out!

# House coming down

They're pulling down the house
At the corner of the Square,
The floors and the ceilings
Are out in the air,
The fire places so rusty,
The staircases so dusty,
And wallpaper so musty,
Are all laid bare.

It looks like a dollshouse
With the dolls put away,
And the furniture laid by
Against another day;
No bed to lie in,
No pan to fry in,
Or dish to make a pie in,
And nobody to play.

*Eleanor Farjeon*

Do you like old houses? Why/Why not?
Do you like new houses? Why/Why not?
Some old buildings can be repaired and used again, while others are too broken down or ugly to repair. What are the buildings like round you? Are they old or new? or are they a mixture of old and new?
Do you think the places round you look nice or could they look nicer?

◁ Do you help to put the rubbish out? What do you think happens to the rubbish you throw away? How could you make sure that there is less to throw away?

*Shel Silverstein*

# Pollution

The air was crisp and still
And as the boat sailed past,
    the water stirred
To cause a flutter of wings
But then it died.
A smell had come.
Pollution
The water swirled and smacked
    against the wall
And left a slick of oil.

*Lesley Samuels*

The water looked nice but it smelt horrible. What was wrong with it? What does pollution mean? How do you think water might get polluted?

## The little witch

A lost little witch spills a trail of magic through a city and makes it beautiful:

The big city was dark. Even the streetlights were out. All day people had gone up and down, up and down; cars and trams and trams and buses had roared and rattled busily along. But now they had all gone home to bed, and only the wind, the shadows and a small kitten wandered in the wide still streets.

The kitten chased a piece of paper, pretending it was a mouse. Quick as a wink he leaped after it, and then forgot it because he had found something else.

"What is this?" he asked the wind, "here asleep behind the rubbish bin. I have never seen it before."

"Ah," said the wind, "it is a witch . . . see her broomstick . . . but she is only a very small one."

The little witch heard the wind in her sleep and opened her eyes. Far above, the birds peered down at the street below.

"Let me see!" a baby sparrow peeped sleepily.

"Go to sleep!" said his mother. "I didn't hatch you out of the egg to peer at witches all night long." She snuggled him back into her warm feathers. But there was no one to snuggle a little witch, wandering cold in the big empty streets, dragging a broom several sizes too big for her. The kitten sprang at the broom. Then he noticed something.

"Wind!" he cried. "See! – wherever this witch walks, she leaves a trail of flowers!"

Yes, it was true! The little witch had lots of magic in her, but she had not learned to use it properly, or to hide it, any more than she had learned to talk. So wherever she put her feet mignonette grew, and rosemary, violets, lily of the valley, and tiny pink-and-white roses . . . all through the streets, all across the road . . . Butterflies came, from far and wide, to dance and drink.

The little witch laughed, but in a moment she became solemn. She was so alone. Then the kitten scuttled and pounced at her bare, pink heels, and the little witch knew she had a friend. Dragging her broom for the kitten to chase, she wandered on, leaving a trail of flowers. She pointed up at the city clock tower, and it became a huge fir tree, while the clock face turned into a white nodding owl and flew away!

The owl flew as fast as the wind to a tall dark castle perched high on a hill. There at the window sat a slim tired witch-woman, looking out into the night. "Where, oh where is my little baby witch? I must go and search for her again."

"Whoo! Whoo!" cried the owl. "There is a little witch down in the city and she is enchanting everything. What will the people say tomorrow?"

The witch-woman rode her broomstick through the sky and over the city, looking eagerly down through the mists. Far below she could see the little witch running and hiding in doorways, while the kitten chased after her.

Down flew the witch-woman – down, down to a shop doorway. The little witch and the kitten stopped and stared at her.

"Why," said the witch-woman, in her dark, velvety voice, "you are my own dear little witch . . . my little lost witch!" She held out her arms and the little witch ran into them. She wasn't lost any more.

The witch-woman looked around at the enchanted city and she smiled. "I'll leave it as it is," she said "for a surprise tomorrow."

Then she gathered the little witch onto her broomstick, and the kitten jumped on, too, and off they went to their tall castle home, with windows as deep as night, and lived there happily ever after.

And the next day when the people got up and came out to work, the city was full of flowers and the echoes of laughter.

*Margaret Mahy (abridged)*

**Songs**

*Tinder-box:* 47 The tidy song, 48 Let it be, 45 I would like to be, 66 May there always be sunshine

*Subject index:* Caring for our surroundings

**Stories**

*Dinosaurs and All That Rubbish* M. Foreman (Hamish Hamilton)
*Green is Beautiful* M. Rogers (Andersen Press)
*Hare and Badger go to Town* N. Lewis (Andersen)
*Miss Hendy's House* J. Drake (Brockhampton Press)
*Hunter and his Dog* B. Wildsmith (Oxford University Press)
*The Little Boy and the Big Fish* M. Velhuijs (Abelard-Schuman)
"The Pines" from *The First Margaret Mahy Story Book* (Dent)
*Quickhoney* G. Hurle (Methuen)
"The Trees" from *The Third Margaret Mahy Story Book* (Dent)
*Where Are You, Duck?* (Church Information Office Benjamin Books)

# Separation

**Objectives**
☐ To think of times when we are separated from people and places we love
☐ To explore feelings of loss

Many things can cause children to experience feelings of loss and alienation – separation from people they love and are dependent on, moving house away from friends and familiar places, coming to school for the first time.

**Starting points**
○ Ask the children if any of them have recently experienced separation of some kind. Perhaps a parent has been away from home, they have just moved house or started school. Ask one or two of them to describe how they felt.

○ Invite an adult who was an evacuee or refugee during the Second World War to talk to the children about their experiences.

○ Sing *You and I* or play a recording of *The leaving of Liverpool* or *The wreck of the John B* and discuss the words.

○ Sing *I've just moved into a new house* and use it as a starting point for discussion about moving home. Invite some of the children to read out written work on moving home (see classroom activities).

## Gone

In a big house across the way,
Lived my friend, Jane, until today,
Six men this morning, in a van,
Came after breakfast, and began
To pack up all the beds and chairs,
The nice red carpet on the stairs,
And all the things I used to see,
When Jane invited me for tea.

They took the dishes and the plates,
And packed them into wooden crates.
They took Jane's toybox, dolls and all.
They took the big clock from the hall.
They took the carpet, tied with strings,
And pots and pans and kitchen things.
They took the sofa where we played
(And where I slept, the night I stayed).

Cupboards, chests and kitchen stools,
Cooker, fridge and gardening tools,
Jane's red bike – I don't know how
They got them in that van. But now
They've gone, and shut the big front door,
And I can't call there any more.
It's sad to think that, from today,
I'll never go to Jane's to play.

Have your friends ever moved away? How did you feel?
How could you still stay friends with them? (Write letters, visit, telephone.)

## India

Now I am in England
I think of the days in India.
I remember the tall eucalyptus trees.
There was a lawn to the left of the eucalyptus trees.
To the left of the lawn there were flowers and fruit trees.
Also there was a tomato patch with bright red tomatoes.
In front there was a verandah with a cool floor.
I used to play with my cousins underneath the verandah.
Oh! I really miss those warm sunny days.

*Hartash Dale*

my mummy lives in London and I miss her I feel like crying too and when I go there next time Im going too the zoo and my mummy is pretty and she puts me and Glenn in the bath I love my mummy and she loves me too. the end. zoe mitchell 6

90

# Emmie and Chips

On a hot summer evening when Emmie and her little dog Chips were walking home Emmie said, "The holidays are nearly here and soon we shall go to the sea and have a lovely time together."

Emmie thought and thought about the sea-side. How she'd need a bottle for her orange juice and her yellow hat against the sun. "You need a hat you know, when the sun's hot," Emmie told Chips. "And I shall take my red swim-suit and my rubber ring for swimming." And Emmie put them on and stared at herself in the mirror and longed for the holidays to come.

"You'll like it at the sea, Chips," Emmie said. "We'll roll on the sand and splash in the sea and we'll play together all day long."

But when Emmie went to the sea-side Chips didn't go with her. The lady at the house had said "No Dogs Allowed" and Chips had to be left behind with granny.

Emmie sat on the beach and watched the waves and a little boat, sailing in the sunshine. But she was so sad without her little dog.

"Never mind," said dad, "you can play with the children tomorrow."

But Emmie wouldn't be comforted.

The next morning the sun shone and the sky and sea were blue. "Come and swim," called a little boy. But Emmie stood at the water's edge and just cried and cried.

All day long she thought about Chips. She imagined him all alone, perhaps fastened to a chain and with no-one to play with. And Emmie wouldn't talk to mum or dad or anyone.

But the next morning dad didn't have breakfast as he usually did with mum and Emmie. "He won't be long," said the lady at the house. And she smiled and winked a little wink.

Suddenly, Emmie heard a special sound and she ran to the door.

And Chips had come.

Chips barked and Emmie laughed and there was a lot of licking and cuddling while mum and dad and the lady at the house just smiled and smiled.

"Thank you for bringing Chips for me," said Emmie to her dad. And down on the sand ran Emmie with Chips scampering after her.

But Chips ran away from the waves and while Emmie floated and splashed in her rubber ring he sat in her yellow sun hat where he felt safe.

Then, as the hours went by, Chips learned that the waves wouldn't hurt him and soon he was playing in the water with Emmie all day long.

So Emmie and Chips had their holiday together after all just as Emmie had planned.

*Peggy Blakeley*

## Classroom activities
### Language
☆ Use the poem *Gone* as the starting point for accounts of the children's own experiences of moving home.

☆ Get the children to describe their first day at school, a stay in hospital, an occasion when their parents went away, or when they themselves were away from home. What happened? Who looked after them? What did they like or dislike about the experience? How did they feel afterwards?

☆ Ask the children to write a letter to a friend they know. Pretend they have moved to another part of the country. Describe what they liked doing best with them. Say why they miss them and suggest a way of meeting again.

### Songs
*Tinder-box:* 49 Ladybird, 50 Puff the magic dragon, 51 I've just moved into a new house, 55 You and I
*Subject index:* Sadness, Separation

### Stories
*Charley, Charlotte and the Golden Canary* C. Keeping (Oxford)
*Harry by the Sea* G. Zion (Bodley Head)
*In Bed* B. Gilroy (Macmillan)
*Janey* C. Zolotow (World's Work)
*Lost in a Shop* R. Palmer (Macmillan)
*Moving Molly* S. Hughes (Armada)
*Mrs Cockle's Cat* P. Pearce (Kestrel)
*Sally Moves House* N. Snell (Hamish Hamilton)
*Susanne's Parents Get Divorced* B. Erup (Black)
*The Trouble with Donovan Croft* B. Ashley (Oxford)

# Disappointment

**Objectives**
☐ To think of times of disappointment
☐ To consider how we feel and how we behave

**Starting point**
○ Discuss with the children what it means to feel disappointed. For instance, they would feel disappointed if they had come to school expecting something exciting to happen – a party or puppet show – and then had been told that it wasn't going to happen after all. What other occasions do they find disappointing? A group of children could read out their written work.

○ Read *A broken promise* and discuss how Ben felt and showed his disappointment. How did he feel when he realised that he had been given a picture of a dog instead of a real one? Was he right to be angry with his grandparents? Do the children think they intended to disappoint him? Have the children ever been really disappointed like this? What happened? How did they feel? What did they do?

**Classroom activities**
☆ Ask the children to write about a time when they have been disappointed. How did they feel? What did they do?

**Songs**
*Tinder-box*: 53 Why does it have to be me, 56 Try again
*Subject index*: Disappointment, Sadness

## A broken promise

The post had come, and it was all for Ben. His father had piled it by his place for breakfast. There were also presents from May and Dilys, Paul and Frankie, and his mother and father. They all watched while, politely, he opened their presents first of all, and thanked them.

He was not worrying that there had been no dog standing by his place at the breakfast-table. He was not so green as to think that postmen delivered dogs. But there would be a letter – from his grandfather, he supposed – saying when the dog would be brought, by a proper carrier, or where it could be collected from. Ben turned eagerly from his family's presents to his post.

He turned over the letters first, looking for his grandfather's handwriting; but there was nothing. Then he looked at the writing on the two picture-postcards that had come for him – although you would hardly expect anything so important to be left to a postcard. There was nothing. Then he began to have the feeling that something might have gone wrong after all. He remembered, almost against his will, that his grandfather's promise had been only a whisper and a nod, and that not all promises are kept, anyway.

He turned to the parcels, and at once saw his grandfather's handwriting on a small, flat one. Then he knew for certain that something was wrong. They would hardly send him an ordinary birthday present as well as one so special as a dog. There was only one explanation: they were sending him an ordinary present *instead of* the dog.

"Open it, Ben," said his mother. He cut the string round the parcel and then unfolded the wrapping-paper.

They had sent him a picture instead of a dog.

And then he realised that they *had* sent him a dog, after all. He almost hated them for it. His dog was worked in woollen cross-stitch, and framed and glazed as a little picture.

There was a letter which explained: "Dear Ben,

Your grandpa and I send you hearty good wishes for your birthday. We know you would like a dog, so here is one . . ."

There was more in the letter, but, with a sweep of his hand, Ben pushed aside letter, packing-paper, string and picture. They fell to the floor, the picture with a sharp sound of breakage. His mother picked it up. "You've cracked the glass, Ben, and it's a nice little picture – a little old picture that I remember well."

Ben said nothing, because he could not. His mother looked at him, and he knew that she knew that, if he hadn't been so old, he would be crying.

"Did you expect a *real* dog?" Frankie asked suddenly.

Everyone else answered for Ben, anyway. His mother said, "Of course not. Ben knows perfectly well that Granny and Grandpa could never afford to buy him a real dog."

His father said, "And, anyway, you can't expect to keep a dog in London nowadays – the traffic's too dangerous." Ben remembered the cat scuttering from under the wheels of the car that morning, and he hated his father for being in the right. "It isn't as if we had any garden to let a dog loose in," went on Mr Blewitt; "and we're not even near an open space where you could exercise it properly."

Ben's hands, half-hidden by the wrapping-paper, that his mother had picked up from the floor, clenched into angry fists. Mrs Blewitt, still watching him anxiously, took the letter again to skim through the rest of it. "They say they hope you won't be disappointed by their present – well, never mind that – and – why, Ben, just listen! – they ask you to go and stay with them again as soon as you're able. Isn't that nice? You always like that. Now, let's see when you might go . . . Not next week, but perhaps the week after, or perhaps even –"

On this subject Ben had to speak. "I don't want to go there," he said. "I don't ever want to go there again. I shan't."

*Philippa Pearce*

# Death

## Objectives
☐ To think about our feelings when someone dies
☐ To discuss how we come to terms with someone dying

This is a sensitive subject. Children nevertheless often think about it and may welcome the opportunity to share their thoughts and feelings. (No classroom activities are given for this section.)

## Starting points
○ You may like to lead into the subject through talking with the children about the deaths of pets. Many of them will have had a pet who has died or been killed. Explain that everything that is alive has to die but that the death of someone you have loved can make you very sad at first. Later on it becomes possible to remember them without feeling unhappy.

## Songs
*Tinder-box:* 54 Babes in the wood, 66 May there always be sunshine
*Subject index:* Death, Ghosts

## Stories
*Cathy's Story* C. Brighton (Evans)
*Flowers for Samantha* L. Parr (Methuen)
*Nonna* J. Bartoli (Harvey House)
*A Taste of Blackberries* D. Buchanan Smith (Heinemann)
*The Tenth Good Thing About Barney* J. Viorst (Collins)
*That Dog* Nanette Newman (Heinemann)

## Grandad

*Grandad's dead*
*And I'm sorry about that.*

He'd a huge black overcoat.
He felt proud in it.
You could have hidden
A football crowd in it.
Far too big –
It was a lousy fit
But Grandad didn't
Mind a bit.
He wore it all winter
With a squashed black hat.

*Now he's dead*
*And I'm sorry about that.*

He'd got twelve stories.
I'd heard every one of them
Hundreds of times
But that was the fun of them:
You knew what was coming
So you could join in.
He'd got big hands
And brown, grooved skin
And when he laughed
It knocked you flat.

*Now he's dead*
*And I'm sorry about that.*

*Kit Wright*

## Grandad

A quiet man,
A thinking man,
Always down in his shed
Working on a broken clock
Or fixing a car instead.
A quiet man,
A thinking man,
But now he's dead.

*Rebecca Bazeley, aged 11*
*Fitzjohn's Primary School*

At first all of us feel very sad when someone we love very much dies, but as time passes we are able to look back and remember the things we enjoyed so much about them.
What did the people who wrote these poems remember about their grandparents?
What did they like about them?

# Birthdays

## Objectives
☐ To think why we celebrate birthdays
☐ To consider why our own birthdays are special
☐ To think about the anticipation and excitement of birthdays
☐ To think how we can participate in someone else's birthday

Celebrations for the children's birthdays can be held regularly in school. One could be held each week for the children whose birthdays have fallen during that time. Make birthday badges or rosettes using house number signs for the children to wear during the day. Light candles and sing birthday songs.

The material in this theme could be used for a special assembly when the reasons for celebrating birthdays might be looked at more closely.

## Starting points
○ Set up a birthday display. Some children could design cards, others could bake a birthday cake and decorate it. Decorate the walls with paintings. You could choose to celebrate the birthday of a school pet or pick a time when a number of birthdays can be taken together – the end of the summer holiday would be a good time. Discuss the meaning of the word *celebration*. What occasions do the children celebrate? Why do we celebrate birthdays? What do the children enjoy about their own birthdays? What do they enjoy about other people's birthdays.

○ Discuss birthdays which are celebrated nationally and internationally – the birthday of Jesus, the Prophet Muhammed, Guru Nanak, and so on. How are these birthdays celebrated?

○ Discuss the meaning of anniversary. List some of the different kinds of anniversary we celebrate – the birthdays of famous writers, artists and composers, the foundation of societies or buildings, independence day celebrations, jubilee celebrations, and so on.

## Classroom activities
### Language
☆ Ask the children to write about one of the following: My most unusual birthday present; The very special secret; Granny's birthday.

## What someone said when he was spanked on the day before his birthday

Some day
I may
Pack my bag and run away.
Some day
I may.
– But not today.

Some night
I might
Slip away in the moonlight.
I might.
*Some* night.
– But not tonight.

Some night.
Some day.
I might.
I may.
– But right now I think I'll stay.

*John Ciardi*

Do you ever feel like running away from home? Why? Why wouldn't you?

## Between birthdays

My birthdays take so long to start.
They come along a year apart.
It's worse than waiting for a bus;
I fear I used to fret and fuss,
But now, when by impatience vexed
Between one birthday and the next,
I think of all that I have seen
That keeps on happening in between.
The songs I've heard, the things I've done,
Make my un-birthdays not so un-

*Ogden Nash*

## Birth

It was about five-thirty. Mrs Swann had left. The room looked squared up, Nan shut her eyes, so I went upstairs to where my two children were asleep. Marie stirred awake and spoke to me. She told me that she had dreamt of baby cries.

"Yes, you dreamt and you heard. Our baby has been born."

"No? . . . honest, Dad? What is it?"

"A boy."

"Larry, oh Larry!" she cried. "Waken up! What do you think – baby has come! And it's a boy."

"What's he like, Dad?"

"Well, he's not bad. Perhaps not so lovely as either of you . . . but I'm sure you'll like him. He's more beautiful than any baby except you two. He's big; Mrs Swann guessed he was more than nine pounds."

I sat on Larry's bed. It was dark, but not black.

"Isn't it funny, Dad – he doesn't know what he's come to. He doesn't know I'm his brother, or that Marie's his sister."

"I really wanted a girl, Dad; but now he's born I'm glad it's him, and that he's a boy."

"I wonder what he'll think of us?"

"He'll like you – I'm sure he will."

I gave a hand to each child.

"Now children, I must go to work this morning, and I want you to help while I'm away. I'll be back at dinner-time, it's Saturday. Your Mum must stay in bed; so what I want is for you to do some jobs – will you?"

"Yes, Dad."

*Bill Naughton*

## A riddle

One can bear it,
Two can share it,
But for three
It never can be.     *(a secret)*

What have secrets got to do with birthdays?
Do you think a surprise is spoilt if you give the secret away?
Do you like to guess what's in your parcels before you open them? Would you like to know what's in them before your birthday or save them for the day? Why?
Have you ever had to keep a special secret for someone else's birthday? Did you find it hard to keep?

# Eeyore's birthday

"That's right," said Eeyore. "Sing. Umty-tiddly, umty-too. Here we go gathering Nuts and May. Enjoy yourself."

"I am," said Pooh.

"Some can," said Eeyore.

"Why, what's the matter?"

"*Is* anything the matter?"

"You seem so sad, Eeyore."

"Sad? Why should I be sad? It's my birthday. The happiest day of the year."

"Your birthday?" said Pooh in great surprise.

"Of course it is. Can't you see? Look at all the presents I have had." He waved a foot from side to side. "Look at the birthday cake. Candles and pink sugar."

Pooh looked – first to the right and then to the left.

"Presents?" said Pooh. "Birthday cake?" said Pooh. "*Where?*"

"Can't you see them?"

"No," said Pooh.

"Neither can I," said Eeyore. "Joke," he explained. "Ha ha!"

Pooh scratched his head, being a little puzzled by all this.

"But is it really your birthday?" he asked.

"It is."

"Oh! Well, many happy returns of the day, Eeyore."

"And many happy returns to you, Pooh Bear."

"But it isn't *my* birthday."

"No, it's mine."

"But you said 'Many happy returns' –"

"Well, why not? You don't always want to be miserable on my birthday, do you?"

"Oh, I see," said Pooh.

"It's bad enough," said Eeyore, almost breaking down, "being miserable myself, what with no presents and no cake and no candles, and no proper notice taken of me at all, but if everybody else is going to be miserable too –"

This was too much for Pooh. "Stay there!" he called to Eeyore, as he turned and hurried back home as quick as he could; for he felt that he must get poor Eeyore a present of *some* sort at once, and he could always think of a proper one afterwards.

*A. A. Milne*

Why was Eeyore so sad?
How would you feel if someone forgot your birthday?
Do you remember other people's birthdays?
What could you do to make their birthday a special day?

# Little Clotilda

Little Clotilda
Well and hearty,
Thought she'd like
To give a party.
But as her friends
Were shy and wary,
Nobody came
But her own canary.

*Anon*

How do you think Clotilda felt when no one but the canary came to her party?
What do you enjoy about your birthday?
Who helps you to celebrate it?
What do your friends do on your birthday?
Do you mind if someone forgets it's your birthday?

# A witch poem

The witch my sister from over the
    sea
Wonderful presents has sent to me.
A whistle to blow and a bell to ring,
Silver ropes for a shining swing,
A golden lion that will play and purr,
Dancing slippers of silver fur,
And, sharp as a needle, bright as a
    pin,
A mouse that plays on the violin.

*Margaret Mahy*

**Mathematics**

☆ Make a birthday graph.

**Art**

☆ Get each child to design and make a party hat for themselves.

☆ Design wrapping paper and print it. The children could choose a special person to design their paper for – their mum, dad, pet, friend – and make a design particularly suited to that person.

**Drama**

☆ Get the children to sit in a circle and silently choose a present they would like for their birthday. Each mime their present in turn. Can the others guess what it is?

**Songs**

*Tinder-box:* 59 Birthday song, 65 One two three
*Subject index:* Birthdays

**Stories**

*Bear's New Baby* S. and J. Berenstain (Collins)
*Benjamin's 365 Birthdays* J. Barrett (Puffin)
*A Birthday for Frances* R. Hoban (Faber)
*Kate's Party* J. Solomon (Hamish Hamilton)
*Little Gorilla* R. Bornstein (World's Work)
*Mr Rabbit and the Lovely Present* C. Zolotow (Puffin)
"Mrs Mallowby's Birthday" from *The Faber Book of Nursery Stories* ed. B. Ireson (Faber)
*Momoko's Birthday* C. Iwasaki (Bodley Head)
*Nippers* series: *Plenty of Room* L. Berg and *Ricky's Birthday* J. Wilson (Macmillan)
*Paul's Christmas Birthday* C. and D. Carrick (World's Work)
*A Tale of an Egg* K. Tolmie (Oberon Press)
"The Tick Tock Party" from *The First Margaret Mahy Story Book* (Dent)
*That Baby* L. Berg (Macmillan)
*What Happened at Rita's Party* P. Breinburg (Kestrel)

**Information books**

*Birth of a Duckling* H. Isenbart (Dent)
*The Chicken and the Egg* (Oxford Scientific Films and G. Whizzard Publishers)
*How You Began* H. Spiers (Dent)

# Homecoming

## Objectives
☐ To think why we celebrate homecomings
☐ To think about how we celebrate them

## Starting points
○ Play a recording of *Sailing* (Gavin Sutherland) or sing *Welcome home* and ask the children about the song's meaning and how it makes them feel. Ask them about their experiences of being away from home and longing to be back. What does feeling homesick mean? What things do we miss about home? Some of the children could read out their written work on this subject (see classroom activities).

## Classroom activities

### Language
☆ Write a letter to welcome home a special friend or relative. Ask the children to say why they have missed their friend.

☆ Tell the story of Ulyses returning to Ithaca from Troy, or discuss the return of the astronauts after the moon landing. Get the children to use their imaginations to write about a dangerous adventure from which they have just returned safely home. How did they feel? Who welcomed them home? What did they do to celebrate?

☆ Ask the children to write a description of how home looked when they got back from holiday. Did it seem different? (smaller, bigger, and so on).

☆ Describe a celebration meal for someone who has returned home after a long absence. Ask the children to think what that person would most like to do and what they would most enjoy eating.

## Songs
*Tinder-box:* 60 Welcome home
*Subject index:* Homecoming

## Stories
*Molly Moves Out* S. Pearson (Bodley Head)

---

Mum'll be coming home today.
It's three weeks she's been away.
When dad's alone
all we eat
is cold meat
which I don't like
and he burns the toast I want just-brown
and I hate taking the ash-can down.

He's mended the door
from the little fight
on Thursday night
so it doesn't show
and can we have grilled tomatoes
Spanish onions and roast potatoes
and will you sing me "I'll never more roam"
when I'm in bed, when you've come home?

*Mum's reply*

If you like your toast
done just-brown
then take it out
before it burns.
You hate taking the ash-can down?
Well now you know
what I know
so we might as well take turns.

But now I'm back,
yes let's have grilled tomatoes
Spanish onions and roast potatoes
because you know
when I was away
I wanted nothing more
than be back here
and see you all.

*Michael Rosen*

---

## Sad ... and glad

The sun has gone down,
Leaving an empty sky
   Above the hills
   Above our town.
Street-lamps switch on.
   Buses swish by.
Strangers are laughing.
My friends have gone in:
   I'm alone –
It's time to go home.

Someone runs to the post,
   Leaving an open door –
   A family
Makes itself toast
   Round the fire
Down a long corridor.
   It's chilly,
And I've been out all day:
   I want my tea.
It's time I was home.

They're calling in Tommy
   (I wish he was me);
   On the allotments
Bonfire smoke rolls
Sluggish, blue-grey.
I'm still streets away:
   This time of year,
   This time of day,
     Makes me sad
And glad – to get home.

*Brian Lee*

Why did the child feel sad?
Is there a particular time of day, type of weather, which makes you feel sad?
What was he looking forward to at home?
Why do you like to get home?

What did the child miss about his mother?
Has someone who looks after you ever gone away? What happened? How did you feel?
What was it like when they came back? Were you pleased, sad, cross with them, didn't care?

# Halloween

## Objectives
☐ To find out why Halloween is celebrated
☐ To explore how it is celebrated
☐ To think about its meaning

Halloween, meaning *Holy Eve*, is the night before All Saints' Day (November 1st). In the old Celtic calendar, October 31st was the last night of the old year, thus Halloween used to be a New Year celebration. People believed that with the passing of the old year all kinds of spirits went abroad. It was a night of transition from old to new and therefore a night of danger. Light with its power over darkness and evil played an important part in warding off the evil spirits – hence the Halloween lanterns which are a well-known feature of the festival. It was also a time for mischief and masquerade and in some places children still dress up and play *trick or treat* on neighbours. As with other New Year festivals, it was a time to sweep away the evil which had accumulated in the old year and start out fresh in the new.

## Starting points
○ Ask the children what they know about Halloween. What happens? How do they celebrate it? (Customs will vary in different parts of the country). Explain simply the background to Halloween.

○ Ask them about witches. What do they think witches are? What powers do they have? Do they think they really exist? Explain that a long time ago many people believed in them and some people still do today. Halloween was the night when witches and other spirits were about and the people had to think of ways of scaring them away. What did they do?

○ Discuss fear of the dark, and the comfort of light in the darkness. Ask them to try to imagine what it would be like without electric lights, street lamps, and so on. The nights would be very dark as candles and lamps are not very strong. How do they think people in olden times felt the morning after Halloween? – relieved, safe, joyful?

○ Find out about the background to customs such as apple-bobbing, dressing up, turnip lanterns, and so on.

## Halloween

Who raps at my window?
Who in a white sheet
Runs across the midnight lawn
Without the sound of feet?

What moon grows in the East
So huge and dusky red?
Who howls from the chill within the hill
Where the farmer's hound lies dead?

The dry leaves twist and rattle
Alive in an evil spell.
Down by the pond the man who drowned
Tolls a wavering bell.

The wind has hardly wakened.
Yet flapping through the air
Fly shapes with wings and bony things
And form with jagged hair.

Who blows at my candle?
Whose fiery grin and eyes
Behind me pass in the looking glass
And make my gooseflesh rise?

Who moved in that shadow?
Who rustles past unseen?
With the dark so deep I dare not sleep
All night on Halloween.

*Marnie Pomeroy*

How do *you* feel on Halloween night?
Why was the person in the poem too scared to go to sleep?

## Mixed brews

There once was a witch
Who lived in a ditch
And brewed her brews in the hedges.
She gathered some dank
From the deepest bank
And some from around the edges.

She practised her charms
By waving her arms
And muttering words and curses;
And every spell
Would have worked out well
If she hadn't mixed the verses.

Not long since
When she wanted a Prince
To wake the Sleeping Beauty,
A man appeared
With a long grey beard
Too old to report for duty.

With a magic bean
She called for a Queen
Who was locked in the wizard's castle.
There came an old hag
With a postman's bag
And threepence to pay on the parcel.

What *comes* of a witch
Who has hitch after hitch?
I'm afraid that there's no telling
But I think, as a rule,
She returns to school
And tries to improve her spelling.

*Clive Sansom*

What did the witch try to use her spells for?
Why did they go wrong?
What happened?

○ Read *Aunt Nasty* and talk about good witches and bad witches. What would a good witch use spells for? What would a bad witch use them for? Do the children think that people are likely to be all good or bad. *Aunt Nasty* tried very hard to be completely bad but she didn't quite manage. What is a spell? How would the children make one and what would they like to do with it?

○ Ask different classes to prepare Halloween food, costumes, games, and decorations and bring everything together for a Halloween Party. Invite parents to take part. Have a fancy dress competition, prepare Halloween food, make lanterns and play games.

### Classroom activities
### Language
☆ Spells. Ask the children to imagine they are a very old witch teaching an apprentice witch a new spell. Write instructions bearing in mind

  what the spell is for,
  what ingredients are needed,
  how much of each,
  how to make the spell,
  what magic words are needed to make it work.

Think of some magical objects – a cloak, ring, hat, broomstick, carpet, lamp, boots, wand. What powers would the children expect each to have? – a cloak might make you invisible, a ring could give you three wishes, a hat might give the power of knowing what others are thinking. Ask the children to choose one of the items and describe how they would use it. You could give them specific problems to solve by magic.

  You are late for school and the bus
  is stuck in a traffic jam.

  You have forgotten to bring your gym shoes
  and you know the teacher will be angry.

Ask them how they would solve the same problem if their magic didn't work. Why might the magic have gone wrong? (They may not have used the correct procedure for making the magic work.) How could they improve their spelling? (Close their eyes and turn round three times while reciting the alphabet backwards?)

98

## Aunt Nasty (extract)

*Toby and Claire's aunt is not just an aunt – she is also a witch. One day a letter arrives to say that Aunt Nasty is coming to stay. The family go to meet her at the airport:*

When they got home Aunt Nasty went straight to her room. She smiled at the sight of the foxgloves and the woody nightshade, but she did not say thank you.

"I will have a cat-nap," she said, stroking the raggy black fur collar she wore. "I hope the bed is not damp or lumpy. I used to enjoy a damp bed when I was a young witch, but I'm getting old now."

Then she shut the door. They heard her put her suitcase against it.

"What a rude aunt!" said Toby.

"She has to be rude, because of being a witch," said Mother. "Now, do be nice quiet children, won't you! Don't make her cross or she might turn you into tadpoles."

The children went out to play, but they were not happy.

"I don't like Aunt Nasty," said Claire.

"I don't like having a witch in the house," said Toby.

The house was very very quiet and strange while Aunt Nasty was there. Everyone spoke in whispery voices and went around on tiptoe. Aunt Nasty stayed in her room most of the time. Once she came out of her room and asked for some toadstools. Toby found some for her under a pine tree at the top of the hill . . . fine red ones with spots, but Aunt Nasty was not pleased with them.

"These are dreadful toadstools," she said. "They look good but they are quite disappointing. The brown, slimy ones are much better. You can't trust a boy to do anything properly these days. But I suppose I will have to make do with them."

That was on Tuesday. Some smoke came out of

the keyhole on Wednesday, and on Thursday Aunt Nasty broke a soup plate. However, they did not see her again until Friday. Then she came out and complained that there was not enough pepper in the soup.

At last it was Sunday. Aunt Nasty had been there a week. Now she was going home again – this time by broomstick. Toby and Claire were very pleased. Mother was pleased too, and yet she looked tired and sad. She went out to take some plants to the woman next door. While she was out Father came in from the garden suddenly.

"Do you know what?" he said to Toby and Claire. "I have just remembered something. It is your mother's birthday today and we have forgotten all about it. That is what comes of having a witch in the house. We must go and buy birthday presents at once."

"But it's Sunday, Daddy!" cried Claire. "All the shops will be shut!"

"What on earth shall we do?" asked Father. "There must be some way of getting a present for her."

"A present!" said a voice. "Who wants a present?" It was Aunt Nasty with her suitcase, a broomstick and a big black cat at her heels.

"Oh, look at the cat!" cried Claire. "I did not know you had a cat, Aunt Nasty."

"He sits round my neck when we ride in the bus or the plane," said Aunt Nasty proudly. "It is his own idea, and it is a good one, because people think he is a fur collar and I do not have to buy a ticket for him. But what is this I hear? Have you really forgotten to get your mother a birthday present?"

"I'm afraid we have!" said Father sadly.

"Ha!" said Aunt Nasty fiercely. "Now I never forgot my mother's birthday. Tell me, can you children draw?"

"Yes!" said Toby and Claire.

"Can you draw a birthday cake, jellies, little cakes, sandwiches, roast chickens, bottles of fizzy lemonade, balloons, crackers, pretty flowers, birds and butterflies . . . and presents too?"

"Yes!" said Toby and Claire.

"Well then, you draw them," said Aunt Nasty, "And I will cook up some magic. Where is the stove? Hmmm! I see it is an electric stove. It is a bit on the clean side, isn't it? An old black stove is of much more use to a witch. Mind you I've got no use for the witch who can't make do with what she can get. I will work something out, you see if I don't."

Claire drew and Toby drew. They covered lots and lots of pages with drawings of cakes and balloons and presents wrapped in pretty paper.

Aunt Nasty came in with a smoking saucepan. "Give me your drawings," she said. "Hurry up, I haven't got all day. Hmmmm! They aren't very good, are they? But they'll have to do. A good witch can manage with a scribble if she has to."

She popped the drawings into the saucepan where they immediately caught fire and burned up to ashes. A thick blue smoke filled the room. No one could see anyone else.

"This smoke tastes like birthday cake," called Claire.

"It tastes like jelly and ice-cream," said Toby.

The smoke began to go away up the chimney.

"I smell flowers," said Father.

Then they saw that the whole room was changed. Everywhere there were leaves and flowers and birds only as big as your little finger-nail. The table was covered with jellies of all colours, and little cakes and sandwiches. All around the table were presents and crackers and balloons – so many of them they would have come up to your knees.

Best of all was the birthday cake. It was so big there was no room for it on the table. It stood like a pink and white mountain by the fireplace. The balloons bounced and floated around the room. The tiny birds flew everywhere singing.

"Well, I must be off," said Aunt Nasty. "I've wasted enough time. The saucepan is spoilt by the way, but you won't mind that. It was a nasty cheap

one anyhow."

"Won't you stay and wish Mummy a happy birthday?" asked Toby. "She would like to say thank you for her birthday party."

"Certainly not!" said Aunt Nasty. "I never ever say thank you myself. I don't expect anyone to say it to me. I love rudeness, but that is because I am a witch. You are not witches, so make sure you are polite to everybody." She tied her suitcase to her broomstick with string and her cat climbed onto her shoulder.

"Goodbye to you anyway," she said. She got on her broomstick and flew out of the window, her suitcase bobbing behind her. She was a bit wobbly.

"Look, there is Mummy coming now," said Father. "Let's go and meet her."

They all ran out into the sunshine shouting "Happy Birthday!" Toby had a quick look up in the air for Aunt Nasty. There far above him he saw a tiny little black speck that might have been Aunt Nasty or it might have been a seagull. He was not quite sure. Then he took one of Mother's hands, and Claire took the other, and they pulled her, laughing and happy, up the steps into her birthday room.

*Margaret Mahy*

If a witch on sagging broom
Passes through your living room,
DON'T BE SCARED
If you're polite, she may decide
To take you for an evening ride.

*Margaret Vogel*

☆ Ask the children to think of words beginning with the letters W.I.T.C.H. to describe witches. Draw word pictures onto cut out witch's hats, cauldrons or broomsticks, e.g.

Wicked
Icy
Terrible
Cackling
Horrific

### Art

☆ Discuss where a witch might live, who might live with her, what furniture she would have, where she would keep her broomstick, spell ingredients, and so on. Make a class collage or individual collages of a witch's home.

### For fun

☆ Play Halloween games.

### Songs

*Tinder-box*: 61 Halloween is coming

*Subject index*: Fear, Ghosts, Halloween

### Stories

*Go Away, Stay Away* G. Haley (Bodley Head)
*Heggerty Heggerty and the Dreadful Drought* E. Lindsay (Hamish Hamilton)
*It's Halloween* J. Prelutsky (World's Work)
*Mr McFadden's Hallowe'en* R. Godden (Macmillan)
*Nightmares* J. Prelutsky (Black)
*Simon and the Witch* M. Stuart Barry (Lions)
*A Witch in the Family* Z. K. Snyder (Beaver)
*The Witch's Garden* L. Postma (Hutchinson)

# Diwali

## Objectives

☐ To explore Diwali – who celebrates it and why
☐ To explore how it is celebrated
☐ To consider the meaning of some of its different aspects

Diwali is the Hindu festival of lights. It is celebrated every year in the last week of October or the first week of November. Four days of festivities precede the culmination of the festival on the fifth day, Diwali.

Central to the festival is the story of Prince Rama and his wife Sita. Rama was chosen by his father as heir to the kingdom of Ayodhaya (Aa-yoh-dja). However, as the result of a plot by his stepmother to gain the throne for her own son, Rama was sent into exile. After fourteen years of danger and adventure in the forest, Rama returned to take the throne. As he approached Ayodhaya the sky became bright with the light of thousands of lamps which the people lit in every window and on every building to welcome him home.

In India, Diwali is also the time for celebrating the gathering of the harvest and the end of the summer rains. The skies are clear and the stars shine brightly. For many it marks the beginning of the new year symbolised by Rama leading his people out of darkness into light. Businesses close their accounts and open new books, children are given new clothes and presents and houses are thoroughly cleaned. It is a time for visiting friends and relatives, dancing, fireworks, playing games and eating special foods. Lights are put in all the windows and along the walls of buildings. Even the rivers are alight with candles in little paper boats. Diwali is celebrated all over the world wherever people of the Hindu faith have settled.

## Starting points

○ Invite a member of the Hindu faith into school to talk to the children about Diwali – how and why it is celebrated. Give the children an opportunity to ask questions afterwards.

## The story of Rama and Sita

A long, long time ago in the kingdom of Ayodhaya in India there lived a king called Dasaratha. Dasaratha was a good and wise king who ruled his people well. The land was rich and the people lived happily. But as time passed the king grew too old to look after the kingdom any more and he decided to pass the work on to one of his sons.

Now the king had three wives, who each had sons. In fact his third wife had twin boys called Lakshmana and Shatrugnha. His second wife had a son called Bharata and the son of his first wife was called Rama. They were all close friends with each other and all grew up strong and brave, but the first son, Rama was the favourite of them all. His father loved him dearly, all his brothers gladly followed his leadership, and the people were happy knowing that one day Rama would be king and that he would rule as wisely and well as his father.

So one day, as everyone expected, the old king gathered his people together and told them that Rama was to be their new king. They all cheered happily and started to plan a great celebration. But one person was not so pleased for Rama. His stepmother Queen Kaikeyi was jealous that her son, Bharata, had not been chosen and she began to form a plan. Many years before, she had saved the old king's life in a battle. He had been so grateful to her that he had promised her two wishes. Now the Queen went to the king and said, "My Lord, do you remember when I saved your life?"

The king was surprised and said rather impatiently, "Yes, yes, of course I remember, my dear. But don't bother me now – I have so much to plan for with Rama about to be king."

"If you remember me saving your life," said the queen, "you must also remember that you promised me two wishes. At that time I did not need the wishes but now the time has come for me to use them. You must grant me these two things. Firstly you must make my son, Bharata, king of Ayodhaya

instead of Rama, and secondly you must send Rama and his wife Sita away from this land for fourteen years so that they cannot interfere with my son's reign."

The poor king was stunned to hear these words. He begged his wife to say that she did not really mean them, but the queen was determined to have her way, and broken-hearted he sent for Rama to tell him what he was forced to do.

Rama comforted his father saying, "Dear father, Bharata my brother will make an excellent king in my place and I shall be happy living in the forest – after fourteen years I shall return."

But his father could not be comforted. He knew that he would not live long enough to see his son again.

When Lakshmana, Rama's brother and closest friend heard the news he was furious and shouted that he would kill anyone who tried to stop Rama being king. But Rama calmed him saying that he must obey his father. Lakshmana finally agreed but said that he would not be parted from his brother and would go with him and Sita into the forest.

Together they packed the things they needed for their journey and said their farewells to the broken-hearted king. The people wept to see them going and followed them to the edge of the kingdom where the great forest began. Sadly they waved goodbye as Rama, Sita and Lakshmana disappeared into the forest.

Now, while all this had been happening, Bharata had been away visiting his grandfather. He knew nothing of what had happened. He returned to the palace to find everyone weeping. The old king his father had died and Rama was nowhere to be found. His mother ran to him joyfully telling him what she had arranged for him. But Bharata grew angry and raged at his mother when he heard what she had done. He ran out along the path Rama and the others had taken into the forest and searched and searched for his brother. At last he found him deep in the forest.

"Come back, Rama," Bharata begged his brother, "I don't want to be king in place of you. Come back and be king as our father wished you to be."

But Rama said firmly, "No, Bharata, I cannot. I must carry out our father's promise to your mother. Go back to the palace and take your place on the throne."

Bharata pleaded with him to return, but Rama was determined. Finally Bharata agreed to let him go but he picked up Rama's sandals and said, "I shall go back but I shall not be king. These sandals shall be placed on the throne and everyone will know that one day Rama will return to be king."

Why did Prince Rama have to leave home and live in the forest?
What do you think of the way Rama's stepmother behaved?
Do you think the king should have kept his promise?
What do you think of Rama's behaviour?
Why was Bharata so angry with his mother? Did he want the throne for himself? Why not?

Together the three lived in the forest in a beautiful hut which Lakshmana built for them. They were happy living off the fruits of the forest, and the animals of the wild came to them without fear. They saw few other people but occasionally they met wandering holy men whom they welcomed warmly into their home. Mostly they had the birds and beasts of the forest for company.

The days did not all pass quietly and the three had many adventures. Wild demons inhabited the lonely places of the forest and loved to torment the holy men. Rama and Lakshmana fought many battles with them to keep the forest quiet and peaceful. But their greatest battle was still to come.

Far away on the island of Lanka, lived the demon king himself. His name was Ravana and as soon as he heard that a beautiful woman was living in the forest he became determined that he would capture her and make her his wife.

One day a golden deer leapt through the forest past the hut where Rama, Sita and Lakshmana lived. Sita at once thought it the most beautiful deer

she had ever seen and Rama promised her she should have it for a pet. Quick as a flash he bounded after the deer and followed it deep into the forest. But as he ran further and further from the hut he realised that he had fallen into a trap and that he had left the others behind in danger. Drawing his bow he shot the animal. As the deer fell, to Rama's amazement, it cried out for help in Rama's own voice.

Far away at the hut, Lakshmana heard the voice of Rama calling him, and Sita begged him to go to her husband's help. Lakshmana was suspicious but reluctantly he ran off in the direction of the voice, calling to Sita to stay by the hut where she would be safe.

As soon as Lakshmana had gone, Ravana, king of the demons, appeared before the hut disguised as an old man.

"Help me, help me." he cried to Sita, "I am old and weak and cannot walk". Kind-hearted Sita left the hut and walked quickly towards the old man to give him her arm.

But immediately the old man turned back into his true form – the ten-headed wicked king of the demons. Ravana seized Sita and carried her off to his chariot hidden in the trees. Away they flew, up into the sky and across the seas to Lanka.

Too late the brothers ran back to the hut only to find it empty and Sita gone. Rama was terrified for his wife's safety.

"Come, Rama," said his brother, "We must find Sita. We shall search together."

Gratefully Rama thanked his brother for his support and the two at once left their old home and began the search for Sita. They travelled for days, weeks and months never finding any trace of her. But one day they met the monkey people and Hanuman, the commander of the monkey army. Before long with the help of the monkey army they learned that Sita had been stolen away to the Island of Lanka where she was being held prisoner by Ravana. Now Lanka is an island many, many miles →

○ Place diva (special lights – see classroom activities) on tables and window ledges in the hall, which can be decorated with the children's class work. Light the diva while singing *Diwali*. The story of Rama and Sita could be read, performed as a play, and discussed.

○ Discuss homecomings. How did Rama and Sita feel as they returned home after fourteen years? (This can be linked with the work in *Homecomings*).

○ Talk about the qualities of darkness and light, fear of the dark, the comfort of light. What other celebrations involve burning candles?

○ Discuss harvest. Ask the children what they know of harvest celebrations. Why is it a time for farmers to work hard? Why might they worry about gathering the harvest quickly? Why is it a time to celebrate?

Finish assemblies on Diwali by wishing each other a Happy Diwali – *Diwali Mubaraka* (Gujerati).

### Classroom activities

#### Language

☆ Ask the children to retell the story of Rama and Sita in writing and paintings.

☆ Discuss and list words for light – bright, shining, etc. Write out the words and display them in the shapes of brightly coloured diva or candles.

☆ Design a new and exciting firework. Describe what happens when it is lit. What does it look like? What noise does it make? Make a class collage of the children's designs. (Use the occasion to talk about the safety code for fireworks.)

away from India. How could anyone get there?

"I shall go," cried Hanuman and with one giant leap he flew up into the air and across the sea to Lanka. There he found Sita, frightened and unhappy surrounded by demon women guards. Hidden in a tree, Hanuman waited his chance and when Sita sat nearby he dropped into her lap Rama's ring, which he had taken as a token. Joyfully, she looked up and saw Hanuman. She quickly hid the ring, knowing that Rama must be nearby and waiting to save her.

Meanwhile, Rama, Lakshmana and all the monkeys were busy building a huge bridge of boulders across the sea to Lanka. At last the bridge was ready and Rama, Lakshmana and the monkey army started to cross. When the demons saw them coming they hurriedly formed themselves into an army and made ready to defend their city. A great battle followed. Rama, Lakshmana and the monkeys fought fiercely and bravely against all the magic and trickery which Ravana and his demons used against them and finally, after many dangers and adventures, they won. Rama and Sita were together again.

And now the fourteen years of Rama's exile were over. He along with Sita, Lakshmana and Hanuman, accompanied by all their new friends stepped into a wonderful flying chariot, which the gods had given them, and set out for home.

As the chariot approached Ayodhaya, Rama's people heard of his coming and lit lamps in all their windows and along all the walls of their houses to light the travellers' way out of the dark forest and welcome them home.

Bharata was overjoyed to see his brother again and immediately started preparations for Rama's coronation. Everyone was happy again – even Queen Kaikeyi, whom Rama forgave for the wrong she had done him so long ago.

And so it is that every year since then, people have celebrated Rama's return from the dark forest by lighting lamps at Diwali time.　　*Traditional*

## Art

☆ Decorate the classroom with Diwali flowers. Cut flower shapes out of card and cover them with coloured tissue paper screwed up into balls. Hang them from the ceiling.

☆ *Rangoli*: this is the art of decorating the floor at the entrance to a house with patterns in rice flour as a symbol of welcome. Rangoli means "a pattern in colour." They are especially important during Diwali. There are plenty traditional designs to choose from but nowadays there is scope for experimenting both with the patterns and the materials. Use any materials – powder paint, chalk, cereals, seeds, flowers. If you have an understanding caretaker each class can paint its own Rangoli pattern outside the classroom door, using thick powder paint. Otherwise they can be mounted on card and displayed on the walls. The traditional medium, rice flour, was used so as to offer food to the ants, birds and squirrels, and as a sign of thanksgiving.

☆ Decorate the walls with a frieze of Indian dancers (use tissue or thin materials to give a 3D effect), peacocks or elephants.

☆ *Diva*: these are the traditional oil lamps lit during Diwali. Children can make them by moulding clay, plasticine or pastry dough into small bowls. Let them experiment with the shape – they could form the clay into boats – but ensure that each has a firm base. Pour a little clarified butter (ghee) or any vegetable oil into the diva and twist a little cotton wool, dipped in the oil, into a wick. Night lights, painted glasses or jam jars can also be used and can be fun to make.

**Songs**
*Tinder-box*: 62 Diwali

**Stories**
*The Prince of Ayodhya* (Nehru Library for Children)
*Ramayana* (Oxford)
*The Story of Prince Rama* B. Thompson (Kestrel)
*The Story of Rama and Sita* J. Troughton (Blackie)

**Information books**
*Diwali Foods* available from Minority Group Support Service, Coventry
*Gopal: His Life in India* D. Darbois (Chatto)
*A Hindu Family in Britain* (Religious Education Press)
*India* Z. Lindsay (Black)
*Rangoli: Floor Patterns Book* available from Independent Publishers, 38 Kennington Lane, London SE11
*Ravi of India* Hardy and Aruna (Lutterworth)
"Something to Celebrate" Project: *Diwali* (Bedfordshire Education Service Resources Centre, Acacia Road, Bedford)

**Videocassettes**
*Merry Go Round* series (BBC) – extract on a Gujerati family celebrating Diwali in Britain
*Something to Celebrate* (ITV *Finding Out* series)

# Christmas

## Objectives
☐ To explore Christmas – who celebrates it and why
☐ To consider some of the different meanings the festival has for people
☐ To explore Christmas activities

Christmas celebrates the birth of Jesus, the founder of the Christian faith. Before his birth the Jews had for a long time expected the coming of a saviour, but they believed it would be a warrior who would free their nation from their enemies. Instead, Jesus was born into a humble carpenter's home and founded Christianity on the teaching of love and peace. Like other festivals Christmas has significance on many levels. It celebrates the birth of Christianity, it is a time of great hope and longing for peace, a time of giving and receiving, and for children it is a time of special excitement and anticipation.

## Starting points
○ Invite a Christian minister into school to explain what Christmas means and how it is celebrated. Give the children time at the end to ask their own questions.

○ Ask the children how many of them celebrate Christmas and invite a few to describe what they do on Christmas day. Discuss their responses and explore what they feel is important about Christmas.

○ Discuss the activities which take place before Christmas and on the day itself. How do the children take part? How do they feel? What do they most look forward to?

○ Make a display of the children's art work.

○ Talk about presents. Why do we give them? How do the children feel when they give a present to someone? Ask about Father Christmas – who is he? where does he live? Do they believe in him? (Read a story about the origin of the Father Christmas legend).

## Long ago in Bethlehem

Long ago when Mary and Joseph set out on their journey to Bethlehem they had to walk because there were no cars or trains or aeroplanes. But they had a little donkey, so that helped. Sometimes Mary had a ride to rest her feet.

It was often cold, especially at night, and the journey took a long time. They were thankful to see the lights of Bethlehem – little oil lamps that flickered and glowed through the darkness. But by the time they wandered down the street searching for a place to stay Mary was very weary. Joseph knocked on one door after another but everyone said "No room."

And by this time even the little donkey was tired. So there was nothing for it but to walk on and keep trying. Joseph told Mary not to worry. "We'll find somewhere to stay soon," he said, "You'll see." And Mary tried to smile though her back ached and the little donkey kept stumbling over the stones.

At the Inn the man said he'd no room in the house either but that Mary and Joseph could make a bed in the stable in the back yard if they liked. So they thanked the man and went in. Joseph said it wasn't much of a place but at least it was warm and they'd make do. And Mary had her baby there.

It was bitter cold out on the hillside. The stars were bright but the wind was chill and the shepherd blew on his hands and crouched under his blanket to try to keep warm. The sheep huddled together to keep out the cold and they mostly went to sleep. But the shepherds were wakeful. They had to be, to keep a look-out for any sheep that might stray away and get lost. It was quiet and peaceful but very, very cold.

But all at once the sky lit up. One of the stars shone out like a great ball of light and from all around the sky came sounds – as if the winds were singing and calling.

The bright light startled the shepherds and frightened the sheep who ran away down the hill. But the shepherds stood close together and stared fearfully at the star. By now it lighted up the sky and the grass and the sheep with a golden glow.

When they had come to their senses, one shepherd said "I'm sure I heard a voice telling of a new king being born and I think we should go down into Bethlehem to see if he has come."

And off they went, shepherds and sheep with the star to guide them.

They had to search. They were looking for a king with a golden crown, but the star led them to a stable in the back yard of the Inn. And when they found him they could hardly believe their eyes – a little baby lying in a manger among the hay.

"Not much of a place for a king," a shepherd said softly.

But Joseph smiled and Jesus slept and Mary was content.

*Retold by Masahiro Kasuya*

Why was Mary so tired?
How do you think she felt having to leave her home when she was expecting a baby and there was nowhere to stay?
How did the shepherds know that something very special had happened?
Why were they surprised when they found the baby?

## Classroom activities

### Language

☆ Ask the children to think of someone they would like to make a present for, then to think carefully what that person would most like. Ask them to write a description of the present giving their reasons for choosing it.

☆ Talk about letter-writing – how a letter should be addressed, set out on the paper, and so on. Then ask the children to write a letter to Father Christmas saying what they would like as a present and why they feel they deserve it.

☆ Write an account of the best part of Christmas day.

☆ Make a list of words to describe how the children feel on Christmas Eve and on Christmas day after they have opened their presents.

### Mathematics

☆ With the children, make a wall chart showing their favourite presents. Make a survey of the class first to find out the four most popular toys – ask the children to devise a way of finding this out.

How many more children would like leggo than would like a train set? . . .

### Art

☆ Ask the children for ideas for Christmas cards. Discuss what the children feel are the most important things about Christmas and use one of these as a theme for their card. They could use cut out card shapes, e.g.

## Christmas in Uruguay

For me, Christmas means my mother. That may sound strange, coming from a grown man, but it's true: she's eighty years old, but still very much the centre of our huge family – all seventy of them! – and of all our Christmas celebrations.

My home city is the country's capital, with more than a million inhabitants. The shop windows are dressed up for the festival, but the real Christmas atmosphere is to be found in the home. Our house is flat-roofed, painted white, and has a tiny garden at the back crammed with vines, lemon trees and tomato plants.

Everything is noise and laughter at Christmas. And with seventy people, you can imagine what I mean by noise. There is always someone singing, the television is on in one corner of the room, the record player is blaring away in another, the children are letting off fireworks everywhere, and we are all playing jokes on each other – it's chaos!

All the windows and doors are open, of course – apart from the fact that the house just can't hold us all, it's summer and the weather is very hot.

We tuck into a huge feast on the evening of December 24th. The centre of the feast is a roast pig – a whole one! All the family gives something: cold meats, Russian salad, chickens, ravioli, and for dessert pineapple flan, fresh fruit salad and pastries. The survivors finish off with coffee!

The children all bring a little present for their grandmother, but the adults usually club together to buy her something special. As I said at the beginning, my mother is still the centre of affection for everyone. It is she who cares about us all, who has the right word for each one of us and a gentle sense of humour that encourages us and gives us strength. The family often meets at her house: there are so many of us, there's always a marriage, a christening, or a birthday to celebrate. Christmas brings home to me the richness of *family* life, with its love and tears and laughter.

Who is the most important person for you at Christmas time?
What do you eat for Christmas dinner?
When do you give your presents?
Is your family as big as this?
Who do you celebrate Christmas with?

## Mrs Hooligan's Christmas cake

As I sat in me window last evenin'
A letterman came unto me.
He had a nice little neat invitation,
Saying 'Won't you come over to tea?'
I knew it was Hooligan sent it
So I went for our friendship's sake,
And the first thing he gave me to tackle
Was a slice of Mrs Hooligan's cake.

There were plums and prunes and cherries,
Raisins and currants and cinnamon too.
There were nuts and cloves and berries
But the crust it was nailed on with glue.
There were caraway seeds in abundance,
'Twould give you a fine head-ache,
'Twould kill any man twice to be eatin'
A slice of Mrs Hooligan's Christmas cake.

Miss Mulligan wanted to taste it,
But really it was all no use.
She worked at it for over an hour
But couldn't get any of it loose.
Till Hooligan went for the hatchet,
And Kelly came in with the saw.
That cake was enough, by the power,
To paralyse any man's jaw.

*Traditional Irish*

## The legend of the spiders

At Christmas time, people told stories of the Christ Child coming again to visit the earth. A German legend tells how, one Christmas Eve, the Christ Child came to a farmhouse where the family all lay asleep in bed; the house was dark; the doors and windows were closed. Outside in the snow, some spiders were crying bitterly. The Child asked them what was the matter. The farmer's wife had cleaned the house for Christmas, and turned them all out to live in the barn. The spiders had seen the Christmas tree brought into the house from the forest, planted in a pot, and placed in the living room. Now they wanted to see it with the shining decorations, lights, sweets and toys hanging from its branches.

The Christ Child opened the door of the house, and told the spiders they might go wherever they wished, and see everything they wanted to see. The spiders scurried in, and went straight to the tree. They clambered up and down, all over its laden branches, and examined everything. Then they went happily back to the barn. The tree was covered from top to bottom in grey spiders' webs, but the Child touched the tree and blessed it, and all the threads turned to gold.

*German legend*

### A mixed blessing

Old Father Christmas
Landed on the roof-top,
Climbed down the chimney,
Tiptoed through the room;
Filled all the stockings,
Leaving sooty footprints
Right across the carpet,
So go and get the broom!

*Elizabeth Hogg*

The letters of Christmas

candle  holly  robin  icicle  Snow  tree

mistletoe  angel  Santa with his Sack

Jennifer Graham Aged 6

☆ Take each letter of Christmas and illustrate it (see opposite).

☆ Sing *The Twelve Days of Christmas*, talk about the words then ask the children if they can suggest alternative presents for each day (a Caribbean version is given in *Mango Spice*, published by A. & C. Black). Ask each to illustrate their choice of present or make a class decoration together. Cut out a large circle of card for each day, paint them and hang them from the ceiling.

☆ Make Christmas tree decorations.

**Songs**
*Tinder-box*: 63 Mary had a boy-child
*Subject index*: Christmas

**Stories**
*A Christmas Fantasy* C. Haywood (Brockhampton)
*The Christmas Story by Father Christmas* I. Gantscher (Neugebauer)
*The Little Shepherd Boy* P. Blakeley (Black)
*Lotta's Christmas Surprise* A. Lindgren (Methuen)
*Mog's Christmas* J. Kerr (Collins)
*Mole's Family Christmas* R. Hoban (World's Work)
*Plain Lane Christmas* C. Walter Hodges (Dent)
*The Silver Christmas Tree* P. Hitchins (Bodley Head)
*The Smallest Christmas Tree* P. Blakeley (Black)
*Stories for Christmas* A. Uttley (Faber)
*The Twelve Days of Christmas* B. Wildsmith (Oxford)

**Information books**
*Celebrating Christmas* ed. S. Tompkins (Christian Education Movement)
*The Christmas Book* S. Baker (Macdonald)

# Chinese New Year

## Objectives

☐ To explore why and how Chinese New Year is celebrated.

☐ To link this with New Year celebrations elsewhere

☐ To think why New Year is so widely celebrated.

Chinese New Year – the Spring Festival – falls on a day between mid-January and mid-February. The date changes because the Chinese calendar is lunar. It is the most important festival of the Chinese year and can last up to a fortnight. On New Year's Eve the whole family tries to be together for a special reunion meal. On New Year's morning dumplings are the traditional breakfast. Everyone dresses in their best clothes, and goes out visiting friends and relatives. Children receive presents of sweets and money wrapped in red paper packets and have fun with games and fireworks. Houses are given a spring cleaning and decorated with flowers of prosperity, red and gold New Year scrolls and hangings. The festivities go on for many days including, games, plays, dances and the very popular Lion Dance.

## Starting points

○ Ask a member of the Chinese community to come into the school to talk to the children about the New Year festivities, and answer their questions.

○ Ask the children about how they celebrate New Year. What activities do they take part in? What preparations are made? What customs do they have? Explain that in different parts of the world New Year falls at different times. In parts of India it is the day after Diwali. In Britain it is the 1st January. In China it falls on a day between 20th January and 20th February. Why do they think New Year is an important time to celebrate – it might mark the end of harvest, the beginning of Spring. Why might it be at a different time in different parts of the world? (Depends when growing season starts or ends, what kind of calendar is followed, etc.)

○ Find out more about the Chinese cycle of twelve years each named after a different animal – rat, ox, tiger, hare, dragon, snake, horse, ram, monkey, cockerel, dog, pig. People are believed to have the qualities of the animal in whose year they were born.

## New Year with Hsiao Ming

The chubby four-year-old boy was playing in the garden when his mother called him. "Hsiao Ming! Hsiao Ming! I have good news for you," she says. "Father is coming home tomorrow for Chinese New Year. Aren't you happy?" She picks him up in her arms and gives him a big kiss on his rosy cheeks.

It is two days before Chinese New Year, or Ko Nien as it is called in China, and Father always comes home to celebrate it with Hsiao Ming and his mother. The little boy cannot remember his father very well, but Mother tells him that Father works on a big ship that sails around the world.

It is always a happy time for Hsiao Ming when Father returns. There are lots of sweets and good things to eat and plenty of firecrackers to play with. And his uncles and aunts always give him little red packets with money inside.

"Mama, tell me the story of Nien the wicked monster again," he begs.

His mother sits down and puts Hsiao Ming on her lap. "Once upon a time," she says, "there lived a wicked monster called Nien. Everyone in the village was terrified of Nien because each year, on New Year's Eve, Nien would come out of his den to hunt for food. Then people would stay indoors and bolt their doors and shut their windows.

"But Nien was afraid of three things. He was afraid of red, he always ran away when he saw fire, and the noise of firecrackers made his hair stand on end. So on New Year's Eve people painted all their doors red and lit a lot of firecrackers hoping to scare Nien off.

"The next morning when the people woke up and looked out of their windows, Nien was nowhere to be seen. So they put on their best clothes, ate plenty of cakes and sweets and celebrated Nien's disappearance. Everyone rejoiced that the wicked monster would not come back to the village for a whole year, until next New Year's Eve. And now that they were safe and sound, children visited their uncles and aunts and friends to wish them a Happy New Year, and each time they did this they received red packets with money in them. That is what Ko Nien means, Hsiao Ming, and that is how we will celebrate it."

The little boy loved to hear his mother tell him the story of Nien. Later in the day he helped Mother with the preparations for New Year. Together they swept the house clean, tidied up all the rooms and put things in their proper places. Then Mother made some little cakes for the New Year, and in the afternoon Hsiao Ming helped Mother decorate the living room walls by hanging up pretty New Year cards that they received from friends.

The next day was New Year's Eve and an even busier day for Mother. Hsiao Ming remembered the story of Nien and decided to light a few firecrackers outside the house, just in case Nien was prowling around.

Suddenly he heard a voice call him from behind. A tall, sunburned man who knew his name was watching him. A little shy and frightened, Hsiao Ming ran into the house. "Mama, Mama," he called.

His mother came running out of the kitchen, her hands covered with flour.

"Welcome home, dear," she said to the tall stranger. "Hsiao Ming, your father is home," she said to the little boy.

"Papa," said Hsiao Ming shyly. Then his father came towards him, lifted the little boy up in the air and swung him around and around.

That evening Mother laid such a feast on the table and Father, Mother and Hsiao Ming sat down for the reunion dinner that is eaten once a year in all Chinese homes when the whole family is present.

Next morning a burst of firecrackers woke Hsiao Ming up.

"Happy New Year," said his mother as he opened his eyes.

"Get up quickly, Hsiao Ming," said Father. "We are going to visit your uncles and aunts, and then we are going to see the lion dance."

The little boy scrambled out of bed. Mother helped him into his new clothes and the family went out. Many of the houses they passed on the way had "Happy New Year" and "Peace in the New Year" written on the doors in red and gold letters.

Hsiao Ming greeted his uncles and aunts and bowed to them. And they all wished Hsiao Ming and his parents a Happy New Year. His aunts offered him a bowl of tasty red and white dumplings filled with nuts and sugar. They told him that the Chinese eat dumplings in the New Year because their round shapes mean that the family will be strong and united. When it was time to go to the lion dance, Hsiao Ming had both pockets filled with sweets and red packets of money.

The lion dance had not started, but the streets were packed with people waiting for the dancers. All around the crowds firecrackers were going off. There was a bamboo pole sticking out of the window of a tall building. At the end of the pole a long string of firecrackers was hanging down. When someone lit one of the firecrackers, they all started

to go off. Bing! Bang! Bing! Bing! Bang! Smoke and sparks flew everywhere.

Suddenly Hsiao Ming heard the sound of trumpets, cymbals and drums. "The lion dance is here! The lion dance is here!" he shouted, clapping his hands.

A large, friendly, shaggy lion trotted up, followed by a smaller lion. Hsiao Ming watched the dancers' feet underneath their lion costumes. The lions swayed with the music. They shook their heads up and down. They rolled over and stood on their hind legs. When the music stopped, they bowed and trotted off. Everyone clapped. They were happy to see the lion dance because the Chinese believe that, together with the dragon and the phoenix, lions bring good luck and prosperity.

When Hsiao Ming and his parents got home that evening, Mother put the little boy to bed. It was already very late, but Hsiao Ming did not feel sleepy. He was thinking of the lion dance, the fireworks, the red packets he received from his uncles and aunts and the good time he had had today with Mother and Father. And as he shut his eyes he mumbled, "When will it be Chinese New Year again?"

## The legend of the New Year animals

It was decided that each animal was to have a year named after it. The twelve animals argued and argued about who should be first until the gods told them they must race across a big river. The animal who reached the opposite bank first would be the winner.

The animals lined up along the bank. Then, ready ... steady ... GO! they jumped into the river and were off. The ox soon swam out ahead of the others and made strongly for the other bank but the clever rat jumped on his back and was carried along too. Just as Ox reached the other bank and was stepping out of the water, Rat leapt off his back onto the bank and declared himself the winner.

One by one the others joined Ox and Rat on the bank: first Tiger, then Hare, Dragon, Snake, Horse, Ram, Monkey, Cockerel, Dog, and last of all Pig.

And that is how the Year of the Rat became the first year of the Chinese calendar and how all the others followed after.

| | | |
|---|---|---|
| Rat | — 1972 | — 1984 |
| Ox | — 1973 | — 1985 |
| Tiger | — 1974 | — 1986 |
| Hare | — 1975 | — 1987 |
| Dragon | — 1976 | — 1988 |
| Snake | — 1977 | — 1989 |
| Horse | — 1978 | — 1990 |
| Ram | — 1979 | — 1991 |
| Monkey | — 1980 | — 1992 |
| Cockerel | — 1981 | — 1993 |
| Dog | — 1982 | — 1994 |
| Pig | — 1983 | — 1995 |

### Classroom activities

☆ Devise a Lion Dance. The real Lion Dance is very strenuous and skilled requiring trained athletes to perform it, but the children could perform their own version in class without too much difficulty. If possible, show the children photographs or a videocassette of the real thing first or invite a member of the Chinese community to describe the dance to the children and tell them about its origins and significance. A lion head can be made using a cardboard box painted and decorated with brightly coloured tissue and metallic paper (see the back cover). Attach a length of material to the box. The children can take turns to take the lion's head and lead the dance, the others following behind. Accompany the dancing with the song New things to do using plenty of cymbals and drums.

☆ Design a Chinese New Year Card.

☆ Make a display of Chinese articles: chopsticks, bowls, fans, lanterns, and so on.

☆ Ask the children what they know about the signs of the Zodiac. List the signs with them. Why is the Zodiac similar to the Chinese New Year animals. Do they think that you can really tell what someone is like from the month or year in which they are born? Why? Why not? What is a horoscope? Make a class collage of the twelve animals or of the signs of the Zodiac.

### Songs
Tinder-box: 58 New things to do
Subject index: Festivals

### Stories
A Sky Full of Dragons M. Whatley Wright (Abelard-Schuman)
Sweet and Sour C. Kendall and Yao-Wen Li (Bodley Head)

### Information books
Chinese Childhood M. Fawdry (Pollock)
Chun Ling in China N. Fyson and R. Greenhill (Black)
Goodbye Hong Kong, Hello Glasgow (Glasgow NAME publication, c/o 17 Cranworth Street, Glasgow G12)
Phoenix Bird Chinese Take Away K. Mackinnon (Black)
"Something to Celebrate" Project: Chinese New Year (Bedfordshire Education Service Resources Centre)

# Trinidad Carnival

**Objectives**
- [ ] To explore the origins of Carnival
- [ ] To find out how and why it is celebrated

Carnival's origins in Europe stretch back beyond the Christian era to ancient rites performed to frighten away the demons of winter and welcome in the spring. With the rise of Christianity the festival was absorbed into the Christian calendar and became a two-day period of merrymaking preceding Ash Wednesday, the beginning of Lent. The word Carnival is derived from the Latin *carne vale* meaning "farewell to the flesh" and Carnival was the time for one last bout of feasting and enjoyment before entering upon a period of fasting and repentance during Lent.

The festival was established in Trinidad by the French planters who settled there from the late 18th century onwards. After emancipation in 1834 the Afro-Caribbean people of the island made the festival their own drawing on the European masquerade costumes, music and dance and adding to them a distinctively African influence.

Today local carnivals are celebrated all over Trinidad and Tobago in small towns and villages but the main Carnival celebrations take place in Port of Spain and centre on a highly sophisticated masquerade in which thousands of people take part. It is one of the largest and most spectacular community festivals in the world.

Carnival lasts three days:
*Dimanche Gras* (the Sunday before Ash Wednesday) – a day for dancing and parties lasting long into the night.
*Jour Ouvert* – all morning people dance in the streets to the music of their favourite steel bands.
*Mardi Gras* – the highpoint of Carnival when thousands join in playing 'mas' (masquerade) and the great masquerade procession makes its way to Queen's Park Savanna where competitions are held to choose the Carnival King and Queen, the best steel band, Calypso King, and so on.

The costumes range from the very simplest, which are produced in large numbers for the members of the masquerade band, to the most elaborate one-off creations, which may take months to prepare. Masquerade bands vie to outdo each other in the

## Carnival in Trinidad

Romance in the tropic air
Here and there and everywhere
Everyone is on the go,
Pans to tune, costumes to sew;
Money lending
Wire bending
Metal sheeting
In the beating
Bleachers building,
Coaches gilding.
Miles of gold and silver braid
Heralding the masquerade.

Sensuous calypso beat
Echoing through every street,
Youth and age alike will be
Gyrating round in ecstasy
Steelbands clashing
Jab-jabs lashing
Robbers cracking
Coons click-clacking
Witches croaking
Jesters joking
Imps and devils on parade
All part of the masquerade.

Ancient monarchs, ladies fair,
Dragons belching red hot air,
Grotesque moko-jumbies tall
Red Indians, wigwams and all
Groggy fellow
Strumming 'cello
Police chasing
Children racing
Parents hissing.
Lovers kissing.
Devotee and renegade –
All part of the masquerade.

Share our nation's festival,
Heritage of great and small,
Most exciting of them all:
Blaze of glory – Carnival.

*Nydia Bruce-Solomon*

## Carnival of dreams (extract)

*This is a story about Carnival in Britain. On Carnival day Mrs Carval and her two sons Elroy and Clint go to visit Auntie Nella, Uncle Tosh, and Cousin Benjoe for lunch before joining the big parade in the afternoon. Everyone is getting ready to take part except Mrs Carval who is feeling sad despite Carnival. The day before she thought she had won the pools but found she had filled in the wrong coupon:*

Elroy skipped along the pavement to Auntie Nella's house. "Come in," she said. "I had a feeling that you would come round. The table is laid for six, and there's plenty of good things to eat."

Elroy could hardly wait for his lunch. But he was made to wait until Uncle Tosh, Benjoe, and Clint came back from the school hall.

He walked around the table looking at everything. There were dishes of rice and peas, fried fish and curry goat. There were salted mackerel and boiled green bananas. There were fresh vegetable salads, sweet potato pudding, and iced carrot juice to drink.

It seemed to Elroy as if he had waited a year by the time they sat down to eat. He felt ravenously hungry, and gave himself large helpings of rice and curry.

Auntie Nella's cooking was excellent. Elroy tried some of everything and asked for seconds of most. When his mother saw him having seconds of salad she could hardly believe her eyes. She shook her head and said, "Hunger is the best sauce."

After lunch, everyone was busy dressing up for the big parade. Auntie Nella and her family were dressed as Space People, and were going in a Space Ship with the Martian Steel Band. Clint and Elroy were going with the Happy Wanderers, a tribe of fierce Indians.

When they were all ready, they stood outside in the street waiting for the decorated floats to arrive.

Mrs Carval, in her everyday clothes, stuck out like a sore thumb. They waited for what seemed hours. The street was so crowded that they thought the floats would never come.

Elroy looked at his mother. She was left out of the fun. He remembered their plans when they thought they were rich. He felt so sad for her.

"Mum," he said. "Why don't you dress up? Surely Auntie Nella could find you something to wear for Carnival!"

"It's too late," she replied. "Much too late."

"Nonsense," said Auntie Nella. "Come on. Join in the fun. Let's go and look for something you can wear."

Mrs Carval thought for a moment about the football coupon and not winning the pools. But they no longer mattered. The two women went back indoors.

Elroy could just see a float at the top of the street. "Clint," he shouted. "Our float is coming. I can see it."

Clint craned his neck. "I can't see anything," he said.

"Our float is coming," said Benjoe. "The Space Ship is coming."

And so it was. People crowded round it. Everyone said that it was one of the best floats in the Carnival. Benjoe climbed in and then climbed out again. He had forgotten his helmet, and went back to his house to get it. "Mum," he called. "Open the door. I want my helmet, and the Space Ship has arrived. Come on, we have to go!"

The door stayed shut. So, to help the two women along, all three boys started calling together. Then the Happy Wanderers arrived and the excitement mounted.

At last the door opened and out came a space woman with all her space gear. Nobody would know who she was. A few minutes later, Mrs Carval came out, and the crowd said, "Ah!"

"Smashing!" Elroy exclaimed. "My mum looks smashing!"

The onlookers clapped and cheered because she was wearing Jamaican National Costume. She looked just right in her long, plaid skirt and white, embroidered, off-the-shoulder blouse. She looked so attractive in a headscarf that matched her skirt, and with ear-rings like little hoops dangling from her ears.

"Where shall I go?" she asked. "I'm neither a space woman nor an Indian."

"Come with me, Mum," said Elroy proudly. "You look lovely, and you will have a lovely Carnival!"
*Beryl Gilroy*

intricacy and splendour of their costumes choosing themes such as *Birds of Paradise, Danse Macabre, Underwater Extravaganza*, as well as the much older traditional characters such as *Moko Jumbie, Pierrot Grenade* and *Jab-Jab*.

**Starting points**

○ Talk about the word masquerade. Have the children ever heard it before? Do they know what it means? Have they ever played dressing up games? Who did they pretend to be? What do they enjoy about dressing up? You may like to talk about the background to masquerade. In the old Roman Saturnalian festival which probably influenced the later development of Carnival the social system was deliberately turned topsy turvey. Servants changed places with their masters, wore their clothes and were served at table by them. Later on similar customs took place on Twelfth Night when a Lord of Misrule was chosen to direct the mischief and merrymaking on this one night of the year when all normal social conventions were overturned.

○ Make a display of posters, photographs and children's paintings of Carnival to decorate the walls of the assembly hall. (Posters can be obtained from the High Commission of Trinidad and Tobago and slides and photographs from the Commonwealth Institute, Kensington High St, London W8.)

○ Explain the origins of Trinidad Carnival and what happens there today (show a filmstrip if possible). Have any of the children been to carnivals in this country? What other local celebrations have they taken part in? (Street parties, May Day festivals, etc.) What happened? Who took part? Who arranged it? In what way is the celebration of Carnival different from that of Christmas? (Celebrated together by the whole community rather than as a family festival.)

○ Choose a suitable time of year – end of term or Mardi Gras itself – to put on your own school carnival. Alternatively a class on its own may like to prepare a masquerade procession and present it to the rest of the school. A school carnival would be ambitious but possible and could involve competitions like those held in Trinidad Carnival. Each class might prepare a masquerade on a different theme and prepare their own music for the

procession (see classroom activities). You may like to choose the theme of spring for your carnival since the festival has old links with this.

**Classroom activities**
**Language and music**
☆ Explore the music of Trinidad. Its best known elements, which both play an important role in Carnival, are calypso and steel band music.

The calypso is an improvised song which comments, often humourously, on topical events. During the run up to Carnival, the Calypsonians practise in calypso tents in preparation for the Calypso King competition in which they will be judged on the wit and humour of their words and on their ability to improvise. Find some examples of calypso to sing with the children (see *Tinder-box 23* 'Work Calypso' and others included in *Ta-ra-ra boom-de-ay* and *Mango Spice* published by A. & C. Black). Discuss what you would like your calypso to be about and try devising one together or individually. Use the melody from the calypso you have been learning or compose your own. Younger children could write a Carnival poem.

You may be lucky enough to have a steel band in school, otherwise there may be one which performs locally. Enquire whether the band would be willing to play in school or if a group of children might attend a rehearsal. Failing this, recordings of steel band music are fairly easy to obtain from a library or from the Commonwealth Institute (see address above). Explore the origins of the steel band. Steel drums were preceded by Bamboo Tambour drums – lengths of bamboo cut to different sizes to give different pitches. The children could experiment with assorted cylinders in different materials to make their own Bamboo Tambour drums for accompanying Caribbean music and songs. Steel drums developed shortly after the Second World War when it was discovered that by hammering different sized dents into the end of an oil drum a wide range of notes could be obtained. The first fully-fledged steel band quickly followed and since then steel bands have become extremely popular.

Making a steel drum is a highly skilled task but it may be possible to find someone who can demonstrate it and explain the different instruments of the band (there are four sizes, each with a different range of notes and a different function).

**Art**

☆Paint a Carnival frieze. Each child can paint a picture of themselves in the costume they would like to wear (discuss ideas for these first), then mount them on the walls to make a gaily coloured procession. With some research you may be able to find out the background to some of the traditional Carnival figures such as *Pierrot Grenade* and *Moko Jumbie*.

☆Hold a competition for the most original, the funniest and the best decorated costumes, or for the child who makes himself or herself the least recognisable! Discuss possible themes with the class first. It may help to provide the children with a basic outfit in thick paper or card which they can then use their imaginations to decorate (see p. 108).

Alternatively the class might combine their efforts to make a more elaborate centrepiece for their masquerade.

**Dance**

☆Devise a dance to perform during your masquerade procession.

**Songs**

*Tinder-box:* 64 Everybody loves Carnival Night

*Subject index:* Celebration, Festivals

**Stories**

*The Carnival Kite* G. Hallworth (Methuen)
*Carnival of Dreams* B. Gilroy (Macmillan)
*Nini at Carnival* E. Lloyd (Bodley Head)

**Information books**

*Carnival Frieze* A. McKenzie (Oxfam) available from the Ujamaa Centre, Oxfam Education Department, 14 Brixton Road, London SW9
*Seven of Us* A. Henley (Black)
*The Steelband* T. Noel (Commonwealth Institute)
*Trinidad Carnival* a magazine featuring the costumes of each year's Carnival (Key Caribbean Publications Ltd, Fernandes Industrial Centre, Laventille, Port of Spain, Trinidad)

**Filmstrip**

*Caribbean Carnival* (USPG, 15 Tufton Street, London SE1)



# Acknowledgements

**Jennifer Andrews** for her poems 'Seaside' and 'Summer morning'. **E. J. Arnold & Son Ltd** for 'Trog and the fire' by Ben Butterworth. **Asian Cultural Centre for Unesco** for 'New Year with Hsiao Ming' from *Festivals in Asia* published under the Asian Copublication Programme being carried out by the Asian Cultural Centre for Unesco, Tokyo. **Atheneum Publishers** for Lilian Moore's poems 'Ants live here' and 'Waking' from *I Feel the Same Way* © 1967 by Lilian Moore; the extract 'Jethro makes friends with a jumbie' from *Jethro and the Jumbie* by Susan Cooper, © 1979 by Susan Cooper, a Margaret K. McElderry Book, Canadian rights controlled by Atheneum Publishers. **ATV Network Ltd** for 'Boxes' and 'Crossing the bridge' by George Moore from the series *Over to You*. **Sheila Banfield** for 'India' by Hartash Dale. **Rebecca Bazeley** for her poem 'Grandad' from *Hey Mister Butterfly* published by ILEA. **BBC Publications** for 'Underneath my feet' by Richard Greening from *Play School: Humpty's Rhymes*; 'The legend of the spiders' from *Stories and Rhymes* Autumn 1979. **Bell & Hyman Ltd** for 'Hearing and seeing' from *Fables from Africa* collected by Dr Jan Knappert; 'I Wonder' by Jeannie Kirby from *Come Follow Me*. **A & C Black (Publishers) Ltd** for 'Carlo the crocodile makes his escape' from *Carlo the crocodile* by Anna Fodorova; *Emmie and Chips* by Peggy Blakeley; *Everybody said no!* by Sheila Lavelle; *Hanuman* by A. Ramachandran; *Joachim the dustman* by Kurt Baumann and David McKee; *Long ago in Bethlehem* by Masahiro Kasuya; *Onito's hat* by Kimiko Aman and Peggy Blakeley; *The Singing Bird* by Barbara Resch; *The Smallest Christmas Tree* by Peggy Blakeley; extracts from *What are you scared of?* by Hanne Larsen – 'I'm afraid of a man who looks strange', 'I get very frightened when my mum and dad quarrel', 'I'm scared to cross the road on my own', 'Sometimes I'm afraid that my mum and dad don't love me any more'. **Blackie & Son Ltd** for the extract from 'All along the street' by F. J. Teskey; the extract entitled 'Birth' from *A roof over your head* by Bill Naughton; the summary and extract from *There's no such thing as a dragon* by Jack Kent; *What made Tiddalik laugh* by Joanne Troughton. **Basil Blackwell Publisher** for *A boy and his robot* and *The giant child* from the *Rights of Children* series. **Bedfordshire Education Service Resources Centre** for 'The legend of the New Year animals' from 'Something to Celebrate' Project: *Chinese New Year*. **Cambridgeshire Education Department** for 'Brownies' by Susan Mangam and 'June 9th' by James McFadyzean from *At the Rainbow's Foot: an anthology of poems written by children from Cambridgeshire and the Isle of Ely* (out of print). **Cassell Ltd** for 'The Sycamore Tree' by Jonathan Always from *Passport to Poetry II* edited by E. L. Black and D. S. Davies. **Centerprise Trust Ltd** for 'A pigeon' by Marion Sheen, 'In the dark' by Julie Cashman, 'Me, I'm myself' by Pat Kirk, 'Pollution' by Lesley Samuels and 'Stepney' by Rosemarie Dale from *Stepney Words I and II* edited by Chris Searle. **Chatto and Windus Ltd** for the extract 'Jethro makes friends with a Jumbie' from *Jethro and the Jumbie* by Susan Cooper. **William Cole** for 'For sale' by Shel Silverstein © 1972 Shel Silverstein. **Curtis Brown Ltd** for 'The Adventures of Isabel' by Ogden Nash © 1936, 1963 by Ogden Nash. **Daily Mirror Children's Literary Competition 1967** for 'Anger' by Yvonne Lowe. **Judy Daish Associates Ltd** for 'The Park' by Olive Dehn. **J. M. Dent & Sons Ltd** for the extract from 'The Boy Who Went Looking for a Friend', the extract from 'The Playground', and 'A Witch Poem' from *The First Margaret Mahy Story Book*; 'Aunty Nasty' (abridged) from *The Third Margaret Mahy Story Book*; 'The Little Witch' (abridged) by Margaret Mahy. **Niru Desai** for 'The mouse with seven tails'. **Andre Deutsch** for 'The Ugsome Thing' (slightly abridged) from *Ten Tales of Shellover* by Ruth Ainsworth; *The cat who thought he was a tiger* by Polly Cameron; 'A riddle' from *Riddles, Rhymes and Rigmaroles* by John Cunliffe; 'Horrible things' from *Seen Grandpa Lately* by Roy Fuller; 'Father says', 'Late last night' and 'This is the hand' from *Mind your own business* by Michael Rosen; 'I'm the youngest in our house' and 'Mum'll be coming home today' from *Wouldn't you like to know* by Michael Rosen. **Dinosaur Publications Ltd** for the extract from *David and His Sister Carol* by Althea. **Dobson Books Ltd** for 'Bump' from *The Little Pot Boiler* by Spike Milligan. **Doubleday & Company Inc** for 'I am Cherry Alive' from *Summer Knowledge: New and Selected Poems 1938–1958* by Delmore Schwartz © 1958 by Delmore Schwartz. Reprinted by permission of Doubleday & Company Inc. **The Estate of Ogden Nash** and **A. P. Watt Ltd** for 'Winter Morning' and 'Between Birthdays' by Ogden Nash. **The Estate of Alfred Noyes** and **William Blackwood (Publishers)** for 'Daddy fell into the pond' by Alfred Noyes. **Faber and Faber Publishers** for the extract entitled 'The two guinea pigs' from *A Bad Child's Book of Moral Verse* by Charlotte Hough; 'Folks' and 'My Brother Bert' from *Meet My Folks* by Ted Hughes; *Mark and his pictures* (abridged) by Carol Odell. **Aileen Fisher** for 'Noses' and 'The Seed' from *Up the Windy Hill* by Aileen Fisher, published by Abelard-Schuman, New York 1953. Copyright renewed 1981. **Phyllis Flowerdew** for 'Mr Marcus Able and the birds' from *Poetry is All Around* by Phyllis Flowerdew published by Oliver & Boyd. **Fontana Paperbacks** for 'Grandad' from *Rabbiting On* by Kit Wright © 1978 Fontana Lions. **Ginn & Company** for 'The litter bug', © J. Rintoul 1968, from *Ten to two*, Book 5 of *Poems for Me* by Kit Patrickson, published by Ginn & Company Ltd. **Frederick Grice** for 'Dildrum, King of the Cats' from *Folk Tales of Lancashire* and 'The Men of Lorbottle' from *Folk Tales of the North Country* published by Thomas Nelson & Sons. **Grosset & Dunlap Inc Publishers** for 'The Friendly Cinnamon Bun' from *The Pedaling Man and Other Poems* by Russell Hoban © 1968 Russell Hoban, published by Grosset & Dunlap Inc New York NY 10010. **Hamish Hamilton Ltd** for the extracts 'Bad news' and 'The pit heap', from *Old Dog New Tricks* by Dick Cate; the extract from *The bad-tempered ladybird* by Eric Carle. **Harcourt Brace Jovanovich Inc** for 'Growing Up' from *The Little Hill* by Harry Behn © 1949 Harry Behn, © 1977 by Alice L. Behn. **Harper & Row Publishers Inc** for 'It is grey out . . .' from *Near the Window Tree: Poems and Notes by Karla Kuskin* © 1975 by Karla Kuskin; 'I woke up this morning' from *The Rose on my Cake* written and illustrated by Karla Kuskin © 1964 by Karla Kuskin; 'Just me, just me', 'The Loser', 'Magic', 'Rain', 'Sarah Cynthia Sylvia Stout', and 'What a day' from *Where the Sidewalk Ends: The Poems and Drawings of Shel Silverstein* © 1974 by Shel Silverstein; the summary and extract from *Big sister and little sister* by Charlotte Zolotow; 'Rain sizes' from *The Reason for the Pelican* by John Ciardi © 1959 by The Curtis Publishing Company, a J. B. Lippincott book. 'What someone said when he was spanked on the day before his birthday' from *You Know Who* by John Ciardi © 1964 by John Ciardi, a J. B. Lippincott book. **Harper and Row** and the **Lutterworth Press** for 'Christmas dinner' from *Farmer Boy* by Laura Ingalls Wilder. Text © 1933 by Harper & Row Publishers Ltd; renewed 1961 by Roger L. MacBride. **Harvey House Publishers** for *Whose Garden?* (slightly abridged) by Marilyn Kratz. **Heinemann Educational Books** and the **Estate of James Reeves** for 'Vicary Square' and 'The Wind' by James Reeves. **Anita Hewett** for 'The boy who trapped the sun' (slightly abridged) from the BBC programme *Something to Think About*. **David Higham Associates Ltd** for 'Bedtime' and the extract 'House coming down' from *Silver, Sand and Snow* by Eleanor Farjeon, published by Michael Joseph; 'Friends' from *The Secret Brother* by Elizabeth Jennings, published by Macmillan. **Hodder & Stoughton** for 'Crosspatch' (abridged) by Margaret Baker from *Tell Them Again Tales*; 'Mr Wolf and his tail' from *Folk Tales* by Leila Berg; 'The two giants' (slightly abridged) by Michael Foreman; 'Johnny's pockets' by Alison Winn. **Elizabeth Hogg** for her poems 'Capability Tim', 'Favourite colour', 'Mixed blessings', 'Ups and downs' and 'Very odd jobs'. **Steve Hoyle** for his story 'Leon and the Sumwitch'. **Inner London Education Authority Learning Materials Service** for 'The Park' by Rochelle Beman of Simon Marks Primary School and 'Shadows' by Kamala Panday of Granton Primary School from *Hey Mister Butterfly* edited by Alasdair Aston, © ILEA 1978; the extract from 'Starting School', from *Make-a-Story*. **Jacaranda Wiley Ltd** for *The giant child* and *A boy and his robot* from the *Rights of Children* series, published in Australasia by Jacaranda Wiley Ltd. **Johnston & Bacon Ltd** for 'The little old lady' by Rodney Bennett from *Fresh Flights*. **Paddy Kinsale** for his story 'Ranjit and the tiger'. **Alfred A. Knopf** for 'Good morning when it's morning' and 'Hello's a handy word' from *Nuts to You and Nuts to Me* by Mary Ann Hoberman, Canadian rights controlled by Alfred A. Knopf. **Brian Lee** for 'Sad . . . and Glad' © Brian Lee, first published in *A First Poetry Book* compiled by John Foster, Oxford University Press 1979. **The Literary Trustees of Walter de la Mare** and **The Society of Authors** as their representatives for 'Me' and 'Miss T' by Walter de la Mare. **The Lois Lenski Covey Foundation** for 'Sing a song of people' from *The Life I live* by Lois Lenski © 1965 by The Lois Lenski Covey Foundation Inc, reprinted by permission of the copyright owners. **Edward Lowbury** for 'Secrets' from *Green Magic* published by Chatto & Windus Ltd. **Lutterworth Press** for the extract 'A traditional Japanese house' from *How They Live Now – Kiku of Japan* by Juliet Piggott. **McClelland and Stewart Ltd** for the extract from *Winnie the Pooh* by A. A. Milne, Canadian rights controlled by McClelland and Stewart Ltd. **Macmillan Education Ltd** for the extract from *Carnival of Dreams* by Beryl Gilroy. **Macmillan Publishing Inc** for *The Little Brute Family* by Russell Hoban © 1966 by Russell Hoban and *The Stone*

*Doll of Sister Brute* by Russell Hoban © 1968 by Russell Hoban. **Eve Merriam** for 'Grownups' from *There is No Rhyme for Silver* © 1962 by Eve Merriam, and for 'Sometimes' from *Catch a Little Rhyme* © 1966 by Eve Merriam. Reprinted by permission of the author. **Methuen Children's Books** for 'Chitra makes a curry' by Ursula Sharma from *Allsorts 6* edited by Ann Thwaite; the extract entitled 'Eeyore's birthday' from *Winnie the Pooh* by A. A. Milne, 'The End' from *Now We Are Six* by A. A. Milne; the extract from 'The very first story' from *My Naughty Little Sister's Friends* and 'The very old birthday party' from *More Naughty Little Sister Stories* by Dorothy Edwards. **Milton Road Infants School** for children's handwritten work. **Oxford University Press** for *The Most Beautiful Child* by William Papas © 1973; 'Out of School' from *Tomorrow is My Love* by Hal Summers; the extract entitled 'Such a stubborn mule!' from *Tales of the Hodja* retold by Charles Downing. **Oxford University Press Australia** for 'Today' by Cathy Thompson from *Once Around the Sun*. **Philippa Pearce** for the extract from 'Lion at School' © 1971 Philippa Pearce, first published 1971 by the British Broadcasting Corporation. Permission granted by the author. **Penguin Books Ltd** for 'Growing', 'Know-alls', 'Don't go, Miranda' and 'Look out!' by Max Fatchen from *Songs for My Dog and Other People* by Max Fatchen, Kestrel Books 1980, pp. 12, 27, 50–51, and 57, © 1980 by Max Fatchen; 'Sweet Dreams' and 'The People Upstairs' by Ogden Nash from *Custard and Company* by Ogden Nash, Kestrel Books 1979, pp. 80 and 105, © 1979 by the Estate of Ogden Nash; the extract 'A broken promise' from *A Dog So Small* (pp. 14–18) by Philippa Pearce, Longman Young Books 1962, © 1962 by Philippa Pearce; 'The hardest thing to do in the world', and 'Rodge said' by Michael Rosen from *You Tell Me* by Roger McGough and Michael Rosen, Puffin Books 1981, pp. 38 and 17, © Penguin Books Ltd 1979 (for the collection) © Michael Rosen 1979 (for his poems). **A. D. Peters & Co Ltd** for 'I was sitting in the sitting room' from *Gruesome* by Roger McGough from *You Tell Me*, Puffin Books, 1981, p. 48. **Marnie Pomeroy** for 'Halloween'. **The Putnam Publishing Group** for 'A Dreadful Sight' from *All Together* by Dorothy Aldis, © 1925, renewed © 1953 by Dorothy Aldis; 'My brother' from *Hop, Skip and Jump* by Dorothy Aldis, © 1934, renewed © 1961 by Dorothy Aldis; 'Little' from *Everything and Anything* by Dorothy Aldis, © 1925–27, renewed © 1953–55 by Dorothy Aldis. **Russell & Volkening Inc** for 'Hello's a handy word' and 'Good morning when it's morning' by Mary Ann Hoberman from *Nuts to You and Nuts to Me*. **Clive Sansom** for his poem 'Mixed Brews'. **Santley Junior Mixed School** for 'Brixton Market' and 'An interview with the school caretaker'. **Janet Smith** for her poem 'Auntie Alice'. **The Society of Authors**, literary representative of the Estate of Rose Fyleman for 'Wanted' by Rose Fyleman. **Suffolk County Council** for 'My Mum' by Angela Lowett. **D. C. Thomson & Co Ltd** for 'Gone' reproduced from *Twinkle Annual 1980* © D. C. Thomson & Co Ltd. **Viking Penguin Inc** for 'Sneaky Bill' by William Cole from *Oh, That's Ridiculous* edited by William Cole © 1972 by William Cole. **Frederick Warne (Publishers) Ltd** for 'My face' from *Round About Eight*. **John Wiley & Sons Canada Ltd** for *The giant child* and *A boy and his robot* from the *Rights of Children* series, published in Canada by John Wiley & Sons Canada Ltd. **Mrs Iris Wise** and **Macmillan, London and Basingstoke** for 'The Wind' from *Collected Poems* by James Stephens. **The Women's Press** for 'As I was sitting', 'My dad's work', 'My mother repairs radios', 'Speaking English' and 'Things about my neighbourhood' from *Come With Us: Children Speak for Themselves* published by The Women's Press. **World Council of Churches** for 'Christmas in Uruguay' (abridged) from their magazine *One World* No. 32, December 1977. **World's Work Ltd** for 'The friendly cinnamon bun' from *The Pedalling Man* by Russell Hoban, © 1968, published in the UK and British Commonwealth by World's Work Ltd; 'The Guest' and 'Tear-Water Tea' from *Owl at Home* by Arnold Lobel © 1975, published in the UK and British Commonwealth by World's Work Ltd; the summary and extract from *Big Sister and Little Sister* by Charlotte Zolotow © 1966, published in the UK and British Commonwealth by World's Work Ltd.

The author and publishers wish to thank BBC Publications for their permission to use in the themes *Water, rain and snow* and *Sun and fire* some ideas for classroom activities from programmes in the series *Something to Think About* (1980).

Every effort has been made to trace and acknowledge copyright owners. If any right has been omitted, the publishers offer their apologies and will rectify this in subsequent editions following notification.

# Index of stories

# Index of poems

# Subject Index

## to 15 A & C Black song books

This index arranges songs from 15 books under 65 subject headings. Some songs appear under more than one heading. Within each subject, songs are listed alphabetically by song book, so that *Alleluya* songs come first, in numerical order, then *Apusskidu*, and so on.

An index of this sort can never be comprehensive. Both the subject headings and the lists of songs are really selections; teachers and other users may wish to make their own additions.

Our thanks are due to Deborah Gillingham and Enid Deakin, both of Holy Trinity School, Weymouth, who suggested this index and made suggestions towards it.

The drawings are by Toni Goffe.

For details of the A & C Black song books and other music books, please write to A & C Black, Howard Road, Eaton Socon, Cambs.

| | | |
|---|---|---|
| AL | Alleluya | *77 thoughtful songs* |
| AP | Apusskidu | *56 songs for children* |
| CG | Carol, gaily carol | *43 Christmas songs for children* |
| FR | Flying a Round | *88 rounds and partner songs* |
| GS | Game-songs with Prof Dogg's Troupe | *44 songs and games* |
| HA | Harlequin | *44 songs round the year* |
| JB | Juke Box | *33 pop songs* |
| JH | The Jolly Herring | *77 folk songs and pop songs* |
| MB | Merrily to Bethlehem | *44 Christmas songs* |
| MS | Mango spice | *44 Caribbean songs* |
| OK | Okki-tokki-unga | *56 action songs* |
| SH | Sing hey diddle diddle | *66 nursery songs* |
| SS | Someone's singing, Lord | *59 hymns and songs* |
| TA | Ta-ra-ra boom-de-ay | *55 songs for everyone* |
| TB | Tinder-box | *66 songs for children* |

## Action songs

all the songs in *Okki-tokki-unga*, and *Game-songs* plus:

If you're happy, AP 1
My ship sailed from China, AP 7
Clap, stamp, slap, click, FR 33
Old Bill Jones, FR 71
The locomotion, JB 3
Ol Mas Charlie, MS 16
Pull away, me boy, MS 24
Bring me half a hoe – Angelina, MS 26
Charley Marley, MS 35
River to the bank, Covalley, MS 36
Manuel Road, MS 37
Brown girl in the ring, MS 38
Here we go round the mulberry bush, SH 37
Ring-a-ring o' roses, SH 38
Make a face, TB 3
Kaigal – Hands, TB 4
I've got a body, TB 5
Work calypso, TB 23
Let's pretend, TB 25
Slowly walks my grandad, TB 28
Mysteries, TB 40
Weather song, TB 41
Majā pade – Let's all be happy, TB 57

## Anger

There was a little girl, SH 39
I lift up my finger, TA 39
The angry song, TB 9
Don't you push me down, TB 26
Why does it have to be me? TB 53

## Animals

see also **Birds, Nature, Prehistoric animals**

Where have the seals gone? AL 36
The Wombling song, AP 27
Song of the Delhi Tongawallah, AP 36
Rabbit ain't got, AP 37
The animals went in two by two, AP 38
Going to the zoo, AP 39
The hippopotamus song, AP 40
Tiger, tiger, AP 41
Where, oh where has my little dog gone? AP 42
Daddy wouldn't buy me a bow-wow, AP 43
Five little frogs, AP 44
Frog went a-courtin', AP 45
Down in Demerara, AP 46
The bear went over the mountain, AP 47
Ferdinando the donkey, AP 48
The kangaroo song, AP 49
Katie's garden, AP 50
Apusski dusky, AP 51
The elephant, AP 52
Gobbolino, the witch's cat, AP 53
A windmill in old Amsterdam, AP 54
Maggon, the bad-tempered dragon, AP 55
Risha, rasha, rusha, AP 56
Little donkey, CG 3
Softly sings the donkey, FR 15
Song of the frogs, FR 21
Frogs' festival, FR 22
Kookaburra, FR 29
Country life, FR 60
Rowdy round, FR 65
Monster stomp, GS 31
Down on the farm, GS 41
English country garden, HA 22
Caterpillars only crawl, HA 26
Bright eyes, JB 29
The Jolly Herring, JH 1
Pete was a lonely mongrel dog, JH 13
Bob the pedigree sheepdog, JH 14

## Halloween, witches

see also **Ghosts**

There was an old witch, AP 17
Gobbolino, the witch's cat, AP 53
Make a cake, GS 30
Halloween's coming, HA 35
Spooky, HA 36
Halloween is coming, TB 61

## Happiness

Raindrops keep fallin' on my head,
 AL 58
If you're happy, AP 1
The clown, AP 35
Up on the roof, JB 16
Good morning, starshine, JB 21
I can see clearly now, JB 28
Knees up, Mother Brown, OK 6
O Lord! Shout for joy! SS 4
Stand up, clap hands, shout thank
 you, Lord, SS 14
Let's all go down the Strand! TA 7
Lazy coconut tree, TA 18
Pack up your troubles, TA 32
When the red, red robin, TA 33
The happy wanderer, TA 34
When you're smiling, TA 35
Ob-la-di, ob-la-da, TA 44
Majā pade – Let's all be happy, TB 57

## Historical people and events

The fifth of November, HA 38
Settle–Carlisle railway, JH 8
The broadside man, JH 11
MacPherson's farewell, JH 28
Turpin hero, JH 31
The Ellan Vannin tragedy, JH 38
The Marco Polo, JH 49
Sing, John Ball, TB 32

## Hobbies and sports

Shoot! shoot! shoot! AP 28
One potato, two potato, AP 31
Kite flying high, FR 16
Sledging, HA 4
Roller skating, HA 23
Football crazy, JH 15
Messing about on the river, JH 72
Fishing, OK 31
The cricket match, TA 25
Stewball, TA 27
The happy wanderer, TA 34

## Holidays

The train is a-coming, AP 23
Take me to the seaside, HA 27
A holiday in Spain, HA 28
I do like to be beside the seaside, TA 3

## Home

Moving on song, AL 39
When Father papered the parlour, AP 34
A windmill in old Amsterdam, AP 54
Coal-hole cavalry, JH 9
If it wasn't for the 'ouses in between,
 JH 43
The miner's dream of home, OK 28
At half past three we go home to tea,
 SS 58
Island in the sun, TA 17
Jamaica farewell, TA 22
Home on the range, TA 40
A house is a house for me, TB 13
Place to be, TB 34
I've just moved into a new house,
 TB 51

## Homecoming

She'll be coming round the mountain,
 AP 26
Travellin' light, JB 13
Whip jamboree, JH 53
Sailing, JH 70
Janey gal, MS 30
Dis long time, gal, MS 32
At half past three we go home to tea,
 SS 58
We're going home, SS 59
Welcome home, TB 60

## Houses

The building song, AL 59
Right said Fred, JH 4
Hosanna! MS 25
The wise man and the foolish man,
 OK 29
A house is a house for me, TB 13
Skyscraper wean, TB 36

## Imagination

see **Make-believe**

## Jobs, work

The bonny blue-eyed sailor, AP 9
The guard song, AP 32
The fireman, AP 33
When Father papered the parlour,
 AP 34
The clown, AP 35
Lollipop man, FR 7
The umbrella man, HA 25
Harvest, HA 31
Right said Fred, JH 4
Hole in the ground, JH 5
Drill ye tarriers, drill, JH 6
Indeed I would, JH 7
Settle–Carlisle railway, JH 8
Coal-hole cavalry, JH 9
This old hammer, JH 10
Fling it here, fling it there, JH 40
Land of the old and grey, JH 42
The drunken sailor, JH 44
Pay me my money down, JH 51
Penny Lane, JH 67
Hill an gully, MS 23
Pull away, me boy, MS 24
Day oh! MS 27
Miss Polly, OK 17
Can you tell me? OK 55
Little Boy Blue, SH 27
Pat-a-cake, SH 44
When lamps are lighted, SS 26
The farmer comes to scatter the seed,
 SS 56
Any old iron? TA 4
Lazy coconut tree, TA 18
Linstead market, TA 19
Keep that wheel a-turning, TA 41
All the nice girls love a sailor, TA 45
There's something about a soldier, TA 46

Work calypso, TB 23
Supermum! TB 24
Let's pretend, TB 25
Ladybird, TB 49

## Make-believe

see also **Nonsense**

Yellow submarine, AP 4
There was an old witch, AP 17
Bananas in pyjamas, AP 20
Battle song of the Zartians, AP 29
Frog went a-courtin', AP 45
Katie's garden, AP 50
Maggon, the bad-tempered dragon,
   AP 55
Be a clown, GS 17
Walking through the jungle, GS 18
The Jolly Herring, JH 1
Pete was a lonely mongrel dog, JH13
Have you seen the ghost of Tom?
   JH 63
The princess, OK 20
Old Roger, OK 21
Let's all play at Indians, OK 26
You can't keep a horse in a
   lighthouse, TA 23
Jennifer's rabbit, TB 14
All alone in my quiet head, TB 17
Let's pretend, TB 25
Puff the magic dragon, TB 50

## Marriages

Daisy Bell, AP 8
Sparrow twitters, AP 13
I'm Henery the Eighth, I am, AP 15
Frog went a-courtin', AP 45
Where are you going to, my pretty maid?
   SH 28
Under the coconut tree, MS 29

## Mechanical things

Wheels keep turning, AP 24
Ticking clocks, FR 25
Keep that wheel a-turning, TA 41
My grandfather's clock, TA 54

## Morning

A better world, AL 60
Good morning, starshine, JB 21
Coal-hole cavalry, JH 9
I jump out of bed in the morning,
   OK 47
The golden cockerel, SS 2
Morning has broken, SS 3
Sun Arise, TB 43

## Musical instruments

Bellringer, pray give us some peace,
   FR 41
Sound waves, FR 59
Calypso, FR 68
The orchestra song, JH 61
Patapan, MB 42
Someone's in the kitchen with Dinah,
   OK 14
The music man, OK 44
Oh, we can play on the big bass drum,
   OK 45

Tom, he was a piper's son, SH 13
Old King Cole, SH 40
Mama don't 'low, TB 21

## Names

Daisy Bell, AP 8
L'il Liza Jane, AP 11
Clementine, AP 12
I'm Henery the Eighth, I am, AP 15
There's a hole in my bucket, AP 16
Lily the pink, AP 19
Michael Finnigin, AP 22
Katie's garden, AP 50
Andrew mine, Jasper mine, CG 28
Algy, FR 1
Old Abram Brown, FR 42
Old Jim John, FR 51
Old Bill Jones, FR 71
Rhyming name song, GS 22
Birthday round, HA 42
The rain song, HA 44
Right said Fred, JH 4
Timothy Winters, JH 12
Pete was a lonely mongrel dog, JH 13
Bob the pedigree sheepdog, JH 14
Football crazy, JH 15
Colonel Fazackerley, JH 23
Casey Jones, JH 35
Dorset is beautiful, JH 39
Sweet Willie, JH 56
Handsome Molly, JH 57
Tantie Mary, MS 2
Dumplins, MS 6
Sammy dead oh, MS 22
Bring me half a hoe – Angelina, MS 26
Water come a me eye, MS 28
Janey gal, MS 30
Charley Marley, MS 35
Knees up, Mother Brown, OK 6
Miss Mary Mac, OK 12
Someone's in the kitchen with Dinah,
   OK 14
Miss Polly, OK 17

Old Roger, OK 21
Hang on the bell, Nellie, OK 22
Cousin Peter, OK 34
Johnny taps with one hammer, OK 37
John Brown's baby, OK 43
Sally Saucer, OK 51
Bobby Shafto, SH 1
Mary had a little lamb, SH 9
Mary, Mary, quite contrary, SH 14
Doctor Foster went to Gloucester, SH 15
Little Jack Horner, SH 29
Little Miss Muffet, SH 30
Don't bring Lulu, TA 2
Dinah, TA 10
If you knew Susie, TA 12
I came from Alabama (Oh Susanna),
   TA 15
Michael, row the boat ashore, TA 30
Keep that wheel a-turning, TA 41
Ob-la-di, ob-la-da, TA 44
Jennifer's rabbit, TB 14
Helping Grandma Jones, TB 27
I've just moved into a new house, TB 51
Birthday song, TB 59

## Nature

see also **Animals, Birds, Flowers,
Gardens, Trees**

Winter rain, HA 8
It happens each spring, HA 15
Can you hear? HA 33
Nature carol, MB 41
I love the sun, SS 12
Think of a world without any flowers,
   SS 15
God bless the grass, SS 27
I love God's tiny creatures, SS 42
All the flowers are waking, SS 48
In the early morning, SS 49
The flowers that grow in the garden,
   SS 53
One two three, TB 65

My grandfather's clock, TA 54
How many people live in your house?
 TB 19
Mama don't 'low, TB 21
Supermum! TB 24
Slowly walks my grandad, TB 28
Ladybird, TB 49

## Rivers

The hippopotamus song, AP 40
Canoe song, FR 19
On the river flows, FR 28
Moon River, JB 4
Messing about on the river, JH 72
Six little ducks, OK 41

## Sadness

Nowhere Man, AL 20
Raindrops keep fallin' on my head,
 AL 58
Crying song, GS 21
Singing the blues, JB 6
Take a message to Mary, JB 9
Raining in my heart, JB 14
I'll never fall in love again, JB 24
Sweet Willie, JH 56
Handsome Molly, JH 57
The water is wide, JH 58
Once I had a sweetheart, JH 59
Ladybird, TB 49
Puff the magic dragon, TB 50

## Sea, ships, sailors

Yellow submarine, AP 4
The bonny blue-eyed sailor, AP 9
The wind blow east, AP 30
Apusski dusky, AP 51
Take me to the seaside, HA 27
The Ellan Vannin tragedy, JH 38

The drunken sailor, JH 44
Can't you dance the polka, JH 45
Haul away Joe, JH 46
Santy Anna, JH 47
The leaving of Liverpool, JH 48
The Marco Polo, JH 49
The wreck of the John B, JH 50
Whip jamboree, JH 53
Sailing, JH 70
Bobbing up and down like this, OK 7
Fishing, OK 31
Bobby Shafto, SH 1
When lamps are lighted, SS 26
I do like to be beside the seaside, TA 3
You can't keep a horse in a
 lighthouse, TA 23
All the nice girls love a sailor, TA 45
Until I saw the sea, TB 38

## Seasons

see also **Christmas, Festivals,
Halloween**

all the songs in *Harlequin*, plus: –

Turn, turn, turn, AL 32
Little birds in winter time, SS 43
All the flowers are waking, SS 48
Look for signs that summer's done,
 SS 54
See how the snowflakes, SS 57
One two three, TB 65

## Senses

Music of the world a-turnin', AL 19
Sing a rainbow, AP 5
Sound song, GS 39, TB 39
Can you hear? HA 33
Fling it here, fling it there, JH 40
Lord, I love to stamp and shout, SS 5
Give to us eyes, SS 18

He gave me eyes so I could see, SS 19
Praise to God for things we see, SS 20
Hands to work and feet to run, SS 21
Until I saw the sea, TB 38
Mysteries, TB 40
Who has seen the wind? TB 44
Talking, TB 52

## Separation

Lullaby for the times, AL 13
When I'm on my journey, AL 30
By the waters of Babylon, AL 68
Take a message to Mary, JB 9
Sealed with a kiss, JB 11
The leaving of Liverpool, JH 48
The wreck of the John B, JH 50
The girl I left behind, JH 55
Zion, me wan go home, MS 11
Rivers of Babylon, MS 12
Water come a me eye, MS 28
Dis long time, gal, MS 32
The miner's dream of home, OK 28
She was one of the early birds, TA 14
The mocking bird, TA 21
Jamaica farewell, TA 22
Don't dilly dally on the way, TA 42
The last thing on my mind, TA 50
Yesterday, TA 52
Puff the magic dragon, TB 50
I've just moved into a new house, TB 51
You and I, TB 55

## Shelter

see also **Home, Houses**

The building song, AL 59
Rabbit ain't got, AP 37
Lodging, I beg you, good man, CG 6
Standing in the rain, CG 7
The north wind doth blow, SH 12
A house is a house for me, TB 13

## Sickness and health

I think I've caught a cold, HA 34
My last cigarette, JH 21
Cerasee, MS 8
Miss Polly, OK 17
For all the strength we have, SS 16
O Jesus, we are well and strong, SS 40
Short'nin' bread, TA 43

## Sleeping, dreaming

All night, all day, AL 75
Morningtown ride, AP 25
Creep up, GS 12
Lullaby of the spinning wheel, MB 13
Lazy coconut tree, TA 18
Jennifer's rabbit, TB 14

## Snow

January, HA 2
Snowflakes, HA 3
Sledging, HA 4
See how the snowflakes, SS 57

## Storms

The wind blow east, AP 30
The north wind, HA 6
The Ellan Vannin tragedy, JH 38
The lightning tree, JH 73

## Story songs

Gobbolino, the witch's cat, AP 53
Algy, FR 1
Allentown Jail, JB 8
Take a message to Mary, JB 9
Right said Fred, JH 4
Hole in the ground, JH 5
Pete was a lonely mongrel dog, JH 13
MacPherson's farewell, JH 28
Hangman, JH 29
Whiskey in the jar, JH 30
Turpin hero, JH 31
The bonnie lass o' Fyvie, JH 33
John Barleycorn, JH 34
Casey Jones, JH 35
The Gypsy Davey, JH 36
The gypsy rover, JH 37
The Ellan Vannin tragedy, JH 38
Fling it here, fling it there, JH 40
The Marco Polo, JH 49
The girl I left behind, JH 55
Sweet Willie, JH 56
The lightning tree, JH 73
Cerasee, MS 8
Sly Mongoose, MS 19
Sammy dead oh, MS 22
Anancy, Monkey and Tiger, MS 41
Anancy and Dora, MS 42
How Monkey shame Anancy, MS 43
Anancy and Fee Fee, MS 44
Okki-tokki-unga, OK 15
'Neath the lilacs, OK 16
Miss Polly, OK 17
The princess, OK 20
In a cottage in a wood, OK 24
Cousin Peter, OK 34
Sucking cider through a straw, TA 9
The cricket match, TA 25
On Ilkla Moor baht'at, TA 26
Stewball, TA 27
Keep that wheel a-turning, TA 41
Don't dilly dally on the way, TA 42
Let him go, let him tarry, TA 48

My grandfather's clock, TA 54
Jennifer's rabbit, TB 14
Puff the magic dragon, TB 50

## Sun

April, HA 17
I can see clearly now, JB 28
The golden cockerel, SS 2
The flowers that grow in the garden, SS 53
Island in the sun, TA 17
Lazy coconut tree, TA 18
Sun Arise, TB 43

## Surroundings

see **Caring for our surroundings, Neighbourhood**

## Times of the day

see also **Morning**

I watch the sunrise, AL 15
All night, all day, AL 75
Something inside me, FR 10
Hey ho! Time to go to bed, FR 14
At half past three we go home to tea, SS 58
Wee Willie Winkie, SH 66
We're going home, SS 59
Song of the clock, TB 7

## Trains

The train is a-coming, AP 23
Morningtown ride, AP 25
To stop the train, FR 55
Casey Jones, JH 35
The runaway train, TA 47

## Transport

see also **Trains**

Bus story, AL 23
Daisy Bell, AP 8
Song of the Delhi Tongawallah, AP 36
A holiday in Spain, HA 28
The Ellan Vannin tragedy, JH 38
Messing about on the river, JH 72
The galloping major, OK 5
The wheels on the bus, OK 32
City beasts, TB 37

## Travelling people

for **Sailors** see under **Sea**

Can't help but wonder, AL 34
Moving on song, AL 39
Trav'lin' round, FR 20
The Gypsy Davey, JH 36
The gypsy rover, JH 37

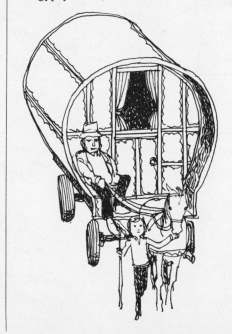

The happy wanderer, TA 34
Side by side, TA 36
So long, it's been good to know you, TA 55

## Trees

O Christmas tree, CG 41
Pussy willow, HA 12
I can see cherries, HA 30
The lightning tree, JH 73
Who has seen the wind? TB 44

## Weather

see also **Rain, Snow, Storms, Sun**

Little wind, FR 45
Weather song, GS 38, TB 41
Ho! Jack Frost, HA 5
The north wind, HA 6
Wonderful weather, HA 14
April, HA 17
Fog, HA 37
The north wind doth blow, SH 12
I love the sun, SS 12
Coming down, TB 42
Who has seen the wind? TB 44

## Witches

see **Halloween**

## Work

see **Jobs**

*SUBJECT INDEX to 15 A & C Black song books.*
© 1982 A & C Black (Publishers) Ltd, 35 Bedford Row, London WC1R 4JH.

Revised 1983